PRAISE FO

A magical encounter with a wolf was in many ways the culmination of Rebecca Wallick's long-time canine love affair. In this insight-filled memoir, Wallick testifies to the power of dogs: to their companionship, the ways they connect us with the natural world, and the solace they provide when life throws us curveballs. Dogs, particularly Malamutes, have literally been Wallick's co-pilots throughout her life as a daughter, trail-runner, attorney, and advocate for the well-being of animals domestic and wild. It's a story worth reading.
 —Claudia Kawczynska, Founder, *The Bark* magazine and Editor-in-chief of *The Bark* and TheBark.com

Sometimes we choose the dog, sometimes the dog chooses us. In *Wild Running*, Rebecca Wallick's honest-to-the-core memoir, the choosing was not only mutual, it was mutually beneficial. Trail-runners, Malamute fans, and those who value nature in general and wolves in particular will all find something to like here.
 —Susan Tasaki, Senior Editor, *The Bark* magazine

Rebecca Wallick's *Wild Running* is a tenderly written and uplifting account of experiencing the wild beauty of nature through trail running with her dogs. Throughout her travels, Rebecca's encounters with wolves and other wildlife remind us of the bond between humans and the natural world and why we must cherish it. If you love dogs and nature, you must read this book.
 —Adrian Raeside, Author of *The World According to Dogs: An Owner's Manual*

Wallick writes a book about a lifetime of running and a lifetime with the dogs of her life. This beautiful book will carry you across much of the West, it will carry you into Wallick's world, it will inspire you to run (or walk or hike) through wildness, and it will inspire you to remember the dogs of your life.
 —Sean Prentiss, author of *Finding Abbey*

I've had a fascination with huskies for most of my life, and even got to experience life and trail running with one for over eight years. I have also had a fascination with wolves since I first moved to the Tetons in the late-90s, which was a very pivotal time in the reintroduction of wolves to the Greater Yellowstone area. I've known of Wallick's love and deep respect for Malamutes for 20 years, meeting her and The Girls (Maia and Meadow) at the Peterson Ridge Rumble, a dog-friendly trail race I organize. With all of that, plus having read her first book, I read *Wild Running* with high expectations.

Wallick is a wonderful storyteller. I really appreciate the chronology of her life and the Malamutes she's had the pleasure of living with in different phases of her life, how those parts came together when she lived in very rural Idaho, and how that sometimes put her and her dogs in very dangerous situations.

Wild Running is part memoir, part Malamute, part Australian shepherd, part wolf, part user-conflict, part ultrarunning, and almost all outdoors and in the mountains. It's flowy and suspenseful, and with a lot of fun along the way, thanks to Opus, The Girls, Finn, Conall, and Chann.

—Sean Meissner, Dog Lover, Running Coach, and *UltraRunner Magazine* columnist

If you've ever loved a dog and found solace on a trail, this book will resonate deeply. I've never met Wallick, yet her writing makes her feel like a trusted friend, a friend with a compelling story to share and an admiration for a misunderstood predator that is sure to have a strong impact on all who read her book.

—Kristina Siladi, Physical Therapist, Runner, Dog Mom

REBECCA WALLICK

WILD RUNNING

Lessons from Dogs, Wolves, and the Natural World

A MEMOIR

Copyright © 2024 Rebecca M. Wallick

All rights reserved.

This book or any portion thereof may not be reproduced or used in any manner whatsoever without the express written permission of the publisher except for the use of brief quotations in a book review.

Printed in the United States of America
First Printing, March 2024

ISBN-13 (print, special edition): 978-0-9913648-4-8

Maian Meadows Publishing
217 Bolton Rd
Cabot, VT 05647

Cover design and formatting: Jane Dixon-Smith
https://www.jdsmith-design.co.uk/
Editing: Susan Tasaki

All photos are part of the author's personal collection unless otherwise noted.

For my father.

And every dog and wolf who has graced my life.

Who's this—alone with stone and sky?
It's only my old dog and I—
It's only him; it's only me;
Alone with stone and grass and tree.
 —Siegfried Sassoon, *Man and Dog*

If you talk to the animals they will talk to you, and you will know each other. If you do not talk to them, you will not know them. And what you do not know, you will fear. What one fears one destroys.
 —Chief Dan George

CAST OF CANINE CHARACTERS

OPUS:
Female Alaskan Malamute
Spring 1985–April 1999

FINN: Male Australian Shepherd
December 18, 2007
(actual date unknown)–

MAIA:
Female Alaskan Malamute
April 9, 1999–June 6, 2013

CONALL:
Male Alaskan Malamute
December 5, 2014–

MEADOW:
Female Alaskan Malamute
May 19, 2001–July 22, 2013

CHANN:
Male Alaskan Malamute
May 11, 2023–

CONTENTS

PRELUDE 1
MAGIC 4
WILD 8
OPUS 15
DISTANCE 23
PUPPIES 27
COMMUNING 38
PERSISTENCE 46
TRANSITION 59
WILDLIFE 68
INTROVERT 77
STONES 86
CONALL 96
SEASONS 99
WOLVES 146
EMPATHY 157
SHATTERED 164
NATURALISM 172
MASCULINITY 181
WOLF-BIRDS 191
STEPS 199
AFTERWORD: GRAY WOLVES IN THE UNITED STATES: A PRIMER 206
CODA: NEMOPHILIST 216
NOTES AND REFERENCES (by chapter) 218
RESOURCES and SOURCES CITED 228
ACKNOWLEDGEMENTS 235
ABOUT THE AUTHOR 237

PRELUDE

Those who love their canine companions—and there are millions of us in the US alone—owe a debt of gratitude to the gray wolf. Every pet dog today carries gray wolf DNA.

So, why so much wolf hate?

That question has vexed me ever since getting my first Alaskan Malamute, Opus, in 1984.

While hiking with Opus, and later, running wilderness trails with the Malamutes who followed her, I often pondered the various theories proposed over the years for when and how early humans first made a connection with wolves, eventually leading to our modern love affair with so many breeds of dogs. How did that happen? I wanted to know, to understand. I knew my Malamutes, so closely related to gray wolves and retaining some wolfish traits and behaviors, provided unique insights, not just on wolf behavior, but also, how the wolf-to-dog transition may have played out (with human help) so many thousands of years ago.

I've bonded with dogs my entire life, starting with the cocker spaniel my family had when I was born. In addition to five Alaskan Malamutes (so far), I've also shared my life, home, and trail running with an Australian shepherd. I've taught puppy obedience classes and, for twenty years (2002–2021), operated an annual, weekend-long dog camp, during which I was able to observe many different breeds in a leash-free, secluded, forested environment. All of those experiences opened my eyes and mind to just how diverse dogs are, and how beneficial to our health and sense of well-being. I also learned how different northern breeds, including Malamutes, are from most other breeds of companion dogs, their traits and behaviors much more wolflike than say, terriers, hounds, or lap dogs.

In 2005, I was abruptly confronted with extreme wolf hate when my two female Malamutes and I moved from Seattle to the Salmon River Mountains of central Idaho. Both dogs were gray and white, and if their tails weren't curled over their backs, they looked like wolves to those unfamiliar with the breed. In Seattle, they had been admired and adored;

no one mistook them for their wild cousins. In Idaho, I was constantly asked (from the safety of a vehicle) if they were wolves. People crossed to the other side of the street to avoid us.

Shocked by this degree of fear, I constantly worried they'd be mistaken for wolves and shot when we ran trails in the national forest. To my bafflement, those attitudes only hardened over time. In hindsight, I now know that my dogs and I had unwittingly landed in the heart—in both time and location—of Idaho's wolf reintroduction effort. It was wildly controversial, with the vast majority of Idaho residents opposed to it.

I kept thinking (and hoping) that if only people opened their minds to understanding wolves, set aside preconceived notions and old myths and followed the science, they might actually appreciate the species' true nature. If they knew wolves want nothing to do with humans, that they aren't a danger to us if we give them space, they might stop fearing and killing them. If only people understood the role wolves play in healthy ecosystems, they might advocate for their conservation, for their reintroduction across the entirety of their former range.

I once asked my father what he thought caused people to fear and hate wolves. "I guess they still believe in fairy tales," he said. Not long after, I started reading and collecting everything I could find about gray wolves and their history and was interested to discover that at least one well-known writer echoed my father's offhand comment.

I told my friends I wanted to write a "wolf book" that would dispel the myths and help create understanding and acceptance. But I'm no expert on wolves. I'm not a wildlife biologist. I've been lucky enough to enjoy a few sightings of wolves in Idaho's forests. I've heard their soul-stirring howls through an open window on a warm summer night. But that's the extent of my real-life experience with them. More than most of the US population, to be sure, but those encounters don't make me an expert. I'm just a woman who loves running with my Malamutes through wild forests inhabited by wolves.

I've always admired wolves and hated seeing them persecuted out of ignorance. Running trails with my Malamutes, our feet and paws on the same ground trod by reintroduced gray wolves, allowed my mind to freely roam, to imagine how ancient humans and wolves may have cooperated and lived close together. Maybe they even ran side-by-side through the forest, as I did with my dogs.

So, I rethought my "wolf book." What if, along with sharing insights gleaned from decades of trail running—the emotional and health benefits of being active in the natural world—I described the joys of living with Malamutes. Would describing their keen senses, behaviors, traits, and characteristics make wolves more relatable to the average person who has never encountered a wolf and probably never will? Maybe I could describe wolves realistically, and factually, while tying in what I've observed in my various Malamutes, the behaviors they inherited from their wolf ancestors undiluted by too much selective breeding for form or utility.

Wolves are intelligent, social, resilient, adaptable, and empathic. So are Malamutes.

Wolves are family-oriented animals and apex predators. So are humans.

Wolves, Malamute, humans: We have more in common that most imagine.

We love our dogs. We have dogs in our lives because gray wolves and ancient humans came together at some point long ago, and that bond led to the domestic dog. What an amazing thing, with a huge and ongoing impact on human societies.

Maybe it's not such a wide chasm to cross, I thought, to ask people to embrace that history, to understand and learn from the positive place wolves have held for thousands of years in most Indigenous cultures, to see their vital role in the health of climate-change-challenged ecosystems today.

It's hard to hate something you come to understand and no longer fear.

Primatologist Jane Goodall wrote, "What you do makes a difference, and you have to decide what kind of difference you want to make." The wolf, for me and so many others, is a symbol of family, loyalty, and wilderness. If my "wolf book" means one less wolf is killed because of human ignorance, I've made a difference.

MAGIC

Running trails in the forest, my dogs and I see a wolf.

In the wild.

Maia, my older Alaskan Malamute, sees him first. She stops, turns, and stares through the trees behind us. I see her tail drop.

Then, following her gaze, I lock eyes with the wolf.

It was July 2006, our first full summer in Idaho. We'd arrived early at the trailhead deep in the Payette National Forest. My two Alaskan Malamutes, Maia and Meadow, and I were eager to start running. The early-morning sun threw long shafts of angled light through the lodgepole pines, and lingering wildfire smoke gave the air a campfire smell. The pattern of sepia light and shadow made the forest feel both dense and spacious. Ruby Creek burbled nearby.

Among the trees, the forest floor was covered in low-growing grasses and wildflowers. There were phlox, its delicate white-lavender flowers providing a cushy carpet and the scent of cloves. Bright orange Indian paintbrush, blue-purple lupine, and tiny blue larkspur added more color. Native huckleberry shrubs, bushy with tiny leaves, lined the trail.

The girls quickly settled into their long-distance trot, which nicely matched my running pace. I watched them moving together along the trail several feet ahead of me, tails feathery plumes of white curled over their hips, waving gently side-to-side as they moved.

I heard a distant raven's caw, but mistook it for a dog's bark until I heard it again. Then Maia spooked a grouse next to the trail. It exploded into the air, wings beating furiously as it lifted from the ground and flew through the trees. My senses sharpened with the sheer joy of running through the forest as well as the knowledge that surprises always lurked.

About a mile in, we heard small branches snapping, the sound of a large animal we couldn't see through the trees. I looked to Maia and Meadow, hoping their body language would tell me what it was. The girls stood still, listening, looking in the direction of the sound as we waited for the tell-tale thump of hooves made by leaping deer or elk. We didn't hear it, but the girls weren't too concerned so I decided not to worry.

"Let's go, girls. It was probably just an elk." Maia resumed her trot, I followed her, and Meadow tucked in behind me. *This*, I thought. *This is what I live for, what makes me happy. Running trails deep in the forest, alone with my dogs.*

Maia and Meadow were less deliberate than I in their approach to trail running. They frequently slowed, even stopped, inhaling scents on the breeze, sniffing a wildlife track, or listening intently to something only they could hear. I continued running, letting them indulge their senses before catching up with me. When they resumed their usual positions, their breathing—lightly panting, tongues out—added a comforting soundtrack to our run.

For four-plus miles, we ran in this casual, easy way. Then, reaching a section of forest so thoroughly burned that no adult trees remained, we lost our shade. The climbing sun was turning up the temperature and the trail had diverted away from Ruby Creek. With no easy access to water for the girls, I decided to turn around.

"Okay, girls, let's go back!" I called out. Ahead of me on the trail, they reacted with joy, turning and dashing past me to retake the lead, then settling into their trot. As much as Maia and Meadow loved running trails, they were always happy when we headed back, relieved to have survived the unknowns of running *away* from the car.

A mile later, the trail brought us close to Ruby Creek again. "Go get a drink, girls." They didn't need much encouragement. Lapping wild water as they slowly walked along the creek bottom, they took their time. Then, back to the trail and running. But within a few yards, Maia, who was just ahead of me, stopped.

Time slows. The wolf stands among the trees, just sixty feet away, directly facing us, watching.

"Maia, stay," I whisper, although she doesn't seem inclined to move. Meadow, observing Maia's body language, turns to look through the trees as well. Her tail drops as she, too, looks directly at the wolf. Telling her to stay, I grab the short loops of climber's rope attached to their collars. Meadow's posture surprises me. She's usually fearless, her tail a plumy flag of confidence when encountering people, dogs, wildlife.

This wolf is new. Different.

Confident that neither girl wants to approach the wolf, I look up again, directly into the wolf's eyes. My heart pounds. I barely breathe.

Sunlight on the wolf's face brings his amber eyes alive. I sense his intelligence, his curiosity. His thick coat resembles Maia's, black-tipped gray, but with brownish tints throughout. He's tall, his long, skinny legs distinguishing him from a Malamute. Relaxed and still, he stands confidently, ears perked, bright eyes studying us.

If there are sounds in the forest, I don't hear them. The world has telescoped to this small patch of land inhabited only by me, my dogs, and a wolf. Nothing else exists.

After what seems an eternity but is only a minute or two, the wolf decides to leave. He turns away and trots—light as air, legs like springs—deeper into the forest. After a few strides, he stops and looks back over his shoulder. Wary, I release the girls' collars and clap my hands together twice, startling both them and the wolf. As wonderful as this encounter is, as rare and magical, I want the wolf to keep moving away before we turn our backs on him.

After he disappears through the dense trees, I'm sorry he's gone and feel badly about breaking the respectful silence of our encounter.

I can barely process what I'm experiencing. Did I imagine it all? My mind races—I'm excited, thrilled, giddy, and grateful. I'm also nervous. Will the wolf follow us, silent among the trees? Was this wolf the animal we heard earlier, perhaps watching us then?

After waiting another couple of minutes, the girls and I continue running along the trail toward the car. At first, their tails are down and they sometimes look behind us or through the trees on either side. As we run a little faster to burn off our nerves, I wonder, *Did the wolf reveal himself to us because my dogs resemble wolves?* Maybe he's a lone wolf, looking for a mate. Or maybe he's a curious yearling, his pack nearby. If so, did other pack members witness our encounter?

The girls' tails soon return to their usual high, confident positions. Their attention focuses on chipmunks and other small forest creatures. They seem to have forgotten about the wolf.

But I don't forget. I'll never forget.

I can't wait to share the experience with my father.

WILD

My father answers a knock on the front door.

"Do you realize your daughter is up in your tree?" a neighbor asks.

Dad steps onto the porch and looks at me sitting on a limb of the maple tree in our front yard. Nodding at the neighbor, my father calmly replies, "Yes."

"Well, aren't you going to do something about it?" the neighbor asks.

"No. She'll come down when she's hungry."

Throughout my childhood, I was a fierce tomboy, tagging along with my three older brothers on foot, bike, and skis. My father encouraged me. The only rule: Keep up or go home.

I had to run. Fortunately, that was something I loved to do—fast as my legs could carry me, pumping my arms, feeling the wind lift my hair from my ears, sneakered feet hitting the dirt or grass with thuds that matched the wildly alive beat of my heart. I became faster and stronger, chasing my brothers as we ran through the woods next to our house with our ski poles, pretending we were downhill skiing as we leaped over fallen tree trunks, making sharp "air" turns. Annual grade school physical-fitness testing included a fifty-yard dash, and I worked hard every fall and spring to beat my previous time. When my father described me to others as a tomboy, I heard the pride in his voice.

After grade school, the word *shouldn't* robbed me of the joy of running.

"You shouldn't run so much. It's not ladylike," my mother's mother admonished.

"Boys don't like girls who can outrun them," added my mother. "You shouldn't be such a tomboy."

Despite my love of running, I didn't try out for track in junior or senior high. In the winter, I continued the alpine skiing lessons I'd started in fourth grade (my father's idea), focusing on slalom racing. When I was a sophomore in high school, my PE teacher suggested I try out for gymnastics. I did uneven parallel bars and trampoline, and while fun, I wasn't a natural. During the summer months, in addition to water skiing and swimming, I rode my brother's old ten-speed bike for exercise and freedom, a way to be alone, to get away from home. I shot baskets with my brothers and father.

Meanwhile, my mother insisted I make the salad for dinner every night, set the table, wash the dishes, vacuum, and clean the bathrooms. My brothers didn't have indoor chores.

By the end of my sophomore year, I had stopped running.

My father, who loved me unconditionally, nurtured and encouraged my athleticism. My mother, however, was always just beyond my reach. A narcissist, she was emotionally distant. A competent but (toward me at least) uninterested caregiver. Not athletic herself, she had no interest in any sport. She wanted me to be like her, pursuing indoor, feminine activities. I tried but consistently failed to interest or please her.

Another difference: Despite my mother's objections, my father insisted children should grow up with pets, especially dogs. In one of my earliest memories, I'm three or four, sitting under our big family-room table, which is covered by a cloth that hangs long over the edges. Rusty, our ginger cocker spaniel, shelters in my embrace, shaking at the sound of thunder. I hold him closely as we both hide, finding safety with each other.

When I was in third grade, we got Trinket, a pet store beagle-mix puppy. I watched my father train her with kindness. Dad taught her an assortment of tricks using carrots as rewards.

Our family dogs also loved me unconditionally. Somehow, despite my young age, I understood how special and important, even crucial, that bond was.

On the eve of my seventeenth birthday, my mother asked my father to leave. It was a week before Christmas, 1973, my junior year. It happened quietly, after I'd gone to bed eagerly anticipating my father's return that night from a two-week overseas business trip. When I got up the next morning—my birthday—I was surprised to see my mother sitting in the family room, face red and puffy, clutching a damp wad of tissues.

"Where's Dad?" I asked.

"Your father left last night."

Somehow, I instantly knew what she meant; I ran back to my bedroom. Eventually, I called the boy I was dating and asked him to come get me. I needed to get away from her.

I wasn't given an explanation by either parent.

The split was a shock to all who knew them, and it devastated me. My birthday and Christmas became symbols of sadness and loss, no longer the happy occasions they always had been. In retrospect, it was probably awkward for everyone. My older brothers were already out of the house, in college or living on their own. They never checked on me, nor did extended family. Dad called me periodically, but I rarely saw him in person. I'd never felt more alone or adrift. My grades suffered, and teachers asked if I was okay.

I kept my grief and confusion to myself, but clung to Dave, my boyfriend, who was two years older. I made it through my senior year, during which my mother used me as her confidant when she started dating and as her chaperone when she went to Las Vegas with her new boyfriend.

The summer I graduated from high school, with my mother's approval and encouragement, I married Dave. It was the only way I knew to escape the trauma of my disintegrating family and the lack of support or interest from anyone. After the wedding, Dave and I moved—with my cat, Blue—to a college town where he had a sports scholarship. I found a full-time job as a bookkeeper. We soon added a shelter dog, a Border collie-mix we named Trigger, to our household. A few months later, Blue's kidneys failed and she died, a keenly felt loss that added to the pile of the others I'd endured.

Dave wanted us to start a family, but I knew—deep inside where little-understood convictions take root and grow—that I didn't want children. Ever. I feared becoming my mother.

I started running again.

In my bones, I also knew I'd made a mistake getting married. My mother was unsympathetic. "You made your bed, now lie in it," she told me. Not wanting to fail, to disappoint her *yet again*, I hung in there with the marriage. But really, I didn't know what to do.

That's when my father reappeared in my life in a significant way: He sent me checks and urged me to sign up for college classes. I took some law and justice and anthropology courses. As my father suspected and hoped, I loved college and decided to pursue a degree.

My inner child was eager to start running again, and in late 1975, I signed up for a recreational jogging class offered by the college. Jogging was a new thing, seen by many as an odd activity. The class covered basics like appropriate clothing, shoes, stride, arm swing, tempo, breathing, and building endurance. After brief lectures on technique, we ran loops around the perimeter of the school's indoor basketball court for two or three sessions. Eventually, the instructor encouraged us to move outside, where we ran on campus sidewalks. That's when it clicked for me: *This feels great. I feel happy. Alive.* Running outdoors brought me brief periods of peace during an unhappy marriage.

Running also gave me confidence.

A year later, after eighteen months of marriage and with several college credits under my belt, I knew I needed to leave. My mother said I was running away from my problems. "You know I love you, but you can't stay with me," she said one weekend when I visited, distraught, hoping for a temporary place to stay while I figured out what to do next. Her words left me feeling helpless and hopeless. Alone, again.

"There's a simple solution," my father told me over the phone later that same weekend. "Move in with me."

That's what I did. As always, my father gave me a soft place to land.

Sadly, I had to leave Trigger with my soon-to-be ex-husband, adding a fresh heartbreak to the list. I didn't miss the marriage, but I sorely missed Trigger, and Blue, already gone. I also learned a lesson that had long-lasting impact on how I approached pets in the future: Getting a dog (or any companion animal) is a commitment for the life of the animal. Unless I knew I could keep it with me throughout its lifetime, I shouldn't have one. Nor should I acquire one jointly with anyone else because I could lose the option to make important decisions about its welfare.

After I moved in with my father, he encouraged me to enroll in college full-time, and paid my tuition so I could do that. He helped me get my life back on track.

I attended the University of Washington, and later got a part-time job to cover food and rent an apartment. As my inner tomboy/athlete re-emerged, I started lifting weights and playing volleyball. And I ran, more than ever before. Embracing the growing trend of road running with zeal, I ran through campus, along the tree-lined streets of Greek Row and nearby Ravenna Park, and around Green Lake, a popular Seattle park with a three-mile running path around the lake. Running became a daily feature of my life, a habit I thoroughly enjoyed. It got me outside regardless of weather, which boosted my mood and cleared my head for studying.

After graduating from UW in May 1980 with a degree in history, I moved to Tacoma, thirty-five miles south of Seattle, where I would attend law school for three years. There, I grew as an athlete. Running, weight lifting, cycling, and swimming were perfect ways to relieve the intense stress of my first year studying law. After joining the local YMCA, I met other runners and trained with them, which led to competing in weekend road races. I also discovered trail running, learning my way around fifteen miles of dirt trails in Tacoma's beautiful forested Pt. Defiance Park. I *loved* running trails.

In August, after surviving my first year of law school, a guy I was dating (a fellow runner) drove me to Mt. Rainier's Sunrise parking area for a trail run. Despite being a native Seattleite, I had never been to Mt. Rainier in summer and was keen to see what all the hubbub was about.

Instead of hiking boots, we both wore the latest running shoe, the Nike Equator. Designed for road running, the Equator featured an aggressive waffle tread and a wide heel for stability. Perfect for trails, it turned out. They were an exponential leap in trail-shoe design, replacing lightweight hiking boots and making trail running easier and safer.

In the parking lot, we strapped on bulky, single-pocket fanny packs more suited for distance hiking. Filled with a water bottle, a PB&J sandwich, a trail guide, and extra clothing, my fanny pack was heavy and bounced against my hip bones with every step. No matter how tight I pulled the waist strap, the pack bounced; I was glad when an uphill section slowed us to a walk.

Despite the distracting fanny pack, when we reached Grand Park, I was gobsmacked. Standing in awe, I drank it all in. I'd never seen anything so beautiful. It felt like I'd stumbled into the opening scene of *The Sound of Music*.

It's said that Grand Park offers the best view of Mt. Rainier, and I found that to be true. We were treated to the sight of the mountain's snow-covered peak, so close it nearly overwhelmed me, taking up most of the blue sky in that direction.

As I learned that day, August is Rainier's peak wildflower month. Hundreds of species bloomed there, a riot of amazing colors, variety, and abundance. While I didn't know their names, I was smitten with them all. Smiling ear to ear, I reveled in a feeling of intense joy as we ran on the narrow dirt trail through the pinks, purples, whites, and oranges, my head swiveling as I tried to take it all in without tripping.

This is so much better than hiking, I thought.

During the remaining two years of law school, my road-running skills grew. Entering several 5K and 10K road races, I did well enough to bring home ribbons and trophies, which gave me positive feedback on my progress. Always eager to push myself, to discover my abilities and limits, I decided to try a marathon, which upped my training distances. A week before the law school graduation ceremony, I ran the Tacoma Marathon and finished with a time of three hours and thirty-six minutes, second woman overall. This was a huge surprise, given that my goal was simply to finish. Despite sore leg muscles, I walked on air for days afterward. The sense of accomplishment was empowering and intoxicating and I wanted more. Running *and* distance. Dirt, trees, *and* wildflowers. All of it.

After graduation in May 1983, my sole job was studying for the three-day Washington state bar exam set for late July. I received some excellent advice from Don, the man who had taken me for that run to Grand Park: Make running part of your bar exam preparation. "The exam is basically a three-day endurance race," he told me. "You need to be fit, physically and mentally. Train for it like you would a race."

I trained hard for the next several weeks, running every morning and studying for the rest of the day and well into the night.

For six hours on day one of the exam, I sat on a plastic chair at one of many tables in a large conference room filled with other aspiring attorneys, my hand cramping from filling bluebooks with handwritten answers. On my way home, I drove to Green Lake and ran three circuits around the lake, a total of nine miles, while mentally critiquing my exam answers. I fell into bed that night exhausted but unable to sleep, mind racing, worried I'd already failed.

The next day I did it again, another grueling six hours of reading questions and writing answers, followed by a run at Green Lake, this time two circuits, or six miles. That night, completely spent, I was able to sleep for a few hours.

The third day of the exam was a half session, the dreaded ethics portion, rumored to be the most-failed part of the test. I walked out feeling good about my answers and celebrated with a single lap around Green Lake, too exhausted to do more. Then the long wait for results began.

In early October 1983, I received the coveted thick envelope[1] in the mail. I'd passed the bar exam in a year when nearly 50 percent failed (and

---

1 A thin envelope contained a one-page letter advising that you had failed the exam. A thick envelope contained a congratulatory letter as well as forms to join the bar association. Every exam taker knew the difference.

more than 60 percent failed the ethics section). I credited my preparation—in particular, running—with giving me an edge.

Officially an attorney, I now needed a job.

OPUS

In December 1983, I moved from coastal Washington, with its ubiquitous green landscapes, mountain peaks in all directions, and abundant clouds and rain, to the "inland empire," the state's relatively flat, open, and often brown (where it wasn't irrigated) agricultural heart. I accepted an associate position with a two-attorney firm, an ideal setting in which to learn how to practice a spectrum of law from true mentors; the firm handled family and criminal law as well as wills and estates. I sorely missed the lush terrain I'd grown up with as I settled into an apartment in Grandview, a tiny agricultural town. My classmates thought I was crazy. Why wasn't I competing for the big law firm jobs in Seattle? I couldn't explain it. All I knew was that I needed to put distance between myself and the family members, other than my father, from whom I felt an increasing estrangement. I also wanted to stand on my own two feet.

I quickly fell in with a group of other young professionals who shared my outdoor passions, especially running and cycling. Spending many early-morning hours training on quiet rural roads, we did 5K and 10K road races together and dabbled in triathlons, swimming laps in the town's outdoor pool to train. We did a marathon together. It was a fun time and I pushed myself to run faster and farther. With no nearby forest trails, trail running wasn't even on our radar, and I missed running on dirt.

One early weekday morning during the autumn of 1984, I was running country roads outside Sunnyside, a slightly larger agricultural town next to Grandview, with my then-boyfriend, John. Sunnyside was surrounded by fields of hops, asparagus, and fruit orchards, with a few acres of mint and a few small dairies. Many of the orchards were being replaced with vineyards, a nod to eastern Washington's burgeoning wine trade and tourism.

The sun was barely above the horizon as birds noisily greeted the day. With no vehicle traffic and only an occasional farmhouse, it felt as though we had the world to ourselves. We talked amiably as we ran an eight-mile loop route.

Suddenly, stealthily, a big wolflike dog started tagging along with us. Long-legged, silver fur with black tips and a hint of a mask around brown eyes set wide above a long, narrow, black-nosed muzzle. Wanting to greet the beautiful interloper, I stopped and turned to face him, calling softly, "Hey pup, hey pup, come here, say hello..." while holding out my hand. Keeping a wary distance, the dog eyed us curiously, then sniffed something in the ditch alongside the road. Rebuffed, John and I eased back into our run. I figured the dog would go home, wherever home was; farm houses were few and far between out there, and we still had three miles back to town.

I was wrong. The dog kept running with us.

Watching him trotting easily just ahead of us, I marveled at his elegant gait. So carefree and bouncy. *Oh, to run so easily!* I thought, envious. Occasionally, he would suddenly veer off the road, jumping across the wide ditch into a field to investigate some movement or smell, then return at a gallop from behind us, catching and passing within a couple of feet to quietly resume lead position.

I thought I was in love with John, but in that moment, I was more in love with the dog, and with the idea of running with a wolflike dog.

I especially loved that he ran with us but stayed independent of us. He was making his own decisions, and on that particular morning, he decided it would be an adventure to hang with a couple of runners. I imagined being an ancient human exploring her world with a wolf companion.

John and I hardly spoke while the dog ran with us. So focused on watching the dog, intrigued by his beauty, by what he might do next, I'd nearly forgotten John was there.

Our route eventually brought us back into Sunnyside proper, where John and I lived in the heart of town. As we began to encounter light traffic, I was sure the dog would reverse course and go home. Worried about cars, I even encouraged him, half-heartedly, to do so. Instead, he stayed close to us, following us right up onto our front porch.

Finally, I was able to touch him, to sink my fingers into his thick, soft coat and say a proper hello. As I cooled down and my heart rate slowly returned to post-run normal, I fell deeply into his bright and curious brown eyes as he panted, doing his own cool-down.

The dog had no collar, no identification. He refused to follow me inside, so while John sat with him on the porch, I fetched a bowl of water and put it down for him. Both John and I had showers to take, jobs to get to; I hoped the dog would still be there when I was done dressing. Rushing out the door to work, I was greeted by an empty porch and a keen sense of disappointment.

The dog made an indelible impression on me, one that stayed with me all day, always in my thoughts. I couldn't get him or our running together out of my mind. It was like I'd converted to some new cult—the Church of Running with Wolf-Dogs—and was overwhelmed with the joy of being accepted. I wanted more.

Perhaps it was time to bring a dog into my life. Not only did I have a visceral need to bond with a dog, I was done with school, I had a good job, was in a good relationship with someone who also loved dogs, and living in a house we'd purchased together. I was ready.

Since the internet had yet to become part of daily life, I went to the town library and checked out the American Kennel Club's hardback book on dog breeds. Browsing through its pages of full-color photos, I felt like an addict taking a hit after a long period of abstention.

Over the next week, John and I talked about getting a dog. He was on board, but the decision was mine; we agreed the dog would be mine as well. I would pay for it and be solely responsible for the costs of food and veterinary care.

Using the AKC book as my guide, I determined that the dog who had run with us was a Siberian husky: independent but friendly and people-oriented, strong with good endurance, intelligent. The only downside: roaming. If given the chance, the book said, huskies will jump enclosures and run off, returning only when they're ready. That certainly rang true, based on my brief experience with the running dog.

Curious about similar wolflike breeds—mostly northern breeds—that would make good running companions, I read about the Alaskan Malamute, listed right after the Siberian husky. Similar in appearance, Malamutes also had great strength and endurance, as well as intelligence. But what really caught my attention: Malamutes were one-person dogs, very attached to their humans. Unlike huskies, Malamutes stayed close to home. They didn't roam. I was sold. I wanted a Malamute.

I quickly learned that Alaskan Malamutes are an uncommon breed. An ancient, or "basal" breed, they are believed to have accompanied Paleo-Eskimo people from Siberia to settle the Arctic some 4,500 years ago. Thought to be bred by the Malimiut Inupiaq people of Alaska's Norton Sound region, they were utilitarian dogs, used to pull heavy sledges and alert to seals and their blowholes. They were also used on hunts, to alert to and distract large predators, like bears.

During the Klondike Gold Rush of 1896, they—along with other sled-dog breeds—were valued for their freight-hauling ability. The historic 1925 Serum Run from Anchorage to Nome and Rear Admiral Richard Byrd's expedition to the South Pole in 1929 made heavy use of the breed as well. During World War I, 450 Alaskan Malamutes were shipped to France to deliver supplies to French army troops isolated in mountain outposts; Mals were later used in World War II (primarily in Greenland) to sniff for mines, carry weapons, and serve as search-and-rescue dogs.

Losses from service in World War II all but eliminated the breed, which had received AKC recognition in 1935. By 1947, it was estimated that only about thirty registered dogs remained.

The day after I'd made the decision to seek a Malamute, the same dog appeared and ran with us again! A few days earlier, John and I had repeated the route, hoping to see the dog, but no luck. Now, here he was! As before, he seemed to appear out of nowhere, as if conjured from the early-morning mist by my desire. He ran with us for a few miles, came back to our house and accepted some water on the porch, then disappeared as effortlessly as he had the time before.

Taking this second visit as a sign validating my decision to get a dog and my choice of a Malamute, I began the process of finding a Malamute breeder. This turned out to be harder than I'd thought. Locally, most folks, including some of my friends in Grandview and Sunnyside, had bird-hunting dogs who were never allowed inside their homes. I vowed to raise my dog the way my father had taught me: as a member of the family, welcome indoors, even on the bed.

Even though Seattle was 175 miles away on the other side of the Cascade Mountain Range, I followed the "pets for sale" ads in the Sunday *Seattle Times* every week with a religious fervor, impatiently hoping. I made phone calls trying to track down breeders in the Pacific Northwest, without luck. Eventually, in the spring of 1985, I saw an ad in the *Seattle Times* for two Malamute puppies, the last two of a litter born near Issaquah, close to where I grew up. After a phone call, I arranged to drive over to see the pups.

I was greeted by a bald-headed young man. He explained that he'd intended to keep the two pups from the litter of six—a male and a female—for himself, but had been recently diagnosed with cancer and realized he needed to find them homes after all. I quickly fell for the female. She was four months old, black and white, and her ears already stood upright. With a striking black mask around her eyes and a black stripe down her long muzzle, she was soft and puppy wiggly. I couldn't resist.

The puppy and I drove back over the Cascades; she rode in a big cardboard box on the passenger seat of my Subaru (this was before plastic shell or wire dog crates were common). It was her first car ride and I tried to calm her with my voice and by stroking her head as she whimpered. I told her I was going to name her Opus, after the penguin in the *Bloom County* comic strip, and as homage to my lifelong love of playing the piano.

So began my love affair with Malamutes, a journey of letting wolflike dogs help me understand and appreciate the natural world.

At a time when I questioned most everything about my life—work, family, relationships—this felt entirely right.

Opus started running with me on country roads when she was about six months old, gradually building up endurance. By 1986, having broken up with John and tiring of small-town life where something as simple as seeing a movie required a forty-five-minute drive each way, I decided that Opus and I needed to return to the Seattle area. For a while, for both work-related and housing reasons, we moved frequently. Because she ran with me, Opus didn't need a large yard for exercise but she did need some fenced outdoor space.

Our first summer back in western Washington, Opus and I started hiking in the Cascades east of Seattle. I'd look at maps or read a trail guide, choose a destination, and we'd head out. Opus gave me confidence and courage to explore remote forest trails by myself, or more accurately, without human companionship. We spent many happy hours in the mountains, finding pristine, green-blue alpine lakes tucked among thick stands of evergreens and scrambles of granite boulders strewn below jagged peaks. Rarely encountering other people, I felt like Opus and I had this vast wilderness to ourselves, sharing it only with the creatures who called it home.

During this time, I also took up cross-country (x/c) skiing, which allowed us to take advantage of our beloved hiking trails in the winter when they were covered with several feet of snow. Opus loved running on snow, and the Cascades had places to ski where she could join me. Her enthusiasm made x/c skiing more fun for me and made the ninety-minute drive from home to access groomed ski trails worthwhile.

During the winter of 1988–1989, Seattle was hit with a significant snowfall—rare, but not entirely unusual. The snow started early in the evening, and accumulated fast enough that I thought it might be fun to x/c ski through the neighborhood. I waited until about ten that night, knowing there would be few cars out that late (Seattleites don't have much experience with driving in the snow and so tend to avoid it). At the time, I was renting a house north of Seattle, and wouldn't normally have gone out alone at that hour, even with Opus. But, with the new snow and people huddled indoors, I couldn't resist. Because I couldn't ski and hold a leash at the same time, I decided to leave Opus home.

I headed out, skiing down the middle of my residential street, thoroughly enjoying the magical scene. Gently drifting snowflakes blanketed my city suburb, creating a welcome hush. Streetlights cast enormous halos of illuminated snowflakes, providing plenty of light for me to navigate; porch lights from houses lining the streets added to the glow.

While gliding first on one ski, then the other, I felt one of my skis briefly catch, as often happened in the mountains when I crossed a pine cone or small twig. Brushing it off, I kept going; then it happened again. Surprised, I stopped and looked down and back at the tail of the ski. On which I saw a pair of large dog paws. Turning my upper body for a better look, I was greeted by a long-legged, gray husky or Malamute, tail wagging happily.

I'd never seen this dog before. Clearly, he was out enjoying the snow, just like me. My skis still facing forward, I twisted as far around as I could, extended my gloved hand, and softly said, "Hey buddy!" Excited at my greeting, the dog rose up on his hind legs and gently placed his front paws on my shoulders to return my hello with a lick to my face. I was so surprised that I fell to the side, butt and shoulders on the snow-covered street. Tail wagging enthusiastically, he planted his front paws next to my right shoulder and gave my face another tongue swipe. Giggling, I watched the dog prance around me as though this was exactly the game he had been hoping to play. Finally, after struggling to get upright on my skis, I dusted snow off my butt and went on my way. I hoped this dog would be my companion that evening, but he trotted off in the opposite direction.

I spent another thirty minutes skiing through my neighborhood, but all I could think about was the dog, how he reminded me of the running dog in Sunnyside, the dog that started my love affair with northern breeds, with dogs that look like wolves. I seemed to attract them as much as they attracted me.

While I didn't set out to do it, somehow, I was creating a life where

I relied upon Malamutes rather than humans for companionship in the outdoors. Though Malamutes are visually intimidating and very good at keeping unwelcome strangers at a distance, most are people-loving and friendly. I enjoyed the quiet interactions Opus and I shared—watching her move gleefully through snow or trot down a dirt trail, sharing her delight in finding a wild stream to drink from or a fresh track to follow. With Opus beside me I was willing to go places I would never have gone alone.

One October weekend, friends invited me to join them on an overnight camping trip in the Cascades. The plan was to hike in on Saturday morning, camp that night, and hike back out Sunday afternoon. That Saturday morning, though, I was scheduled to run a 10K, so we revised the plan: my then-boyfriend Ron would pack in our tent, cooking gear, and most of the food, so all I needed to carry in that afternoon was my sleeping bag, extra clothes, and Opus's food. By the time I arrived, they'd have camp set up and dinner waiting.

I ran the race and did better than anticipated, winning my age group, so I waited around for the awards ceremony to collect my prize. I then went home and showered, put Opus and our gear in the car, and drove to the trailhead, about two-and-a-half hours away. We arrived much later than I had planned; as Opus and I started up the trail, the sun was dropping toward the horizon. On the way, I encountered a couple coming down the trail. They confirmed that a group had set up camp at the lake that was our destination.

Opus and I continued hiking. The trail became steep, switchbacking through scree dotted with short bushes and shrubs. Worried about the waning daylight, I moved as fast as I could with a full pack. Soon, we arrived at a high, sharp ridge. From there, the trail dropped steeply down into thick trees and utter darkness. I could hear my friends' voices and yelled their names several times. No reply. I realized that if they were talking around a campfire, they weren't going to hear me. Stupidly, I had no flashlight; it was in the gear that had gone ahead with Ron.

I spent several minutes on the ridge, frantically calling out, hoping they'd hear me or that maybe one of them would magically appear. With daylight all but gone, I decided the safest thing for me to do was return to the car; at least I was familiar with the trail back. In the light of the rising full moon, I might be able to navigate through the scree and the open hillside below. Heading down toward the lake and my friends through the dense trees, I would have had no visibility.

"Let's go home, Opus," I said. She didn't care where we went as long as we were moving. Like all Malamutes, Opus liked being in the lead and happily started back the way we'd come. Even though I couldn't always see the trail as we went through sections of scree—all the big rocks blended together in the low light—I could follow Opus's fluffy white tail. Curled high over her back, it was illuminated by the moon as if by a spotlight. Opus could see and smell exactly where the trail was. She got us safely off that mountain and back to the car.

DISTANCE

In 1989, at a regular training session with my Seattle YMCA running club, I met a woman who, like me, was in her early thirties and ran trail ultras.

"What's an ultra?" I asked, a little embarrassed that I'd never heard the term before.

"Any race longer than a marathon," she replied. She explained that most races were 50K, 50M, 100K and 100M. She'd run the Western States 100 in California's Sierras, was going to again, and was keen to find local people to train with her on mountain trails east of Seattle.

"I'd love to join you," I offered, shyly, not knowing anything about her—or training for ultras, for that matter. Her legs were muscular and she was impressively fit. I figured she knew some things about running trails, things I could learn. The question was, could I keep up?

Just that simply, my next love affair—with distance trail running—began.

I started running trails in earnest with a small group of new friends, including the woman who initially invited me. A few of us formed a mid-week afternoon training cadre. A larger group of runners met on Saturday mornings, quickly dispersing in small clusters across the mountain, based on pace. At first, I was torn, missing the long Saturday-morning training runs on roads with my YMCA clubmates. Before long, though, the siren call of the forest trails claimed me, and I only ran with my "roadie" friends one day a week after work.

Those early trail-running companions shared invaluable knowledge and training tips. They had run iconic hundred-mile races like Leadville (started in 1983), Vermont (1989), and Wasatch Front (1980). The course for Western States, which in 1977 was the first one-hundred-mile ultra trail race, was the same as that of the Tevis Cup, a one-day equine endurance event started in 1955. In 1974, a man named Gordy Ainsleigh decided to *run* the Tevis Cup. Twenty-three hours and forty-two minutes later, Gordy arrived at the finish line, proving that a runner could cover the entire trail within the competition's twenty-four-hour time limit.

I marveled at the strength and endurance it would require to complete such a feat. It seemed impossible. A marathon? Sure, I'd done a few by 1990. But a hundred miles? On trails?

My friends assured me I could do it, with proper training and commitment. I wasn't so sure. Plus, I didn't want to train so seriously that I couldn't run with Opus. She had first dibs on my time.

Tiger Mountain, a state-managed forest thirty miles east of Seattle and just past the town where I first met Opus, became our go-to place to train for trail ultras. It offered eighty miles of single-track trails across the flanks of its three peaks (Tiger I, II, and III). With our flexible work schedules, our weekday afternoon group ran every week, year-round, for two to three hours each time, depending on daylight. In the first few years, I often brought Opus with me, and she loved it as much as I did.

The larger group met Saturday mornings for longer runs, usually between fifteen and thirty miles. Depending on pace and route, we might be running for four to six hours. Opus stayed home for those. In the summer, when there were no nearby races to attend, a few of us might venture farther east into the Cascades to train. A section of the Pacific Crest Trail from Snoqualmie Pass north—with its steady, six-mile climb to the Kendall Katwalk—was a favorite route. From that vantage point, we were rewarded with spectacular views of Mt. Rainier and jagged peaks in the Alpine Lakes Wilderness; the pristine, blue-tinted, snow-fed lakes sprinkled below those peaks, twinkling like jewels in the sunlight.

In late summer, when most of the lower-elevation snow had melted, Rainier's trails—sections of the Wonderland Trail, as well as trails to Spray Park, Moraine Park, and Grand Park—became our annual pilgrimages. We lived at sea level, and Rainier offered us altitude training, critical because many ultra-distance trail races were run high in the mountains of various western states. Rainier provided challenging, well-maintained trails and unmatched views of glaciers, trees, streams, and wildflowers. We always brought disposable cameras to capture some of this stunning beauty.

I'd found my tribe. Well, my human tribe, at least.

After running my first ultra-distance race in July 1991—Knee Knacker, a thirty-mile event in the mountains of British Columbia—I was hooked. And not just by the challenge and beauty of the course, which I finished with a time of 7:56[2]. It wasn't just the sense of accomplishment, the emotional high; I was hooked on running through new and wild terrain, on meeting other runners and volunteers, and on the camaraderie. The vibe was way more laid-back and friendly than anything I'd experienced even at small road races.

I vividly remember one Saturday morning trail run with Opus in 1992, soon after I started dating Mike. A tall, dusty-blonde engineer and tri-athlete who loved dogs, he had responded to a personals ad I'd placed in a Seattle-area weekly newspaper. Though new to trail running, he was eager to join me. As we headed down the main trail back to the parking area, we encountered a young couple with a miniature poodle hiking up. Mike and I stopped briefly as Opus and the poodle greeted each other. When asked what sort of dog Opus was, I replied, "Alaskan Malamute," adding, as I usually did, "bigger than a husky." After petting the dogs, Mike and I resumed running down the trail, Opus leading the way. As the couple continued hiking up the mountain, I overheard the man say to his companion, "Now that's a *real* dog."

Eventually, Opus started telling me she preferred shorter runs. Unfortunately, at that point I was so in love with trail running and racing that I was increasing the distance and intensity of my runs, going too far for her aging joints. She began easing into running retirement just as I got seriously involved in ultra-distance trail racing. Our runs together were now exclusively midweek morning road outings in the neighborhood. It was a hard transition for me to accept, but my commitment to Opus took precedence over my new addiction. I gave her the exercise and attention she needed, found time to run trails on weekends, and worked as a lawyer, keeping a roof over our heads and food in our bowls.

I loved my new focus on running in the forest on single-track trails, but it was different without Opus. Gone was the quiet contemplation of being with a non-verbal, trail-savvy companion whose body language alerted me to creatures in the forest. To feeling in sync with her and with nature.

---

2 For comparison, my first marathon, in 1983, was 26.2 miles, four miles shorter than Knee Knacker. It took me 3:36 to run.

For the next several years, I played in the forest with my human friends, but something key and elemental was missing.

A sense of safety. That was what I missed. Without Opus, that sense of security in the wilderness with my über-aware dog was gone. The humans talked too much about things like professional sports, things I had no interest in. Birds singing, water burbling, the susurration of wind in tree branches: Nature's orchestra was overwhelmed by human chit-chat and laughter.

Eventually, when Opus was around ten, our runs were replaced by daily walks and an occasional hike. I was still spending lots of time running forest trails, focusing on gaining speed and endurance for ultra-distance events throughout the Pacific Northwest and California. That was my way of coping with not having Opus as a trail companion.

Without her presence and awareness, though, I was running *through* nature, not as a part of nature. I barely observed what was around me. Instead, I focused on myself, my pace-per-mile, my heart rate, how my legs felt, how my feet felt, whether I was overheating.

In her old age, Opus developed some health issues, including non-cancerous tumors in her abdomen and left upper thigh. The tumors caused fluid to collect, resulting in enormous squishy bulges that made it hard for her to get up and walk. The vet drained the fluid several times, only to see it return within two or three weeks.

Finally, the vet recommended surgery to remove them; later, he showed them to me. They looked like small, polished river stones in various shades of pink, sage, and gray. So smooth, even pretty, yet so destructive to Opus. The vet said he couldn't get them all, and warned they might return. They did. And, once more, I asked Opus to endure surgery so we could stay together longer. The second surgery bought her a few good months. But not long after she turned fourteen, the tumors, fluid, and swelling returned. Her mobility was already compromised by aging joints and loss of muscle mass, and I couldn't put her through another surgery and recovery.

With heavy heart, in April 1999, I said goodbye to Opus at my father's rural property, where he and I agreed she would be buried. Her head in my lap, I told her I loved her as the vet injected pentobarbital into a vein in her leg. I couldn't face seeing her in the grave my father had dug with his tractor, so Mike and my father wrapped her in a dog blanket I had crocheted for her years earlier. They laid her in her final resting place, then shoveled the earth over her.

My father planted a dogwood tree over her grave.

PUPPIES

From my home in a Seattle suburb, I traveled west over freeways and then on a ferry across Puget Sound to the unfamiliar undulating country roads of the Olympic Peninsula. Dripping from a recent rain, dense stands of evergreens and ten-foot-tall rhododendrons with enormous red and pink blooms crowded the two-lane roads.

An unseen canine energy was pulling me through this atmospheric landscape, a natural magnet I couldn't resist: a Malamute puppy.

Just when I thought I was lost, I spied the house number I was looking for on a lone roadside mailbox. Turning onto a narrow dirt driveway that meandered through dense, old-growth forest, I headed toward an opening bathed in sunlight. An older, slightly run-down home claimed most of a clearing. Nearby were a handful of worn outbuildings, a large barn, and a small fenced pasture. Old vehicles and machinery were strewn about. *Is this the right place?* I wondered.

Parking, I turned off my car's engine, feeling uneasy until a large Alaskan Malamute loped up to greet me through the car window. Swishing his fluffy tail in welcome, eyes and ears alert, he flashed me a toothy smile. Soon, he was joined by a middle-age couple wearing jeans and warm jackets. Exiting the car, I allowed the Malamute to sniff my hand before I scratched his chin in hello. The couple, charming and friendly, introduced themselves and told me that the Mal I had just met was their stud.

"Would you like to see the puppies?" the wife asked.

With that question, any sense of unease was immediately replaced with excitement.

As I followed the man toward the barn, the woman said to come find them in the house when I was done. I liked that they were trusting me to be alone with the puppies, allowing me time to observe them without any pressure.

Days earlier, I'd read an ad in the *Seattle Times* classifieds listing Malamute puppies for sale. Three months had passed since my heart-wrenching goodbye to Opus. Despite Mike's reservations that it was too soon, that I wasn't ready, the tingle of excitement I felt when I read the ad told me that I *was* ready. Accosting strangers walking their dogs at Green Lake, asking if I could pet their dog because I was so lonely without one, was getting old.

By 1999, buying from "backyard breeders" was considered almost as bad as buying a puppy at a pet store, and I knew to be wary of breeders listing puppies for sale in newspapers. So, when I called in response to their ad, I questioned these breeders closely. They assured me they loved Malamutes and were producing infrequent litters out of love of the breed and as pets, not show dogs. The price they were asking seemed to bear that out: $200, lower than show-dog breeders by half. When they said they bred carefully and selectively, with good temperament paramount, I was sold. It was exactly what I wanted to hear.

On their part, the couple seemed to like that I'd already had a Malamute and knew and loved the breed. They also said I was the first to call, so would get pick of the litter. While that definitely excited me, I was still skeptical; when I set out on that morning, I told Mike I was only going to take a look at these puppies. I wasn't going to fall for cuteness and bring one home that day. I'd wait a few days and go back if I liked what I saw. Mike laughed at that. "You'll come home with one," he predicted.

Preparing for my visit, I'd read up on puppy testing and learned that there were several ways to handle puppies to help determine which was best for you—shy or outgoing, calm or boisterous. The testing involved seeing how a puppy reacted to your touch, to being held off the ground or gently rolled onto its back, and to sudden sounds. I knew I wanted a confident dog, but not an overbearing and aggressive one, nor a shy and timid one. Like Goldilocks, I wanted a puppy who was "just right."

Entering the barn, feeling as giddy as a five-year-old on Christmas morning, I peeked through the opening of the first stall on the left. Roughly twelve feet square, the stall had a two-foot-high plywood barrier blocking the entrance. Its floor was covered in clean, dry straw and eight squirming, wiggling Malamute puppies.

I smiled, holding my breath and watching quietly. Born eight weeks earlier, there were four males, four females. Their coat colors ranged from black and white to gray and white. Adorable fluff balls, they wrestled and tumbled, growling playfully at each other. One occasionally screamed at some sharp-toothed offense committed by a sibling.

The man urged me to step into the stall and join the puppies. Tentatively stepping over the barrier, I stood still, smiling broadly. All puppy eyes turned to me, excitement and curiosity shining bright. Investigating me boldly or shyly, depending on temperament, some lifted a front paw to my jeans-covered shins in welcome. "Me, Me! Play with me!" they seemed to be urging in a chorus of puppy squeals. Then, as quickly as they'd greeted me, they resumed wrestling with each other.

I slowly maneuvered to one side of the stall and sat in the straw with my legs straight out, back against the wall. Once on their level, I instantly became a toy for the puppies to play with. The man quietly withdrew, leaving me alone with eight eager new friends: my version of nirvana.

It hit me just how daunting my puppy temperament-testing task would be. That sheet of paper, with each test listed and a grid for scoring individual puppies, just wouldn't work. There was no way I could put eight individual pups through each test on my own *and* record their responses. Instead, I resolved to rely on observation and memory.

First, I had to identify each puppy: boy or girl, gray or black, shy or outgoing. They were a constantly moving bundle, a busy hive, and I could hardly keep them straight. One thing I could do, however, was discern male from female.

A couple of the boys immediately jumped all over me, playing, biting my jeans, shoe laces, fingers, and each other, wrestling and falling off my legs and coming back for more. They were pushy and aggressive with each other and me. While enjoyable to play with, they eliminated themselves from consideration as too rambunctious.

Focusing on the remaining six, I watched them interact with each other. One black-and-white female retreated to the opposite corner of the stall when I first stepped in, eyeing me warily, avoiding even her siblings. She came off my list, too, as shy and lacking confidence, though she did eventually allow me to pet her.

Of the remaining five, three were female. By then, I was certain I wanted a female, so I spent the next half hour focusing on the three girls: two gray and white, one black and white.

The black-and-white pup was pretty forward, mixing it up with her two equally forward brothers, brawling with them, pushy with her other siblings. I took her off the short list.

That left the two gray-and-white females. Of the two, one hung back. She was slowest of the two to approach me, and did so cautiously. But I noticed she never took her eyes off me, even when one of her more boisterous siblings bullied her. After several minutes, she approached me. I held my breath—I found myself wanting her to like me. To my relief and delight, she was gentle and, eventually, affectionate, letting me touch and hold her, licking my fingers instead of biting them. I picked her up. Such soft fur, such an adorable pink puppy belly! I placed her on my lap and she stayed there for several seconds before jumping off. But she returned again and again, seeking me out. We observed each other equally carefully. She wasn't shy, nor was she overbearing or aggressive. She was a lot like me: calm, inquisitive, open. She was in the middle, temperament-wise, but it was her look of intelligence, her watchfulness, that intrigued me most.

The man returned to check on me and I was surprised to realize that nearly an hour had flown by. As much fun as I was having surrounded by eight gorgeous, playful puppies, I knew I had to make a decision. Take the smart gray girl home?

Yes.

I was that certain. Picking her up, I rubbed her nose with mine and inhaled her wonderfully clean puppy breath. With her nestled gently against my chest, I stepped over the stall's barrier into our new life together.

She and I connected through our eyes. We chose each other.

I named her Maia, after a strong, brave, and wild ancient woman in a novel I'd read.

During her first year, Maia exhibited all of the Malamute traits I'd come to adore after living with Opus. As I started teaching her how to run with me on-leash around Green Lake, I saw that she loved everyone she met, human and canine. She and I became part of a ragtag group who met most evenings at a neighborhood school playground to let our dogs interact off-leash. Maia played well with dogs of all sizes and ages, and I enjoyed watching her make these canine connections.

She thrived, and by the time she was a year old, I began to wonder, *Should I get another Malamute? Have two?* I derived such joy, watching Maia interact with other dogs at the park, seeing how much she enjoyed them. I knew if Maia had a vote on a second dog, it would be a resounding *Yes!*

To see how Maia reacted to living with another Malamute, I volunteered with a local Malamute rescue organization as a foster home. The rescue only sent males to live with us, usually a year or two old and neutered just before arriving. I hosted two, and Maia was besotted with each of them. She enjoyed their companionship and willingly shared her space.

The fact that both of these boys had plenty of testosterone still in their systems when they arrived was not lost on Maia. The rescue advised that females often found unneutered males more attractive. Maia and the foster dogs played all day, both inside the house and outside in the yard. Maia and one of the fosters took to lying next to each other on my bed, wrestling with their open mouths while "talking" their Malamute trash talk. It was delightful to watch. I was as smitten as Maia.

Once I had confidence in Maia's reaction, the idea of having two Malamutes in my life full-time consumed me. But I wanted a trainable puppy, and the rescue's dogs were usually at least a year old when they were surrendered.

I contacted Maia's breeders. They were hoping for another litter soon but sadly, that didn't happen. I waited one more heat cycle (roughly six months), but again, disappointment. So I started looking elsewhere, and eventually found one other Malamute breeder in western Washington. She had a litter of pups that would be ready to go to new homes in about four weeks.

Unlike Maia's breeders, who considered Malamutes pets, bred one litter a year, and focused on good temperament, this woman bred for show. Several litters a year. She had lots of dogs and a constant supply of puppies.

When I visited, the breeder had two female puppies that would go to "pet" homes (rather than to people who intended to show the dogs) because their coats were too thick to meet AKC conformation rules. They were "woolies," she told me. I hadn't heard the term, and I didn't care. Weren't all Malamutes wooly? Thick-furred?[3]

I brought Maia with me so the breeder could meet her. Over the phone, I'd told the breeder that I wanted another female (both of the woolies were female). At first, she said no. "Two females will kill each other," she told me. I assured her that Maia was great with all dogs, male and female. She wasn't convinced and wanted to meet Maia, to see for herself. This was my first experience with someone who breeds dogs for show, so I wasn't aware that their dog world and understanding of dog behavior were drastically different than mine. Because show dogs remain

---

[3] The gene that produces a thicker-than-normal "wooly" coat is recessive but exists in most Malamute lines.

intact, the likelihood of female/female conflict is exponentially higher. And though she occasionally let her dogs in her house, they spent much of their lives in kennels inside a barn, separated from one another; interactions with other dogs and other people were minimal. In short, poorly socialized for life in the human world.

When I visited, I didn't like what I saw. It wasn't that any of the dogs appeared to be mistreated in any way. They were all healthy, well fed, clean, and friendly toward me. But they were this woman's business, not indulged pets; I felt sorry for them. Even more dismaying, the breeder mentioned that two of the show-quality puppies from the litter I was visiting were going to be shipped to "show homes" in the Philippines. When I expressed surprise, given the region's heat and humidity (not to mention the long airplane ride in cargo), she tried to reassure me by saying their kennels would be air-conditioned.

After meeting Maia, she agreed to let me have one of the female wooly pups, although she repeated her warning that two female adults may not get along. Her purchase contract had lots of language about not spaying the puppy for a set number of years in case she (the breeder) wanted the opportunity to breed her later on. I was so desperate for another Malamute puppy that I signed it, knowing full well that I'd have the puppy spayed at an appropriate age. Let the breeder sue me, I figured; the chances of such an event were minimal. I chose the one with a little pink spot just below her black lower lip and arranged to return in four weeks to pick her up.

I named her Meadow.

It turned out I was right about Maia. She loved her new pack mate, accepting Meadow from the start and teaching her how to be a Malamute in the human world. "The girls," as I took to calling them, quickly became besties. They never got in a dispute, even when Maia, with devilish glee, would repeatedly pin puppy Meadow to the ground as they played. For a time, I worried what might happen when Meadow reached adulthood, especially when it became obvious that she was going to be larger and heavier than Maia. Would there be an imbalance, a shift in roles? Would Meadow get mad when Maia pinned her and retaliate? Or would she, the younger of the two, respect Maia's seniority, despite being larger?

The breeder's warnings echoing in the back of my mind, I watched them carefully, supervising their play.

Meadow never once got truly angry at Maia, letting her "win" every time they played, even when both of them—and me, watching—knew

Meadow could dominate if she wanted to. I did notice, though, that Maia didn't push her luck. She seemed to always make sure I was standing nearby, watching and supervising, when she played more aggressively with Meadow. And sometimes Meadow *would* get upset. I could see it in her face, the set of her ears, the way she vocalized, how she'd leap up quickly after Maia released her from a pin. Maybe Maia pinched Meadow's neck just a little too hard, or maybe Meadow just wasn't in the mood. I didn't know. But when I saw the shift in Meadow's body language, I loudly said "Chill!" before things escalated. They'd both immediately stop playing and look at me. And instantly, Meadow was no longer mad.

Yet another thing I love about Malamutes: They don't hold grudges and they forgive quickly.

To outsiders, those who didn't know them as intimately as I did, the girls' play looked completely different, even dangerous. When I took them to off-leash dog parks, they enjoyed greeting people but mostly ignored the other dogs and played with each other. They'd start with their Malamute version of wrestling, gnawing on each other's necks, baring teeth and growling lightly, trying to gain an advantage by rising up on their hind legs for better access to the top of the other's neck as well as downward momentum to assist in a pin. I found it interesting that at the park, Maia rarely actually pinned Meadow; they seemed to understand that she would be vulnerable to other dogs who might not play nicely.

As I stood nearby, watching, smiling, I'd see looks of concern and sometimes shock on the faces of others, so would reassure them. "It's fine; they're playing, they do this all the time." Many of the dogs also seemed concerned and kept their distance. If another dog did approach—some dogs, especially at off-leash dog parks, want to "referee" other dogs' behaviors—the girls instantly stopped playing. Again, they seemed to know how quickly a third, uninitiated dog could blow things up into a misunderstanding, perhaps even a real fight. Once things calmed down, we'd move along and eventually the girls would start wrestling again. I was convinced they enjoyed the reactions of the people and other dogs, almost like they were putting on a show for an audience.

When it came to reading canine body language, Opus had been a great teacher. However, I often needed a few examples before I put two and two together to realize, *Hiker ahead* or *Deer on the trail*. Opus taught me that Malamutes communicate primarily through positions—head and tail, ears, tense or relaxed—rather than vocalization. Unlike many dogs, they rarely bark at strangers or wildlife. Instead, they stop, watch, sniff the air, listen, maybe woof quietly, and decide whether the situation is safe or dangerous.

Maia, and then Meadow, continued to school me in Malamute. Maia had an especially keen awareness of wildlife, and I learned to interpret certain postures to mean a wild animal was nearby, or a human, maybe with a dog, was approaching. Because Meadow tended to bring up the rear during our trail runs, it was a while before I realized she had all the same skills but was comfortable letting Maia take the lead, while she kept us safe from the back.

The girls' interactions and body language intrigued me, and I wanted to understand and anticipate those signals. I wondered if wolf behavior would offer clues. I began reading whatever I could find about wolves, especially those reintroduced in Yellowstone National Park. I started seeing corollaries between what I observed in the girls and wolves.

In a wolf pack, each member knows its own strengths and weaknesses, as well as those of other pack members. Initially, they learn through play; no one pushes the play too far unless they want to be reprimanded or excluded, and, if they balk, possibly injured. Pups are allowed some leeway as they learn their own strengths and weaknesses while growing into their bodies. But when they push too far (as almost all of them do at some point), they're quickly scolded by older pack members. Not hurt, just tutored. With Maia and Meadow, I was the pack matriarch who intervened if one pushed the other too far.

This was the early 2000s, a time of increased study of wolves in their natural habitats. Before that, most descriptions of wolf behavior had been based on observations of captive wolves confined in small enclosures. The idea of an alpha male and beta female roughly ruling the pack, with lots of in-fighting and juggling for dominance, came from those limited observations. Hardly natural, especially since those mating pairs rarely chose each other, but instead, were forced together. The wolves of Yellowstone, reintroduced in the mid-1990s, were thriving. What I read about their behaviors, I often saw reflected in the girls' behaviors.

By the time Maia was a year old, she was a strong runner who enjoyed our forays around Green Lake. At the south end of the lake was a boat house where rowing shells and canoes were stored for local teams and visitor rentals. A public rec center with indoor swimming pool and basketball courts anchored the north end. The rest of the park space consisted of lawns, trees, beaches, and a wading pool. A three-mile, combination paved-and-dirt path circled the lake within this green space, often just a few feet from the shoreline. Bicyclists, skaters, rollerbladers, runners, and walkers, many with strollers, favored the paved path, while the dirt side attracted those eager to avoid pavement. Year-round, there were always lots of people in the park.

Because young Maia was easily distracted by the area's abundant squirrels, I trained her to wear a Halti during our runs. A Halti is a harness that fits a dog's head much like a horse halter; a strap encircles the dog's muzzle and another strap behind the ears holds it in place. The leash attaches to a ring on the bottom of the muzzle strap, just below the jaw. Pulling—by dog or human—gently tightens the strap around the muzzle, and that light pressure is usually enough to stop the pulling. If the dog persists, the Halti and leash together turn its head in the direction of the human, which usually also stops the dog from moving forward. The Halti kept Maia from pulling me off my feet when she spied one of those taunting squirrels. (True to her breed, she was a strong puller, even at a year old.)

Invented by a veterinarian in the mid-1980s, Haltis were still a newish thing in the Seattle area. At first glance, many thought it was a muzzle. (I have to confess that the first time I saw a Halti on a dog, I thought the same thing.) But in fact, that loop around Maia's mouth was usually quite loose and, unless she was pulling, she could fully open her mouth to pant or drink.

From the looks Maia and I often received at Green Lake, I could tell that the Halti, especially on such a large, wolflike dog, frightened a few people. Most, though, weren't scared. Instead, I often heard, "Oh, what a beautiful dog! Can I meet her?" Unless we went very early in the morning, our runs at Green Lake, especially in good weather, were not good training sessions for me because we were constantly stopping so people could meet Maia.

On one run that summer, among all the human and mechanical noise, Maia heard a baby crying. As she pulled me toward the direction she wanted to go, I thought it might be someone she recognized, but no. She dragged me straight to a baby stroller. A woman had stopped on the path and was leaning over a stroller to soothe her crying baby. As we got closer, I could tell Maia was truly concerned. Luckily, the mother was a dog person and didn't mind Maia getting close to the baby when I offered reassurance that my dog was friendly.

Ears perked forward and head tilting side to side, Maia listened intently to the baby's cries, tried to nuzzle the baby with her nose. Realizing that might be a bridge too far, I pulled her back. I was being cautious, cognizant that a total stranger might worry about the safety of her baby. Finally, thanking the mom for indulging us, we resumed our run and I didn't think much more about it.

Until a distinct pattern developed at Green Lake. Maia would spot a baby stroller as we ran or walked and pull me straight toward it. I developed a quick speech for the person behind the stroller: "My dog *loves* babies and would like to meet yours. Is that okay?" Most were delighted. Maia would sniff the baby and sometimes give a quick lick on the cheek, usually to the squealing delight of the child. Positive reinforcement, oxytocin flowing through all the brains: Maia, baby, parent, me.

Otherwise, she simply passed by people unless she heard someone say, "What a beautiful dog!" Then she'd slow to see if they wanted to meet her. (I'm convinced she associated the word *beautiful* with nice people she should meet.)

When Meadow was six months old, I slowly conditioned her to run with us, and by the time she was about nine months, we three were regularly running together. Realizing I couldn't keep two separate leashes from tangling, I bought a coupler: two dogs, one leash. It worked wonderfully, after we all got used to it.

Except when both girls spied one of those taunting squirrels. As adults, Maia weighed eighty pounds, Meadow, ninety. Two strong dogs who already enjoyed running and pulling, they could easily pull me off my feet! I tried using Haltis on both of them, but quickly discovered that if one dog turned her head even slightly, it unfairly cinched the Halti around the muzzle of the other. Discarding that idea, I just got better at anticipating squirrels and anything else that might cause them to suddenly pull on the leash.

One afternoon, "anything else" was a rabbit. We were running near Green Lake when the girls spied one before I did. Rabbit took off running and so did the girls. I held on to the leash as long as I could, but in the end, I couldn't keep up. Rather than fall and be dragged, I let go. The rabbit dove under a portable office trailer. The girls, in their mad dash, didn't coordinate as they neared a telephone pole. Maia went to one side, Meadow the other, and both immediately came to a stop when the coupler hit the pole. Thankfully, there were no injuries to the girls, me, or the rabbit. But, boy, did I learn how vigilant I needed to be, even in an urban park.

Meadow, it turned out, shared Maia's affinity for babies, adopting the same look of worry and concern if she heard one crying. With the two of them together on a coupler, I really worked on my canned speech for parents whenever the girls spied a baby and pulled me directly toward them. I mean, imagine seeing two enormous, fluffy, wolflike dogs towing a small human, making a beeline for you and your child! By the time I finished my quick introduction, we'd be standing near the baby's stroller. Of course, if the child was fearful, I'd immediately pull the girls back and we would continue on our way.

Those days at Green Lake were wonderful and fun.

COMMUNING

"You ran a hundred miles in a day?" my uncle asked at a family Thanksgiving gathering not long after I'd completed the Western States 100 in 1994. Taking a sip of his beer and shaking his head with bafflement, he added, "I don't even *drive* a hundred miles in a day." Aside from my brother Tim, who was a casual jogger, my family saw no point in what they considered my extreme running hobby. Most warned me I'd ruin my knees, wear out my heart, or suffer some other major health issue.

By that point, I was used to my family not understanding why I ran, failing to grasp how good running trails made me feel, or the sense of belonging and acceptance I found out there.

Early into my ultra-racing career, I'd focused on developing speed and endurance. But something unexpected happened. As I found fellow ultra runners to train with, I formed intimate friendships—and as mentioned earlier, I found my tribe.

Moving along trails, over mountains and across streams, in snow, rain, wind, and sun, we easily shared details about our lives with each other even though we were relative strangers. Running in a conga line, one closely following another—or less frequently, side-by-side if the trail was wide enough—doing something a little edgy and potentially dangerous turns out to be a good bonding experience. We shared in ways that would take months or even years of normal social interactions to foster. Reserved by nature, I was surprised at the easy sense of intimacy I found with others on the trails. I had never experienced that in any other social or athletic setting, except, of course, with my dogs. I liked it.

When my training plan called for a thirty-mile run, that was an hours-long investment of precious work-free weekend time. For safety, it was best to run with at least one other person (much as I relied on my dogs, they wouldn't be much help if I fell). I preferred to spend those hours with people I enjoyed, especially Mike. Plus, while out there placing one foot in front of the other for hours on end, I could observe how others handled stressful situations: a trip-and-fall or twisted ankle; foul weather; black bear encounters; losing energy and coordination from lack of food, electrolytes, or dehydration (known as bonking in the world of running); bee stings; errant contact lenses. Telling character traits were exposed. I quickly saw the real person: their good, bad, and ugly. Were they reliable? Empathic? Would they stop to help in an emergency during a race, or run on by? Did they become whiny or cranky when stressed?

On those hours-long training runs, we shared many personal aspects of our lives. Everything from the ups and downs of marriages and relationships to achievements and challenges of children or extended family and work accomplishments or hassles. Sometimes I realized I didn't want to pursue a friendship with someone because those trail hours exposed traits I didn't want or need in my life. Mostly, though, I found a group of people I thoroughly enjoyed and could rely upon—not just on the trail, but in life. I never had to explain my running habit to them. They understood the ultra-running lifestyle, the time and energy required to train, travel to and recover from races or adventure runs, as well as dealing with the physical and emotional impact of a sidelining injury ... all of it.

Something about running itself helped create these unique, strong bonds in such a short time. Moving at a pace and cadence that are not too strenuous (because we had to maintain it for hours on end) allowed us to carry on a conversation, crack a joke, share a personal story, or discuss current events. It was relaxing to move through a beautiful natural setting while expending a steady rate of energy, concentrating just enough to avoid tripping on rocks and roots while also keeping up our end of a conversation. The usual social walls quickly crumbled. Men and women of various ages, backgrounds, and orientations, we were united in our addiction to trail running.

Between 1990 and 2005, I spent countless hours training for and running ultra-distance trail races. Tallying more than ninety ultra-race finishes, including Western States 100, and a few memorable DNFs—runner-speak for "Did Not Finish." During that time, I was also lucky to do some amazing adventure runs. Runs that challenged me mentally and physically. Runs that broadened my knowledge of the world.

For example, in the late spring of 2001, I ran on the Inca Trail in Peru. Flying into Lima, Mike and I met up with a group of fifteen runners from across the US. Our guide service helped us acclimate to the altitude with short runs in and around the city of Cusco. At 11,142 feet, Cusco was once the capital of the Inca Empire. We enjoyed short walking tours, including the baroque Santo Domingo Convent in the town square built by conquering Spaniards on top of the Incan Temple of the Sun, its huge foundation stones still visible.

After we'd adjusted, we spent three days running on the Inca Trail, ending at Machu Picchu. One of the guides, Abelardo, joined us on the trail. A former professor of history at a university in Lima, he was Quechua, one of Peru's Indigenous groups. Abelardo's lectures on the Quechua culture and history, the Incas, the Inca Trail, and Machu Picchu were both fascinating and enlightening.

After covering five easy miles on the first day, we arrived at a clearing at 8,600 feet. Porters had already carried in our food and sleeping and running gear and set up our two-person canvas tents. We were served a delicious dinner of traditional Peruvian foods and wine at an outdoor camp table.

The next morning, the real running began. Covering seventeen miles, we were challenged with navigating three steep mountain passes, each more than 13,000 feet in elevation. While enormous hummingbirds buzzed among the nearby wildflowers, I gasped for breath as I went up and over the first one. *This is what it must feel like on the summit of Mt. Rainier*, I thought. I was barely able to walk the uphills at that altitude. The downhills were better for breathing, but the stones on the Inca Trail were a challenge all their own in terms of footing. Uneven, with spaces in between, they were ankle-twisters, and some stone steps in the steep sections were uncomfortably high for my short legs. Yet, I marveled, our feet were touching the same stone stairs and paths created by the Incas centuries earlier. Along the way, we saw a few archeological sites, strategic Inca fortresses made of stone set at vantage points off the main trail. Mike and I explored most of them, awed by the masterful stonework and views through the windows.

At the end of that long second day, after crossing Dead Woman Pass at 13,800 feet, we arrived at our campsite, a ledge on the spine of a 12,000-foot mountain. Porters had again carried our gear, tents, and food ahead.[4] After dark, a nearly full moon illuminated the even loftier snow-covered

---

4 It was humbling to watch those Andean porters haul seventy-pound loads tied to their backs, straps on their foreheads for leverage, sandals on their feet. They covered exactly the same miles and terrain we did with our lightweight running packs and fancy trail shoes, only faster. One female porter wore a traditional Peruvian skirt.

peaks around us; they looked like huge vanilla ice cream cones floating in the night sky. The stars were so close and vivid, I wanted to pluck them.

Early the next morning, after a fitful altitude-headachy night, I peeked through our tent opening. On the ground in front of the tent were two steaming bowls of water, placed by a porter so we could wash. The sun was cresting over distant Andean peaks and I was on top of the world.

On the third day, we covered ten miles, running through tropical rainforest and seeing more ruins. After nine miles, we arrived at the iconic Gateway to the Sun, or Sun Gate. Here we got our first full view of Machu Picchu, nestled in the jagged, verdant mountains below us. Whisps of thin fog drifted over the scene.

The final mile of trail brought us to the ancient city. Mike, feeling the effects of a flu bug going through the group, called it a day, but I wasn't done. I needed more. I climbed the trail to the top of Machu Picchu Mountain, the taller of the two peaks guarding the ancient city. Alone at the summit, I took in yet another memorable perspective.

The next day, Abelardo gave us a tour of Machu Picchu and told us about its history and significance to the Inca empire; in the background, llamas casually munched the grass around the ruins, keeping the grounds tidy. After two nights in Aguas Calientes, the town just below Machu Picchu, we departed for Cusco. Rather than taking the usual four-hour train ride, our group was surprised by our guide with a scenic flight in a twenty-five-seat Sikorsky helicopter.

Running across the Grand Canyon offered an equally unique perspective on a different sort of history: geological. In the mid-1990s, Mike and I and some ultra-running friends went there three years in a row to do what ultra runners refer to as the Rim-to-Rim-to-Rim (aka, R2R2R, or the Double): from the South Rim to the North Rim and back again. It takes most seasoned runners roughly twelve hours to complete. We covered forty-two to forty-six miles, depending on which of two trails we took on the South Rim side. The elevation change was huge: 20,000 feet.

We always went in early November. There would be snow and ice on the rims, but it wasn't too hot at Phantom Ranch at the bottom of the canyon. The other advantage of that time of year: no mule trains on the south side. Still, the very idea of the Double was daunting, especially because water sources were rare on the north side, requiring careful hydration planning. The emotional reward of completing it, though, was incredible. My entire body ached for days afterward, but my mind was satisfied.

Beyond the sense of wonder I felt running through the grandeur of the canyon all those hours, I vividly remember the first time I trudged up the steep climb to the North Rim. Stopping to catch my breath and give my legs a break, I put one hand against the rock wall into which the trail had been cut. Noticing the striations in the rock, I paid closer attention as I started climbing again, seeing new colors as I went. Umber, dun, gray, dusty pink, even a sort of purple. I was looking at eons of the Earth's history, recorded in layers of sediment.

And running Mount Rainier's Wonderland Trail? What a thrill. A sort of homecoming, given that running in Grand Park while in law school sparked my desire to run mountain trails. In the 1990s, Mike and I joined a small group of Oregon and Washington ultra runners who, for many years, spent time on the mountain every August. The run involved three full days of running, dividing Wonderland's nearly ninety-three miles of trail into three sections—a fun run, not a race. Family and friends transported tents, sleeping bags, food, and extra gear to our Mowich Lake and Cougar Flats campsites; all we had to do was carry enough food and water for the all-day runs through gorgeous wildflowers and forests.

Each of those adventure runs required me to meet and conquer new challenges. In Peru, it was the extreme altitude, which caused headaches and made every step a monumental effort. In the Grand Canyon, radical variations in elevation and temperature and lack of water left me dehydrated and cramping. Rainier taught me pacing ... that I could push through three days of physical exhaustion and lack of sleep, and that determination (and no easy way out) would ultimately get me to the end.

Those runs were my version of fun. I planned. Trained. Started. Pushed myself. Got dirty and smelly. Reveled in the landscape. Took photos. Saw new animals—bighorn sheep, a ring-tailed cat, alpacas. Sometimes, I lost my appetite but forced down enough calories to keep moving. Other times, those calories came right back up. My muscles ached and cramped. I limped. I finished. I learned I was stronger than I thought. I discovered that, with the right mindset, I could endure a lot. I could persevere.

The only thing missing on all of those adventures? The companionship of my dogs.

The physical act of running trails at any pace requires that you simultaneously scan the environment (trail, terrain, wildlife, weather) while maintaining a constant inward focus. Among the things runners mentally monitor are eye-foot coordination; how their feet are hitting the ground; changes in gait or foot placement to avoid tripping on obstacles; joints, muscles, tendons, and skin; heart rate; food and water intake; and when (and where) to pee.

For experienced runners, all this processing goes on constantly but mostly subliminally. As a pilot deeply familiar with normal cockpit readings quickly notices an unusual reading warning of a potential problem, runners learn what's "normal" for their physical state, paying attention only to the atypical signs and signals that give a warning that something's off and, left unaddressed, it could become an emergency. In my case, while my runner's mind processed the physical data, it was also monitoring my emotional content.

Sometimes I had to talk myself into leaving my warm bed, dressing appropriately for the weather, and heading out the door—the hardest part of any run. But, eager dogs, prancing around me as I dressed, anticipating a forest romp? They helped overcome any reluctance. When I started out, my body gently complained as my muscles warmed and I settled into a sustainable cadence (I usually started too fast). Seeing my dogs running ahead of me, light with excitement, eyes, noses, and ears alert, caused me to smile at their joy, glad I made the effort.

Once my heart rate steadied, my mind replayed conversations, actions, thoughts, or worries that had recently plagued me. Dark thoughts tended to emerge first. For this reason, I preferred routes that started uphill because the level of exertion and physical discomfort matched that emotional state. Then the magic happened. After the first mile or so, my body warmed up, became more limber. If it was winter, I'd start shedding excess layers, especially on my hands. My running felt smooth and familiar. Easy. Endorphins kicked in. I felt *good*.

Nature added her own elixir of fresh air, trees, wildflowers, and wildlife, all calming sights and sounds. Those initial troubled thoughts rearranged in ways that allowed me to see them through a wide-angle lens: *It's not as bad as I thought. Maybe I overreacted.* Then came the switch from problems to problem-solving. That allowed me to let the issue go and focus on being in the moment for the rest of the run. The sensation of my feet on dirt (or snow), moving through a beautiful and calming wilderness with my dogs, cleared and opened my mind.

Other times, from the moment I started a run, I was able to effortlessly release any negative thoughts and drift to happy topics. Those were the runs I cherished, times when I was most creative: hatching new writing themes and article ideas, crafting the perfect sentence, seeing new approaches to a stalled book project. My mind flooded with endorphins in this "creativity zone," I barely noticed the physical effort of the run. Some refer to this state as *flow*, and I can testify that it's a fantastic place to be.

Trail running alone with my dogs was key to truly knowing myself. With nature's nudge and my dogs' unfailing positivity, I became adept at working through life's bumps and burns, knowing *this too shall pass* if I just kept running toward my truest, best self.

In "Distance Running Shaped Human Evolution," an article in the November 2004 issue of *Nature*, journalist Michael Hopkin described a theory that early humans developed larger brains because they could run.

That made total sense to me. When covering ground at a pace faster than walking, our senses must sift a lot of information simultaneously in order to remain upright and safe. Not just what's on the ground immediately in front of and beside us, but also, sounds and smells, the weather, wildlife moving nearby or in the distance. A powerful brain is needed to manage all the input.

While moving unrushed on dirt trails through forests or along snow-covered mountain flanks, I had time to truly *see* where I was. I looked at the ground around me, at the plants, wildflowers, and shrubs. I noticed trees previously taken for granted, as well as distant peaks and snow-covered volcanoes. I started asking questions and began memorizing names for alpine lakes, peaks, and ridges; wildflowers; trees; songbirds; and other forest wildlife. Like any life-long resident of the Puget Sound area, I could identify black bears, Mt. Rainier, crows, and blackberries. But how to tell a cedar from a Douglas fir? And what's that bird that we jokingly called the "telephone bird" because its call reminded us of a ringing phone?

Different running friends brought different backgrounds and expertise in the outdoors. One was a birder. Another, a geologist. Several were mountaineers. Like a sponge, I soaked up their knowledge and advice. Yet, it was when I was running alone with my dogs that I enjoyed the best observations. I could stop whenever I wanted to really look at something, unworried about holding someone else back. As we moved through the forest, my dogs and I were quieter than a gaggle of runners carrying on loud conversations. With one or both of my Malamutes in the lead, all I had to do was watch them for a clue about nearby wildlife.

My surroundings fired my brain with sensory input and analysis, one of the reasons I embraced trail running: It was never boring. Each run was different, even if I was on a trail I'd been on many times, because the environment changed with the seasons. *What was that sound? A raven's call? That thumping sound? The drumming of a male grouse! Where is he?* Wildlife encounters invoked thoughts like, *What is that odd scraping sound? Oh my god, it's a black bear cub climbing a tree, and over there is the mama running away; let's turn back!* So many unpredictable and exciting variables with every wilderness run. I was always ready to retreat or change route depending on what we saw, heard, and—in the case of my dogs—smelled.

In spring, song birds joyously sought mates and built nests, foxes and coyotes barked to mates and offspring. The mating scream of a female cougar once made me think a woman was being murdered nearby. In summer, bird songs and calls were constant, mixed with the sudden whoosh of a startled grouse and the thump-thump of deer or elk hooves as they retreated through the trees. In fall, the eerie, high-pitched bugling of rutting bull elk carried for miles. Canada geese honked as they flew south. The screech of soaring bald eagles and the jeers of blue jays filled the void after song birds left on their winter migration. In winter, when snow hushed the landscape, ravens, jays, and the occasional squirrel proclaimed their presence.

Even the sound of my feet against the ground changed with the seasons: squishy and splashing in spring's mud and puddles; a soft patter in summer's dusty dirt; a scuffle through a carpet of fallen leaves and needles in autumn; crunching loudly through crusty snow in frigid winter temperatures.

Constant with all of that sensory input was my breathing and heartbeat, the cadence I moved to: quieter on downhills, faster and louder on the ups.

Running was my body's dance on nature's ever-changing stage.

PERSISTENCE

The mid-August day broke with bright sunlight and wildflowers bursting with color in the high alpine meadows of the Cascades. It was the sort of day every Seattleite cherishes because they're so rare.

Together, Maia, Meadow, Mike, and I were working as trail sweeps for the last twenty miles of the 2003 Cascade Crest Classic, a hundred-mile trail race. Runners had thirty-four hours to complete the big loop course. The race started in the small town of Easton at eight on Saturday morning and ended there at six on Sunday afternoon. Of the sixty runners who started, forty would finish within the final cut-off. Our job was to be the last ones off the course. Along the way, we took down course flagging and markers while keeping an eye on, and staying a respectful distance behind, the last runners, even if they crossed the finish line after thirty-four hours.

This wasn't the first time Mike, the girls, and I had been sweeps for this race. We knew we'd be on the trail for about six hours. We also knew that the eighty-mile aid station where we started (where runners were provided with food and fluids) had a strict cut-off of ten on Sunday morning. If a runner didn't enter the aid station before then, they had to drop from the race. That cut-off let us know roughly when we would start our jobs, following the last official runner to leave that aid station.

We were eager to spend the day in the mountains. Conditions were ideal. Those twenty miles of trail were extremely challenging, with lots of climbing and descending and technical footing on rocks and roots in places. It included the course high point—Thorpe Mountain, 5,840 feet—as well as the lowest point, the finish line, 2,140 feet. I was awed by the racers who managed it after already running eighty miles. The fastest among them had navigated this stretch in the dark with only a headlamp to light the way.

Our plan was to move at a steady but casual pace, more fast-walking than running, covering about four miles per hour. Mike and I talked while we removed ribbons tied to low tree limbs or shrubs. We also took time to absorb the stunning views, from sharp peaks holding snow on their northern slopes to clear mountain lakes in the valleys below. All while watching Maia and Meadow enjoy themselves, unfettered by leashes.

We settled into a rhythm, the girls in the lead, followed by me, then Mike. He and I both knew that—eyes intent on the trail surface to avoid tripping—I often missed strips of flagging; having Mike bring up the rear ensured they were all collected. And I got to watch the girls happily trotting ahead of me, fluffy white tails high over their backs catching the occasional breeze, their senses alert to the sounds, sights, and smells we traveled through. With Mike in the back, Meadow didn't feel the need to bring up the rear.

A couple of hours into the sweep, chatting happily about nothing and everything, running slowly through an open meadow on a slight downhill, I caught a toe on a rock. My feet didn't move far but my upper body's momentum hyperextended my lower back before gravity slammed me face-first to the ground, flat as a pancake. It happened so fast that I didn't have time to cushion my fall with my hands.

The impact knocked the wind out of me.

After a couple of seconds that felt like an eternity, I gasped, refilling my lungs, and did a quick inventory. Was anything broken?

"Whoa. Are you okay?" Mike asked, having witnessed the entire mishap.

"I think so," I replied, cautiously, still not moving. But I knew instinctively that this had been a worse-than-usual fall.

Hearing the commotion, Maia and Meadow returned to me, sniffing my head and face; Meadow offered a quick lick.

Mike knew better than to try to help me up right away. In trail running, falling happens. Rarely does it result in serious injury except to the runner's ego. Scrapes and bruises are common. Most of us prefer to get up under our own power, when we're ready. Mike stood quietly next to me, available to help if I wanted it.

Using my hands, I pushed myself up and back onto my knees and sat on my heels. That felt fine. Nothing hurt in an unusual way. I couldn't see or feel any scrapes. With a hand assist from Mike, I stood and brushed off the dust and dirt from my chest and shorts. We were a long way from any source of help. There was no cell reception in those remote mountains. Besides, it'd be embarrassing to became a distraction for the race director, not only unable to complete our volunteer duties, but also requiring a rescue.

Malamutes have a keen instinct to go from Point A to Point B, and lollygagging is barely tolerated; the girls were eager to get moving. Plus, they loved the attention and treats (bacon!) they got at the aid stations. *Onward!* they said with their impatient body language, pacing around us, tails wagging.

We resumed our usual conga line formation and continued down the single-track trail. It took a mile or so to regain the confidence to run normally. Nothing hurt, so eventually I put the fall out of my mind. Mike and I resumed our usual banter as we pulled flagging, and I enjoyed watching the girls follow their noses a few feet off trail, or stop to drink from the clear-running streams we crossed. The meadow wildflowers—blue lupine, white daisies, orange Indian paintbrush, purple heather—teased our eyes with their beauty while buzzing bees collected their pollen and nectar.

What an amazing day to be running trails in the mountains, I thought. *I'm so lucky. It doesn't get any better than this.*

I couldn't have been more right. Or more wrong.

Roughly two weeks after falling, I noticed a persistent headache. An all-day-long headache that didn't respond to ibuprofen.

I didn't otherwise feel sick.

The headache was worst—quite pronounced and painful—when I ran downhill. On a regular Tuesday morning run, heading down a steep trail in an urban park, I felt an intense pressure in the front of my head, behind my forehead and eyes. It felt like my head would explode with every footfall, and my vision bounced as though I were looking through eyeglasses bobbing on the bridge of my nose. I felt slightly better when I ran on level ground, but the headache and pressure remained, directly related to the pounding of my feet against the ground.

What the hell? I'd never had headaches like this.

I kept running most days, of course. That's what we distance trail runners did. Ran through the pain and trained for the next event. Besides, I'd been running since I was eighteen. It was part of my routine, my identity, and my sense of self-worth. Usually, running made me feel great. But now? Running made my head feel awful.

Something was off, but I couldn't figure out what.

The headache continued for several days, most acute behind my eyes and the bridge of my nose, worse when running but noticeable even when going about my daily routines. Even driving over a pothole provoked an intense and painful pressure. Every jarring motion reverberated.

Yet, I slept well. Amazingly well, in fact. The headache disappeared at night. I would awake each morning headache-free, but within fifteen to twenty minutes after I got up, it came back. Every single day.

I'd never had a sinus infection. Maybe that was it? In early September, roughly two weeks after my fall, I went to a clinic to see if that's what was causing this odd and persistent headache. I saw a physician's assistant, who took a nose swab and gave me antibiotics on the assumption it was an infection.

The swab came back negative. The antibiotics didn't help.

On my next visit, in late September, a physician saw me. Hearing the complaint of persistent headaches and noting that the antibiotics hadn't been effective, she referred me to a neurologist and ordered a magnetic resonance image scan (MRI) of my head.

The MRI and neurologist visit didn't occur until December. By then, my headaches had slowly lessened and mostly resolved. The MRI was "unremarkable."

Between September and December, baffled by my symptoms, I did significant research on Medscape, an online research and continuing education tool for medical clinicians and physicians. (I still had a student account from when I'd briefly returned to university and taken a variety of science and medical prerequisites with the idea of enrolling in a physical therapy program.)

Having a significant health challenge that defies easy diagnosis yet negatively affects your daily life is a powerful motivation to find an answer. Not knowing is almost as bad as the actual symptoms. Those prerequisite science courses had given me enough background to understand and objectively evaluate research articles about various conditions and their symptoms. Most nights found me staring at my home computer screen, entering keywords and poring over research synopses of various conditions. My days were spent struggling to keep up with the demands of my solo law practice, which I'd opened in 1988, in spite of the constant headaches.

I was forty-six years old and in otherwise excellent health, an ultra-distance runner and triathlete. None of this made any sense. I pushed through the pain while pushing for an answer.

One of those nights, while Meadow and Maia snoozed contentedly on my bed in the darkness behind me, I remembered something from an earlier stint volunteering in physical therapy clinics.

At one of the hospital PT clinics, I'd passed the time between patients by looking at textbooks one of the therapists used in her training. Flipping through its pages, I suddenly stopped at the photo of a skinny young girl standing with her back to the camera wearing just a pair of baggy white undies. Her spine was curved, and on her lower back, just above her underwear line, a red circle highlighted a growth of fine "baby" hair near the base of her spine.

"That's me!" I'd thought at the time. I'd never seen or read of anyone with that same growth of hair; I thought I was a solitary freak. From the age of thirteen, I'd been shaving the patch of baby hair on my lower back so it wouldn't show when I wore bathing suits or showered after PE. My parents told me what the pediatrician had told them: It was a birthmark and of no consequence.

The brief textbook article described a condition I'd never heard of: spina bifida occulta. I'd heard of spina bifida, and vaguely understood that it was a failure of the spinal column to close in utero, causing a variety of physical challenges depending on the severity of the defect. Spina bifida occulta, though, was new to me. According to the article, it's a condition in which the spinal column closes in utero, but imperfectly, sometimes resulting in minor neurological deficits.

Suddenly, so much about my body and my life made sense. The hairy patch. My slightly curved spine. Reading about that girl in the book, I thought, *I dodged a bullet.* My spinal column did close and I didn't have any neurological deficits. Just the embarrassing hairy patch.

But now, with my unexplained headaches, I wondered, *Was that true*?

What if my current issue was related to my wonky spine? What if I *did* have a neurological defect? And what if it was manifesting as headaches that dated back to that hard fall on the trail in August?

Maybe the bullet I thought I had dodged had actually nicked me.

Putting those pieces into the overall headache puzzle, my Medscape searches proved far more fruitful. I stumbled upon a condition referred to as Spontaneous Intracranial Hypotension, or SIH.

My symptoms fit perfectly.

Spontaneous Intracranial Hypotension is a condition of low pressure (hypotension) in the head (intracranial) as a result of a low volume of cerebrospinal fluid (CSF). Every day, our bodies create and cycle through fresh CSF, maintaining a constant volume that bathes our brain and spinal column in a cushioning and protective fluid. Often, the reason for the low pressure is unknown (thus the "spontaneous" part of the name), although usually it's the result of a CSF leak through a tear or puncture of the dura mater surrounding the spinal cord.

In layman's terms, if for some reason you spring a CSF leak, your brain stops floating happily within your skull. There's no longer enough fluid pressure to hold it in place against the downward pull of gravity. Instead, it sags when you're standing or sitting, putting pressure at the base of your skull, your neck, and the top of your spinal column. Often, one or more of the twelve cranial nerves—including those connected to your eyes, ears, and face—are impinged upon by the pressure of the sagging brain. All that sagging can lead to symptoms like positional headaches; neck and shoulder pain; tinnitus (ringing or buzzing in the ears); facial muscle drooping; dizziness; light and sound sensitivity; and vague cognitive symptoms like brain fog (muddled thinking, poor memory), low motivation, and a tendency to anger quickly or become easily frustrated.

The Medscape articles I read in 2003 described patients presenting with the key diagnostic symptom of orthostatic or "positional" headaches, which are felt when upright but disappear when prone or supine.

At that time, SIH had only recently acquired a name recognized by the medical profession. The complaints of other, more subtle symptoms hadn't yet been identified as a related cluster that appeared the longer a person experienced a CSF leak. There was precious little research about diagnosing or treating SIH; most clinicians hadn't even heard of it, let alone diagnosed or treated a case.

Over a span of six months, I became a lab rat in the SIH learning curve for the three neurologists who saw me.

My primary care doctor referred me to the first neurologist, who saw me in December 2003. As soon as I mentioned the possibility of SIH to him, he shut me down. I saw it in his dismissive expression. He didn't believe I could still be running if I was leaking, and was skeptical that I had spina bifida occulta. When he asked to see my hairy patch, I showed him the area, saying I had shaved it when showering that morning, as I always did. He determined I didn't have a hairy patch indicative of spina bifida occulta because he couldn't see any hair or stubble. Being of the school that patients who do their own research are hypochondriacs or attention-seekers, he preferred to prove me wrong.

Besides, my head MRI was unremarkable, and my headaches were mostly gone. He threw me a bone by saying if it was SIH, they'd have to do another MRI with contrast to confirm it.

But by then I was feeling almost normal again, so I let it go. I assumed I'd never experience this series of symptoms again. By New Year's Day 2004, I was headache-free. Life was returning to normal and I was ready to put this long mystery-headache chapter behind me. Running with Mike and the girls was fun again.

Then, in mid-January, I tripped and fell while trail running. Not too bad, I thought; certainly not as hard as the August fall. It wouldn't even have warranted remembering. Except that, roughly two weeks later, the positional headaches were back.

This time, putting two and two together, I recognized what was happening and sought diagnosis and treatment right away. With a new neurologist.

Neurologist Number Two took me more seriously, maybe because I printed out the Medscape research describing the condition and handed him copies. He ordered more imaging, another head and upper-spine MRI, this time with contrast.

The results: normal.

Soon after that MRI, I underwent a spinal tap to determine the opening pressure of the CSF in my spinal column. At the time, neurologists speculated that if the opening pressure was lower than "normal" (which fell within a range), that indicated a CSF leak somewhere. They could also test a sample of spinal fluid to rule out other possibilities, like meningitis.

My opening pressure was normal. My CSF fluid was normal.

Despite the normal MRI and spinal tap results, the second neurologist believed me; he agreed that I might have a CSF leak. That was huge, an emotional boost during an incredibly stressful and frustrating time.

To treat it, he ordered a "blind" blood patch, the only medical intervention recommended at that time for CSF leaks. An epidural blood patch (EBP) is a procedure in which a small volume of the patient's blood is injected into their epidural space to stop the leak. It's called "blind" when the location of the suspected leak is unknown. The blood is injected in a best-guess location along the spine, and if it worked, that would be proof that I had a leak. I was game to try.

My blind blood patch was done at the same hospital where the neurologist had an office. I went alone for my afternoon appointment. A nurse ushered me into a small out-patient surgical room, where she asked me to change into a hospital gown, tied in the back so the anesthesiologist could easily access my low back. The room was chilly, clean, sterile, and intimidating. Though I wasn't eager for another long needle poked into my spine, I was determined to see if this would help my headaches. After changing, I sat on a metal chair, tucked the gown under my thighs for warmth, and waited.

Soon there was a knock on the door. The anesthesiologist entered and introduced himself.

"Hop up on the table there," he said, gesturing to a shiny silver surgical platform cushioned by a thin mattress. He then explained to me what was going to happen.

"First, I'm going to draw some blood from your arm," he said in a calm, reassuring voice. He wrapped a stretchy band around my upper arm; upon finding a good vein, he expertly drew enough blood to fill a glass vial.

"Next, I'm going to inject your own blood into the epidural space around your spinal cord. I'll numb your lower back, then insert a needle and inject the blood."

He asked me to lie on my side, knees tucked, facing away from him.

"Are you ready?" he asked.

"As ready as I'll ever be," I said with a small laugh, trying for levity.

"All right. You'll feel some pressure, maybe a little bit uncomfortable, but it shouldn't be painful," he assured me.

As he injected the blood, I did indeed feel pressure. Uncomfortable, for sure, but bearable. Better than the spinal tap.

"The idea is that the blood will float around your dura and be pulled toward any tear by a pressure gradient," he explained as he slowly depressed the plunger. "It plugs the tear by forming a clot."

If this blind blood patch worked, it meant the CSF leak would stop and my positional headaches would disappear. Life would return to normal.

For the next thirty minutes, the anesthesiologist and I made small talk while I remained still, on my side, giving the blood patch time to reach its destination.

"Okay, you're done. You can stand up now," he said, offering his hand to steady me as I carefully stepped onto a small stool and then to the floor.

Standing upright, I instantly noticed my headache was gone. Was it just because I'd spent thirty minutes lying down? Or had the blood patch already worked?

I was stunned at how good I felt, and so quickly. Giddy, even. Almost not believing it, I told him my headache was gone. Going into the procedure, I'd had no idea what to expect, but instant relief wasn't even on my list of best-case scenarios. As I drove home, I sang along to the radio, smiling, headache-free for the first time in weeks, even when my tires hit the potholes that had previously made me think my head would explode.

Plus, the fact the blood patch worked meant I had, indeed, suffered from a tear and a leak. My instincts were validated.

Two days post-blood patch, I noticed a slight headache late in the morning. Day three, a headache started fifteen minutes after getting up and worsened as the day wore on.

My positional headache was back. *Shit.*

It was an immense struggle to not fall into depression. I'd had a brief but glorious taste of normal life, and now it was slowly but inexorably dripping away from me.

After reporting the development to the neurologist—that I felt awesome for a few days but the headache slowly returned—he scheduled a second blood patch.

I went through the same scenario with a different anesthesiologist, a nice-enough guy but not as informative or chatty as the first. The result was the same: I immediately felt wonderful, but my symptoms slowly returned within a few days. To his credit, the neurologist scheduled a third blood patch. The fact that I'd had immediate relief, even if only for a few days, meant we were on the right track.

I was pleased to see the original anesthesiologist when I arrived for my third patch. The process was now routine, so no explanation was required. This time, however, after getting the patch and waiting for it to take effect, he and I had a more specific chat. He was curious about my condition.

Facing away from him and pointing with one hand to the shaved hairy patch on my lower back, I said, "I think there might be some connection between the spina bifida occulta I think I have and the intracranial hypotension."

He didn't respond. I couldn't see his face but didn't want to roll over and mess up the blood patch to look at him. After an awkward minute of silence he asked, "Did your neurologist ever order a low-spine MRI?"

"No," I replied. "Why? What are you thinking?"

"If you do have spina bifida occulta—and you may well have, given that hairy patch—it's also possible you have a tethered spinal cord," he said.

Later that day, feeling great once again, the blood patch working in the short term, I went home and started researching "tethered spinal cord." I learned that if the spinal cord is tethered, it usually means that the very bottom of the cord—called the "cauda equina" because the thick cord splits into several small strands that resemble a horse's tail—has become attached to the innermost layer of dura that surrounds it. Rather than floating freely within the cerebral spinal fluid, it's stuck ... tethered, remaining stationary when the spine moves. A rare condition, it's usually asymptomatic, and often goes undetected for decades, if it's ever discovered.

When a patient receives a blood patch or an epidural anesthetic, or undergoes a spinal tap, the assumption is that it's safe if the needle accidentally pierces the dura because the cauda equina will float out of the way of the needle, preventing a puncture of the spinal cord.

As I left the hospital that day, the anesthesiologist said he would speak with my neurologist. Two days later, I got a call to schedule a low-spine MRI, which showed that I did, in fact, have a tethered spinal cord.

I was grateful that anesthesiologist listened to me. That single piece of information was the last puzzle piece that allowed me to make sense of everything I had been experiencing after falling so hard in August.

The diagnosis also shined a bright light of understanding on many aspects of my childhood. Like those "migraines" that required retreating to my darkened bedroom for a couple of hours midday. And the onset of urinary incontinence around age six, resolving on its own within months. As I grew, as I played hard, my tethered cord couldn't stretch with me, temporarily affecting nerves feeding my head and my bladder.

Luckily, those were the only hints of a problem. I entered adulthood blissfully oblivious to the ticking timebomb that was my spinal cord.

Small dura tears and consequent slow CSF leaks became regular features of my life from 2004 on. While I was still suffering symptoms from the second leak, I saw a third neurologist, a man in his early seventies who was about to retire. He had been an ultra-distance trail runner himself and had a son my age, also an ultra runner. I thought he would understand why I ran through the pain, but I also wanted to make sure running wasn't making things worse. The doctor listened to my story, read through my neuro records, and asked questions. After telling me that he agreed with the diagnosis of SIH, he offered to do something I hadn't thought to ask for. He would write a letter, ostensibly to the second neurologist, saying that I'd consulted him and that he agreed with the diagnosis and treatment.

"I'm going to give you a copy," he said. "You'll have it to present to any new physician you see in the future, wherever you might live." When a copy of his letter arrived in the mail, I was pleased. In addition to a synopsis of my symptoms and diagnostic results, he had noted that I was a "sophisticated patient" who clearly understood my body and who, as an ultra-distance trail runner, tolerated pain better than most, which allowed me to continue running despite the severity of my positional headaches. With that comment, he addressed all the naysayers, like Neurologist Number One, who didn't believe I had SIH because I continued to run.

Complete validation. It felt *so* good.

After the initial diagnosis in early 2004, after the second known leak eventually healed on its own, I might go a few months without a headache, but then I'd trip on a curb, stumble over a tree root and hyperextend my back, or lift something too heavy and a sneaky new tear would occur. A week or two later, I'd notice the tell-tale headaches soon after getting up in the morning, worsening as the day went on, then gradually improving over several weeks as the tear slowly healed itself and my CSF level returned to normal.

As a way of letting those close to me know what was going on with me, I began joking about being "a quart low." During such times, I might be grumpy, would sleep a lot, and needed plenty of alone time, away from irritants.

As time wore on, the tears became more frequent and my dura became slower to seal. Headaches were a constant, eventually joined by tinnitus in one ear, then both, and later, drooping eyebrows, along with all the various emotional symptoms of low tolerance and motivation.

I now understood what was meant by the term "invisible disability." No one would know by looking at me that I was suffering from anything. I dealt with the positional headaches and tinnitus, darkened mood, zapped motivation, and reduced ability to handle daily frustrations, all of which made working full time nearly impossible. Yet I pushed away the term "disability." I wasn't ready to admit, to myself or anyone else, that the changes inside me were *that* drastic. Instead, I would do what my mother taught me: buck up and deal, hide my limitations and feelings.

The constant bright spot in life, the thing that got me through this, was trail running with my dogs, even though running (especially downhill) often made my headaches worse afterward.

After several cycles of tears, leaks, and repairs, I learned to identify and predict some of the subtler symptoms. For example, I became intolerant of loud noises, bright lights, and crowds, impatient with traffic and the common day-to-day challenges of city life. Trying to push through a typical work day, maintaining outward politeness toward clients and colleagues while dealing with persistent headaches, was frustrating and exhausting. Thankfully, I was self-employed, so I had significant control over my schedule. As the leaks and symptoms grew more frequent, I worked less and then, only when symptoms allowed. There were stretches when working even ten hours a week was a monumental struggle. I learned to get by on less income and dial back my expectations.

The leaks made me feel constantly tired. At night, I slept deeply for ten to twelve hours, often waking with a sore back, and dreamed more than usual, an indication that I was spending more time in deep REM sleep. During the day, I got temporary relief if I napped, which gave me enough of a restart to get through the afternoon and evening hours. I felt like I was adopting my dogs' sleep/wake cycles.

With no realistic surgical fix for my tethered spinal cord, the specter of new leaks and regular headaches loomed. A dark cloud obscured my future and dashed any sense of being able to orchestrate my life. Planning travel or scheduling vacations were non-starters. I couldn't predict, come travel day, whether I'd feel good or like shit. More likely, like shit.

I also couldn't fathom running another ultra-distance race. I might feel fine the day I signed up and sent in my race fee, but what if I was suffering leak symptoms on race day? The race would be painful, the headache more noticeable with the pounding of running for hours on end; dehydration would compound the low CSF level and brain sag. Just the thought of that additional pain on top of the aches and blisters of a race took all fun out of even thinking about doing one.

With heavy heart but being realistic, I told Mike he should move on. I couldn't imagine ever again being the partner he deserved. In the autumn of 2004, after twelve years together, he did.

As much as I grieved the loss of Mike, I also grieved the loss of my ultra-runner self. That was my identity, my lifestyle. Long-distance trail running inspired me to get up each morning, to run and train. I set and achieved goals. I looked forward to seeing friends at events. Would I ever enjoy that sense of family and camaraderie at a trail race again?

Some wondered why I didn't just stop running after my diagnosis, especially on forest trails with my dogs, which increased the risk of a trip and, therefore, a new leak. But, I argued, I could just as easily trip while walking along a sidewalk, or create a new tear by lifting something too heavy or twisting my lower back suddenly.

I'd been running throughout my life. I couldn't imagine *not* running. The risk of trail running causing a new leak was one I was willing to take to keep running wild with my dogs.

TRANSITION

In the early 2000s, fantasies of leaving western Washington for a calmer, quieter life frequently filled my brain. By 2004, the second CSF leak and tethered-cord revelation convinced me I had to make significant changes in order to survive, maybe even thrive.

During long, easy runs through forests with my dogs, actual plans took shape in my mind. I wanted a life that would eliminate all the city-life triggers—traffic, sirens, crime, lawnmowers/leaf blowers, loud people—that made my headaches and mood worse. I needed a lifestyle that focused on what still brought me joy: being with my dogs; running trails through forests, mountains, and meadows; seeing wildlife and wildflowers; peace and quiet at home; alone time.

Even before the CSF leaks started, I'd flirted with moving out of state, somewhere in a rural, mountainous area of the inland West. Among other things, I wanted to put physical distance between me and my mother and her constant guilt-tripping and demands to attend all the family gatherings. We had nothing other than DNA in common; I was always the last to arrive and first to leave. I'd miss being near my father—I'd particularly miss his bearhugs—but his remarriage in 1984 had made it difficult for me to spend time with him. His wife was ... challenging; she was, in fact, similar to my mother in her narcissism, but in addition, had undiagnosed and troubling mental health issues and rejected therapy. I needed emotional and physical distance from her, too.

Fundamentally, while I couldn't articulate why it felt crucial to leave western Washington, I knew in my gut that my emotional health depended on getting far away from my long-standing set of big emotional triggers.

In the end, I chose Idaho.

More particularly, the sparsely populated, forested mountains of central Idaho, in the Salmon River Mountain range, home of the Payette National Forest and near the resort town of McCall.

I'd been to the area with friends a few times in the mid-1980s, mostly for white-water kayaking and rafting trips on the Salmon and Lochsa Rivers. But I'd mostly forgotten those experiences until, overnighting in Missoula after two long days of driving through Wyoming and eastern Montana on an exploratory vacation in June 2003, I found myself with twenty-four hours before I had to catch a flight out of Boise back to Seattle. Where to stay?

With that same group of '80s friends, I'd spent two days skiing at Brundage Ski Resort outside McCall. We'd stayed in downtown McCall, on the southern shore of Payette Lake. It so happened we were there during the town's Winter Carnival, an annual ten-day celebration that featured a parade, live music venues, crafts, and snow-themed games. There were elaborate ice sculptures, lots of holiday lights, and tourists. At night, the small downtown looked like a magical movie set, cold and pristine but brightly lit. Add moonlight and stars visible over the darkened lake and mountains beyond, it's no wonder the scene made a strong impression on me.

Now, I decided to see what McCall looked like in the summer. After making a hotel reservation, I grabbed a quick breakfast in Missoula and started driving south. The early part of the drive, which passed through the Nez Perce National Forest in northern Idaho, was gorgeous. Everywhere I looked, I saw evergreens and mountains. For several miles, the two-lane State Highway 12 hugged the curvy Lochsa River, which in June was flowing fast and high. Memories of being "Maytagged" in a Class IV rapid somewhere on the Lochsa—spinning around upside down and underwater in my kayak, grateful when the rapid spat me out—flashed through my mind.

Continuing down Highway 12, I passed through areas of mixed forest, green pastures, and hayfields. After the town of Grangeville, the road climbed to White Bird Pass. There, at 4,245 feet, the wide-open view to the east took my breath away. Endless green rolling hills with few trees, spiny ridges with sharp, much taller peaks in the distance, some still snowcapped.

Quickly dropping almost 2,500 feet, Highway 12 eventually settled in for a long meander alongside the wide, fast-flowing, but mostly rapid-free

Salmon River. The landscape changed to steep, undulating hills rising a couple of thousand feet on both sides of the river. They were mostly brown and barren, with a just tinge of green spring growth and a few short pine trees here and there along ridges.

After crossing into a new time zone (Mountain Time), I drove through Riggins, a tiny town nestled next to the Salmon River where it makes a sweeping bend and the Little Salmon River pours in from the south. A river-rafting mecca, Riggins is constricted to one long narrow strip near the highway. Not here, I thought. Too dry. Virtually no trees. Too closed-in. I began to wonder if I'd already driven through the prettiest part of Idaho.

Leaving Riggins, I continued south toward McCall. The forested Salmon River Mountains rose above and beyond the barren hills I was leaving behind, providing tantalizing glimpses of their rugged beauty. Soon, the road began to climb as it followed a twisting, narrow gorge carved by the Little Salmon River, shadowed by steep hills close to the road. I noticed more and more trees, mostly pines and firs. Crossing into the Payette National Forest—2.3 million acres of high-elevation woodlands, lakes, streams, and mountains—then popping out of the Little Salmon River gorge into Meadows Valley at 3,900 feet, I felt goosebumps on my arms. I'd gone from narrow, serpentine terrain with rock cliffs and steep, tree-covered hills to a wide, lush glacial valley. A handful of miles farther south and the valley opened out even more.

Luxuriant with thick pasture grass, the nearly flat, sixteen-mile-long, five-mile-wide valley was encircled by forested mountains. Ranches with fenced pastures in which black beef cattle lazily grazed dotted the valley's flat bottom. Homes could be seen on the shoulders of the forested slopes on both sides of the valley, partially hidden by tall evergreens. A smile spread across my face.

Continuing roughly halfway through the length of Meadows Valley to the intersection of Highway 12 and Highway 55, I turned left and gained another thousand feet in elevation to reach McCall. Even that portion of the drive—up a narrow canyon, the road steep and curving, sheer cliffs topped with pine trees as it hugged the riotous Goose Creek full of snowmelt—was jaw-dropping gorgeous.

Once home in Seattle, I couldn't shake the feeling of McCall.

I'd assumed that in moving to an area, I'd buy a home in town. But as I started investigating online listings, I was shocked. By mid-2003, housing prices were on the upswing, in a dramatic way, especially in resort areas. That fall, I took my father with me on a road trip to McCall. The real estate agent I'd engaged showed us a few properties in or near town. Both Dad and I were astounded at the asking prices, so high for small, older homes needing upgrades, on tiny lots with little space between neighbors. Nothing appealed to me and we left without making an offer. Though I was discouraged, over the long winter that followed, I continued my online search as McCall and the Payette National Forest slumbered under several feet of snow.

The following spring, remembering how I'd felt when I first set eyes on Meadows Valley, I found a new real estate agent in the tiny town of New Meadows, population three hundred, at the junction of Highway 12 and Highway 55 in the middle of Meadows Valley. He and his firm specialized in properties in Meadows Valley but covered McCall as well. I arranged to meet with him during Memorial Day weekend. This time, I drove to McCall, bringing Maia and Meadow with me for companionship. The next morning, the girls and I drove down into Meadows Valley and met up with the agent at his office. Because I had the girls with me, we took my car. After we'd looked at a couple of homes that didn't do anything for me, I was beginning to feel discouraged again.

"Have you thought about buying bare ground and building?" the agent asked.

"No. What do you have in mind?" I asked, curious but thinking it was a crazy idea.

He suggested that we look at some lots in a subdivision called Timber Ridge. Once there, he pointed me toward two lots for sale. Parking on the field grass of the upper lot, I let the girls out to sniff around as he and I walked the lot. He was explaining the details but I was distracted by what I saw in front of me. Facing west, the five-and-a-half-acre lot had an expansive view, not only across the middle of Meadows Valley, but also to the hills and mountains beyond. I could see the Seven Devils and other peaks on the far side of Hells Canyon and the Snake River that formed the border between Idaho and Oregon.

That evening, after taking the girls for a walk, I called my dad from the motel room.

"Dad. I think I found it. Not a house, a lot. The view is amazing."

"That's great," Dad said. "Think about it before you decide," he advised. "Take your time."

"I can't wait, Dad. The lots are going quickly, and I don't want to risk losing out. I'm going to make an offer tomorrow."

Dad's silence told me he was worried that I was moving too fast. He didn't want me to regret my decision, but he also trusted me.

"You're sure?" he finally asked.

"Yeah, I'm sure."

Before leaving for home the next day, I did indeed make an offer and put down earnest money. The seller quickly accepted my offer, and I became the owner of five-plus acres of unimproved ground in Idaho.

I was committed. And excited.

That my first reaction to unpleasantness in my personal life was to move, to run, to transport myself away, literally and figuratively, wasn't surprising. When shit hit the fan, I always went for a run, removing myself from the situation to find space to think and search for a solution. I moved away from painful relationships and the burdensome expectations of others. I moved—always, inexorably, regardless of cost—toward quiet, calm, peace, and acceptance.

Throughout my life, family and others criticized me for what they perceived as running away from my problems: leaving my teen marriage; avoiding my difficult mother and stepmother; walking away from higher-paying but unfulfilling work to focus on work I felt good about; completely changing my lifestyle to accommodate my invisible neuro-disability (which most of my friends didn't know about).

I'd read the pithy sayings ... *Wherever you go, there you are.* And, *You can run but you can't hide.*

True enough. But I had trouble articulating to family and friends I wasn't doing *that*. I knew in my core I wasn't running away from myself or my problems. I knew the issues I struggled with wouldn't magically disappear if I moved, changed jobs, skipped family gatherings. The issues clung like Saran Wrap, always touching me, constricting my breathing and well-being, wherever I was or how far I ran.

Highly sensitive, I was always keenly aware of issues in my life and relationships. No way could I outrun them all, so I didn't even try. What *was* true: With emotional distance, the stress and internal noise quieted. I could better see and understand my issues. I could approach and maybe even tame most of them. I could set boundaries. I could also better see and articulate my needs, something that became critical after the CSF leak diagnosis. I needed space to reflect, consider, plan, and act. I needed to be the architect of my own life rather than mirror the expectations of others. Being in nature with my dogs allowed the necessary insights and plans to emerge. Running trails with my dogs was running toward my new best self.

After each instance of "running away" from a situation that felt bad or wrong to me, I emerged from the initial sensations of guilt and shame feeling much better. Freer. More myself. Those weren't decisions I regretted, ever.

By my late thirties, I'd begun to trust myself. If my inner voice, my gut, told me I needed to go, to run, to make a big change? I listened. I acted. Carefully, cautiously, often with fear and trepidation and looking for the path that would cause others the least disruption, I made the changes I needed.

Those changes seldom made sense to others. I rarely shared my inner emotional landscape or struggles with anyone. To most of those who knew me, I probably seemed to have my shit together. But when I did make a life change, I was always going toward who I needed and wanted to become rather than toward the expectations of others. So, I'm sure many saw my changes as leaving them behind.

Sometimes change came in baby steps, other times like running easily along a meandering forest trail, and occasionally, with what felt like a mad one-hundred-yard dash to safety. Relocating to Idaho was a mad dash.

Just as I used running to "train" my mind and body for the bar exam in 1983, I used the lessons learned from long-distance trail running and racing as I undertook my biggest and most daring life change to date: starting fresh in a new state where I knew no one.

Plan, but be prepared for the unanticipated, the unexpected.
Adjust goals as you go to address immediate needs.
Train body and mind to deal with unpleasantness, pain,
and disappointment.
Learn how to handle those feelings and sensations because they

will come again.
One foot in front of the other, repeatedly, gets you to the finish line.
Life isn't a race, it's a journey.

Instead of spending my precious energy being mad or feeling persecuted by my own weakened body, I pivoted. Accepted. Changed. Evolved. Grew. And ran in the direction of my lights: dogs and forests.

I acknowledged to myself that I would probably always be on my own. The bonds I had with my dogs had been built on trust and routines in the natural world that most would find odd, or frivolous, even meaningless. Besides, what man would ever find me and my peculiar, rollercoaster of a CSF-leaking lifestyle attractive? How could any man love a woman whose own mother couldn't love her?

I quit looking. I embraced my aloneness.

As I tried to resume my normal routine in Washington, I anxiously planned my new life in Idaho.

I worked as much as I could at my solo practice during the week, depending on CSF levels and mood and the hours I slept. During an active leak, I had precious little time or energy for anything after my morning nature fix with the dogs. Housework could wait. Social phone calls and visits could wait. Appointments could be delayed or cancelled altogether. I had little to no motivation to do anything that wasn't absolutely necessary to stay financially solvent. Grumpy, reacting strongly and quickly to minor irritations, I briefly wondered if I was depressed. But no, I didn't feel hopeless. I knew I would feel better eventually. I wasn't lonely, either. I preferred being alone with my dogs; being alone was easier. But I was sad I'd lost my earlier, more spontaneous lifestyle and I missed my relationship with Mike. I was also sad that my dogs no longer had the energetic, upbeat, outgoing human I used to be.

During the year between buying the Idaho lot and actually moving to Idaho, the girls and I met Mike at Tiger Mountain or nearby Cougar Mountain for a trail run most Saturday mornings. He and I were no longer a couple, but still enjoyed running together with the girls. Those runs helped enormously. My head hurt on downhills, and my eyes often felt like they were bouncing in their sockets, but endorphins and Mike's supportive friendship elevated my mood, at least for a while.

Most of my "free" time was consumed in a blur of planning: hiring a contractor in Idaho to build a home; getting a construction loan to finance it; selling my Seattle home; finishing up my caseload; leaving my legal practice and sole source of income in Washington behind; getting accepted to the Idaho bar and finding new legal work.

During those months, it felt like I was riding a snowball down a steep mountain slope, quickly gaining speed and size (tasks). Scary, but exhilarating.

So many unknowns. So many risks. Some nights I couldn't sleep, thinking about how much could go sideways. But after the lot purchase closed, it was like I'd found a gorgeous new path through the forest. I wasn't sure where it went or how far, or how difficult the terrain was, but I was determined to follow it, one foot in front of the other. Just like an ultra race, I'd see what sort of adventures awaited me and my dogs along the way.

I decided to skip hiring an architect. My basic needs were simple: single level and dog-friendly. A floorplan I found online for $150 had everything I required: a California-style bungalow with three bedrooms, two baths, a sunroom, and an attached two-car garage. Home expos became my go-to destinations. I decided to implement an intriguing heating design, ground loop geothermal heat to an in-floor radiant system, and to have concrete floors throughout, maximizing energy efficiency. (My father made a brilliant suggestion: have the floor stamped with a texture so the dogs wouldn't slip and slide on a too-smooth surface.) Dad helped me work through the design details, which was fun and brought us even closer.

In spring 2005, I took my floor plan and design choices to the general contractor I'd hired. He made some minor changes to the plans, and while he'd never done a geothermal ground loop or concrete floors with radiant heat like I'd chosen, he was game.

All of the research and decision-making helped me mostly ignore the leak symptoms, which came to feel like a sickening, never-ending rollercoaster ride as one leak opened, eventually healed, then another opened, healed, ad nauseam. My good days were quickly outnumbered by leaking days.

In May of that year, to the bafflement of most of my family and friends, I sold my home in Seattle and secured the construction loan I'd need to pay the contractor. After finding a short-term rental near my lot in Idaho, I packed all my furniture—including the 1888 upright piano I'd been playing since age five—into a U-Haul truck. The girls and I made the ten-hour drive in my SUV, a friend following in the truck.

While my house was under construction, the girls and I began exploring our new home territory. Initially, I stuck to a rail trail and Forest Service roads in the Payette near my rental. One day, I stopped by the New Meadows District Ranger Office seeking trail maps and advice.

"Do dogs have to be on-leash on trails?" I asked the young woman in a Forest Service uniform behind the counter.

"Leash?" she asked, clearly startled by my question. "No. No one leashes their dogs in the forest. It's not required."

I could hardly believe my ears. No more worrying about other trail users being upset when the girls were off-leash, or quickly leashing them when someone came along. I couldn't wait to pick up where we'd left off in Washington: running mountain trails, free and wild.

That summer, we explored several trails in the Payette near New Meadows and McCall, learning where water flowed, never venturing more than five miles from a trailhead. The girls gave me the confidence to do this.

After watching the entire construction process—from the bulldozer pushing dirt for the foundation to interior finishing touches—the girls and I moved into our new home in mid-December 2005, on my forty-ninth birthday. Snow on the ground. Best birthday ever.

My new life had begun. It was playing out as I'd hoped: Just me and the girls on an adventure of discovery, health, and growth. Sure, I still had CSF leaks and headaches, but, distracted by the house and the forest, I managed not to dwell on them. It had been two-and-a-half years since that hard fall on a mountain trail started all this change. I could never have guessed or predicted this outcome.

Though I didn't realize it at first, Idaho would teach me the true meaning of "wild." In Idaho's Salmon River Mountains, in the Payette National Forest, every trail run with my dogs was a new lesson in wilderness, wildness, and the incomparable beauty of the natural world, away from most human interference.

WILDLIFE

By the time I moved to Idaho in 2005, I'd been running and racing for thirty years. Maia and Meadow were just shy of their fifth and third birthdays and had plenty of long training runs on their resumes as well, including the Peterson Ridge Rumble in Sisters, Oregon, an eighteen-mile, dog-friendly trail race. I had done some trail running with Opus, but it was after bringing Maia and Meadow into my life that I developed a long-distance trail-running bond with Malamutes.

We usually started our mornings at five-thirty (or before sun-up in winter). One of the girls was usually sleeping on the bed with me. The other would jump onto the bed, hoping that alone would be enough to get me up. If that didn't work, they'd both start breathing heavily, shifting around, becoming excited if I rolled over or moved in any way. *It's working. She's awake. Keep it up*, I imagined them communicating to each other. When I resigned myself to the fact that I was done sleeping and said "Good morning!" the tail wagging, face licking, ear cleaning happiness that was our morning ritual began. If it was Saturday—and I assure you the girls knew what day of the week it was—it was time to head for mountain trails.

Saturday was the girls' favorite day of the week, the day we were more likely to explore a new trail and spend more time running than any other day of the week. If for some reason they couldn't come along (too far or dogs not allowed), I had to sneak into my running clothes and shoes. And yes, they knew running shoes from other shoes, running clothes from work clothes.

Along with the heightened awareness of nature and wildlife that trail running with my dogs brought me, I also noticed a well-earned tiredness that morphed into feelings of calm and peace. Each run delivered a sense of awe—of the forest's natural beauty and the ease with which my dogs and I moved through it—mixed with a keen awareness that something could instantly go wrong, so nothing should be wasted or taken for granted.

A metaphor for life.

This "running with dogs" nirvana didn't happen overnight. I had learned a lot from Opus, but there was an ongoing learning curve for me with the girls. Running with two dogs required us to truly work together as a team, to practice and reinforce skills on every single run. It also required extensive thought, planning, and training. Were they willing and able to run long distances, regardless of my own desire for them to join me? Were their joints and muscles healthy enough to tolerate the loads of a long run? Were they well rested? Could they tolerate the predicted weather (i.e., would it be cool enough)? Would there be enough water? Many of the questions were similar to those I asked myself when nervously toeing the start line of an ultra-distance trail race.

Malamutes are pack-oriented. Since the girls considered me their pack leader (and food provider), they stayed near me on the trail and looked to me for direction. A trait I first observed in Opus and one that has proven invaluable over the years I've been privileged to share trails with them, it cemented me to the breed.

Trail running is a technical sport, sort of like rock climbing, but without harnesses and extreme vertical. To avoid tripping or falling over an unending series of obstacles, attention is primarily focused on footing. While running trails with my dogs on-leash was possible, it was usually far more dangerous for me, and often nearly impossible. Depending on terrain, even on-leash hiking was difficult. Malamutes naturally want to lead and pull and it could be difficult to quickly determine my foot placement when they were running side-by-side on a coupler just ahead of me. After the CSF leak diagnosis, I didn't want to increase the risk of a fall. So, to truly enjoy trail running with my dogs, I worked to develop the mutual trust and skills necessary to run with them off-leash.

Several commands worked for me. "Easy" meant to slow it down a bit, for example on a downhill, so they didn't get too far in front of me. "With me" meant to run beside or close behind me, but not in front of me, so I could better see the trail and control them should we encounter anyone. "Over" meant they should move to the side of the trail to let me pass. "Good lead" told Maia that it was okay to assume the lead position and run ten to fifteen feet ahead of me. "Go drink" assured them that I would wait while they slurped from a nearby stream or lake. A flat, backward-facing palm was the signal not to pass me. And, of course, "stay!" meant don't move until I say "okay." In early training, if I needed to make my own pit stop off the trail, the dogs got a treat when I was finished to encourage them to wait patiently nearby. (I did the same for them, waiting while they peed or pooped, so they never felt left behind or rushed.) As Malamutes, they were naturally inclined to keep their pack together, so it was natural for them to wait if I lagged or stopped.

I constantly talked to the girls as we ran, telling them what good dogs they were. My voice let them know where I was and also warned wildlife that we were nearby. Early on, to reinforce crucial skills, I rewarded them with special "trail" treats, especially when they responded immediately to "come" and "leave it." Training was an ongoing process, every single run. After a few months of consistency, they responded without treat rewards.

The command "leave it" was critical. I knew we would encounter both small and large wildlife on the trail and I didn't want the girls chasing these animals. We had some early failures—hares on Tiger Mountain, and sometimes deer. Those experiences taught me to double down on the training, but also, that when a dog does leave the trail in pursuit of something, most will eventually return to the place they'd left. I learned to wait for them rather than run one direction or the other, calling and hoping to entice them back. I also learned that Maia's compliance with "leave it" decreased slightly after Meadow joined us, a reminder that when there's more than one dog, you have a pack—one followed the other's lead, sometimes without thinking—which required additional effort (and training) to maintain off-leash control of both.

While the girls became reliable trail partners, mostly listening to me, I knew it was foolish to think they would be 100 percent compliant in all circumstances.

During the summer of 2003, I'd had an alarming lesson in the risks of off-leash trail running. We were at Cougar Mountain Regional Wildland Park, a 3,115-acre state park a few miles outside Seattle, near Tiger Mountain. We frequently ran there in the early morning.

One morning near the end of an hour-long run, Meadow suddenly sprinted down a trail, around a curve, and out of sight. Maia, on high alert, quickly followed. I assumed Meadow had sighted a deer that would easily disappear through the undergrowth, at which point the girls would return to me. Instead, when I caught up to them, I saw Maia standing completely still on the trail, tail dropped, looking nervous. Her body language screamed, "Danger! Run to the car!" But what was she worried about?

Meadow, about ten feet off the trail, stood unusually still in the brushy undergrowth, unwilling to return to me or indeed, to move at all. After several stern commands, she reluctantly complied, backing toward me to the edge of the trail. Irritated that she'd chased something, I made her sit next to me. One hand on her collar, I began to dig her leash out of my fanny pack. (Having to run or walk on-leash for a bit was the consequence for not immediately obeying a command to come or leave it.)

Suddenly, I heard a deep roar from behind the tall stump Meadow had backed away from. She had chased an adult black bear! The hair on the back of my neck standing on end, my heart pounding through my ribs, and still holding Meadow's collar, we ran down the trail toward Maia and away from the bear, who clearly just wanted us to be gone. Later, I realized Maia's body language had been screaming "Bear!" but I was too focused on Meadow's disobedience. In Meadow's defense, she was wisely unwilling to turn her back on the bear she had chased. Unwittingly, I made things worse, repeatedly demanding that Meadow come to me, then making her sit on the trail, putting both of us in danger. Fortunately for us that time, black bears are typically shy and non-confrontational.

I already knew Maia, who wanted nothing to do with bears, had excellent ursine radar. Unfortunately, during that morning run at Cougar Mountain, Meadow was in the lead (a rare thing) and saw the bear first. The bear ran (as black bears usually do), triggering Meadow's desire to chase. Apparently, Maia didn't realize what they were chasing until she caught up to Meadow and the bear hiding behind the stump.

That episode taught me to be even more aware of our surroundings and to anticipate, to the extent possible, animals that would entice Meadow to chase. If her nose went up and she sniffed the air with purpose, I'd grab the hand loop on her collar or attach a leash until she and I both knew what scent she'd caught and whether it was an animal that needed a few moments to get away.

I was sure the girls' wilderness skills would transfer to Idaho, but I also knew we were likely to encounter a greater variety of wildlife with greater frequency. And we did. The more we explored new trails and Forest Service roads in the Payette, the more we all learned about Idaho wildlife.

Like that autumn of 2005 when we ran down Goose Creek Falls Trail on a frosty morning. The first mile drops steeply and steadily until the trail reaches a stock bridge across Goose Creek. Crossing the bridge brought us to Goose Creek Trail, right in the middle of its six-mile length from Last Chance Campground at the bottom to Brundage Reservoir at the top. It's a beautiful section of forest, thick with trees and huckleberry shrubs, backdropped by the roar of Goose Creek (especially during snow melt). The trail was too steep, rugged, and challenging for hunters in autumn, and mountain bikers had yet to make the changes that later brought bike tourists to test their skills.

The girls and I descended the steepest early stretch, about a half-mile. Quads burning as I fought gravity, I caught a break when the trail briefly leveled out as it traversed a steep hillside. There were mature evergreens on the uphill side and low shrubs on the downhill side, providing an open view to the next ridge.

My eyes were on the ground; footing was tricky and I didn't want to trip. Suddenly, a flash of movement caught my eye: a white-tailed deer leapt from the uphill side across the trail and ran downhill through the shrubbery. Startled, both girls quickly ran the few yards to where the deer crossed the trail, sniffing the fresh tracks in the dirt, tails wagging, bodies radiating excitement. So close, such fresh scent! Then Meadow plunged her head into the greenery alongside the trail and didn't pull it out right away. Maia moved next to Meadow and did the same. "Leave it, girls!" I shouted, not sure what I was asking them to leave.

Maia backed up, but not Meadow. I reached for Meadow's collar to pull her back onto the trail. That's when I saw the spotted butt of a fawn, legs folded underneath its belly, trying to disappear into the vegetation. Meadow held its tail nubbin gently in her mouth. Not biting, but tasting.

"Meadow, drop it," I said quietly, not wanting to traumatize the fawn even more. Meadow did as I asked and moved back, letting the fawn's tail slip out of her mouth. The fawn was too terrified to move, so I took both girls by their collars and led them down the trail several feet, then shooed them ahead of me. "Let's give that poor baby some space, girls," I said, encouraging them to resume running. Meadow stopped once to look back up the trail where the deer and fawn had been, but they were gone.

I was relieved, but not totally surprised, that Meadow only wanted to taste the fawn's tail. Meadow had a soft mouth; unlike Maia, she never destroyed dog toys. She often carried one of my shoes or socks around the house but never damaged them. On the rare occasions Meadow caught a small wild animal, she always released it alive.

About that same time, Meadow caught a pika as we were running on a dry, lower-elevation trail near Riggins. Maia was ahead of me, as usual, but I then noticed Meadow wasn't right behind me. When I stopped and turned to look for her, I saw her returning to the trail. Her posture was odd and she was slow to come to me. That's when I realized she had something in her mouth. At my command to drop it, she lowered her head and opened her mouth. The pika hit the dirt running and dashed off through the trees on the downhill side, uninjured but probably covered in dog drool. Meadow looked proud.

One early morning in the summer of 2006, the girls and I were running along a new-to-us trail. After a couple of miles, we came to a small lake. I saw two tents pitched near the lake shore, and heard voices, campers starting their day, so I put the girls on-leash. If the campers were cooking breakfast, I didn't want the girls begging, especially if they had bacon. Walking, we approached the campsite. The trail was narrow there, thick shrubs among young trees on both sides. I saw one llama, then a second, tethered to trees alongside the trail, butts and hind legs *on* the trail.

Hoo boy. This was going to be interesting. The girls were both wary of and excited by these new animals and their scent.

"Hello!" I called out. "Runner coming through. I've got two dogs. Can you help me get by your llamas?"

A man appeared and smiled when he saw the girls, who were still distracted by the llamas. After he greeted them, he said, "No worries. The llamas are used to dogs. Go right by them."

I wasn't so sure, but he kept encouraging me. Besides, there was no easy way around them.

"Okay, girls, let's go. Easy, now," I said reassuringly, walking in front of them as we passed by the llamas. The llamas shifted slightly to get a better look at us, but couldn't turn around because of the way they were tethered to trees. Maia seemed frightened and darted by, but Meadow moved more slowly. When her leash went taut, I looked back to see why and caught her with her mouth on one llama's tail nubbin, taking a taste. The llama didn't seem to mind, or at least, it didn't kick her.

Thinking back to the fawn tail-tasting on Goose Creek Falls Trail the previous autumn, I wondered if "tasting" an animal was Meadow's way of learning about them for future reference. I knew from earlier vacations at a dog-friendly dude ranch in British Columbia that Meadow was calm around large ungulates. Curious, she would sniff nose-to-nose with Louis, the horse I always rode, as well as a foal left to graze near the guest cabins in order to become socialized to people and dogs. To my relief, that curiosity and calmness transferred to the Idaho wilderness.

Except for elk. For some reason, Meadow found elk irresistible and always wanted to get near them, to chase them. Fearful they would hurt her, I never let that happen.

By August 2007, the girls and I had run Campbell's Cow Camp Trail a couple of times with friends and their dog, climbing under and over a few downed trees in the process. A primitive trail, it got little use or maintenance except during hunting season. The trail traversed a steep slope, turning in and out of gullies where small streams ran over it or through small culverts underneath. I knew that at least two of the streams flowed all summer, including Squirrel Creek, four miles in, ensuring plenty of water for the girls.

We started early, taking advantage of cooler air. It had been a dry summer and the first trail mile was a dusty one. The girls and I headed for the creek in our usual formation: Maia in the lead, followed by me and then Meadow. The forest was quiet and still except for the noise we were making—footfalls and paws on dirt, breathing deeply from the steady exertion.

We arrived at Squirrel Creek in good time. I stood on the sturdy wood stock bridge a couple of feet above the creek; it was maybe four feet wide and unencumbered by railings. Both girls immediately waded into the creek, which was still running strong and full. I pulled my camera from my pack and took photos of them drinking, cooling their hot paws, tongues long and dripping water. Because it was the start of hunting (bow) season, both girls wore their Do Not Hunt Me vests with some extra neon-green flagging on their collars to be more visible from the front.

After satisfying her thirst, Maia jumped directly from the creek onto the bridge and stood next to me. I stroked her head while we watched Meadow continue to wade and drink. Meadow was like a tanker; when thirsty, she drank lots of water, taking her time, filling up.

Maia turned to look the other way, into the trees. She stood utterly still. Looking down at her hind end next to my right leg, I saw her tail drop.

Slowly, I followed her gaze.

There in the undergrowth, spotlighted by a shaft of morning sunlight breaking through the trees, I saw a cinnamon-colored black bear. It appeared to be foraging, maybe fifty feet away and facing the other direction, apparently unaware of us.

Shit. "Meadow, come. Up, up, Meadow. Come!" I urged *sotto voce*.

I knew Maia wouldn't chase the bear, but I was never 100 percent certain Meadow wouldn't try to introduce herself, so I wanted to put her on-leash ASAP.

To my immense relief, Meadow obeyed and joined us on the bridge; I quickly clipped a leash to her collar. Then, still standing between the girls, I slowly turned around to better see the bear. I had no plan in mind, other than to remain calm and quiet and hope it would continue on its way.

Meadow's tail also dropped as we watched the cinnamon bear.

Since the bear was slowly moving away from our route back to the car, I started planning a quiet retreat. Then Meadow alerted to something on our right, close to the trail we needed to follow to safety.

A cub. A small black version of the cinnamon bear, also casually foraging in the undergrowth while slowly heading in the direction of its mama.

Okay. Don't get between mama and cub. Let the cub keep moving, I thought.

I've never been so impatient for a wild animal to move. *Please, go! Go toward your mama!* But the cub was in no hurry.

That's when I decided to make our presence known to mama bear. I hoped that if she realized we were in the vicinity, she would move away more quickly, convincing her cub to follow.

"Yo, bear!" I called out, not too loudly, but enough to be heard. I startled the girls; they both looked at me briefly before returning their gaze to the two bears.

Mama bear looked over her shoulder at us, then resumed foraging.

"Yo, bear. Keep moving that way, please!" I said, clapping my hands together twice and feeling utterly silly for having such a one-sided conversation.

Mama bear looked toward where her cub was shifting the shrubbery as it slowly moved toward her. She seemed to decide that neither she nor her cub were in any danger from the crazy woman on the bridge.

After waiting another few minutes—it seemed like forever—I decided both bears were far enough away that the girls and I could make our quiet escape back along the trail. As Maia eagerly led the way, tail down and nervous, I kept Meadow on-leash for my own peace of mind. A half-mile later, deciding we were well away from the bears, I released Meadow and we resumed our usual "Malamute sandwich" formation. Before long, Maia's tail returned to its life-is-good position over her back.

"Maia, you're amazing," I told her. Without Maia's initial alert, we might have gotten between mama bear and her cub, a dangerous situation for all concerned.

INTROVERT

Lots of people love to travel, visiting as many cities, countries, national parks, local mountain peaks—whatever their passion—as possible over the course of their lives. I have several friends whose goal is to run a marathon in all fifty states.

Personally, I find traveling both stressful and exhausting. To me, vacation travel is too busy, too fast, providing only a nibble of a particular location's flavors. The effort and expense put into getting to a place outweighs the fun experienced during the short time spent there. With the ever-present threat of a CSF leak and its persistent headaches, tinnitus, and moodiness, I was not at all enticed by the thought of travel.

Prior to the CSF leaks, I'd traveled some, including to Mexico; across two of Canada's provinces; to several US and Canadian national parks; through seven countries and two principalities in Europe (all in one whirlwind, fifteen-day trip in a tiny rental car); and to Peru to run the Inca Trail. Most of the international travel was with Mike, and I'd enjoyed each trip, seeing different countries, cultures, and people, learning about their history. Mike and I were good travel companions. But at the conclusion of each, I'd felt drained and tired and needed to retreat to the solitude of home and forest to recharge my introvert batteries. Besides, I'd missed my dogs.

Such travels proved I'm my father's daughter. Over the course of three decades, his job as a Boeing test pilot regularly took him to many countries around the globe. Who knows how many circumnavigations his air miles added up to? Yet he always said he was happiest when he returned home. His preferred leisure travel was close to home as well, flying into remote lakes in the interior of British Columbia for a few days of trout fishing. Peace and quiet, few people about, out in nature. I accompanied him on several of those fishing trips because I shared his taste in travel and destination. I just skipped the fishing part.

Also like my father, I preferred to revisit favorite places, getting better acquainted each time.

My early knowledge of the natural world derived from my father's lessons. Later, those lessons expanded with the time I spent in forests, observing wildlife, plants, weather, seasons, and how they all interact. I was always a student, hoping someday to become an expert in some tiny part or two of this beautiful, pale blue dot of a planet we call Earth.

After moving to Idaho, my desire to learn about the natural world intensified.

Gaining deep-seated familiarity with any place takes years and multiple seasonal cycles. Once in Idaho, I made repeated visits to specific locations in each season to note the subtle changes, learning which birds call and sing when, and from where; which wildflowers bloom first, or last, and at what elevations; which wild animal is moving, denning, mating, eating, hiding; what the air smells like; what the ground feels like under my feet; where the snow piles and drifts; how the views change.

My trail running slowly morphed to accommodate my new focus and interests. Gone were the Seattle days of group training runs on weekends, of running several ultra-distance races each year, of workouts to maintain speed and endurance. Without a local trail-running community in Idaho, I started running with just my dogs for company. I explored new terrain and remote trails with Maia and Meadow as my trusted guides, confident that their sense of location meant we'd never get lost. Without them, I would never have had the courage to explore alone, so deep in the Payette, so far from help and without cell reception.

I ran whatever pace my dogs and I enjoyed and the CSF leaks permitted, a pace that allowed the girls to follow their noses along fresh deer tracks a few feet off-trail, or me to stop and take photos of them, the wildflowers, the distant peaks. We were all getting older, so a slower pace seemed not just natural, but also wise. It was a big shift in my approach to running, but one I embraced.

Within Idaho's abundant and varied forest wildflowers and berries, I found another version of Mt. Rainier. Virtually all of Rainier's blooming friends greeted me in the Payette at some point in the year, from early snow melt—hello, white trillium and yellow avalanche lilies—to late summer's huckleberries and rosehips. In between, lupine, Indian paintbrush, American bistort, larkspur, penstemon, daisies, sunflowers, asters, shooting stars. I slowly learned their names and where and when they bloomed. I learned to follow the flowers uphill each spring; when those blooming near my home at 4,000 feet were past their prime by May, those at 5,000 feet were just emerging from the snow, on up to the highest elevations at 8,000 feet, where the wildflowers didn't bloom until late July or early August. It was a wildflower aficionado's nirvana.

Lupine were my favorite, maybe because purple is my favorite color. Or maybe because the name comes from lupus, Latin for wolf. Tall, with palm-like leaves at the bottom, they were easy to recognize as the plant first emerged in the spring. Their flowers form a tall cone of multiple small, pea-like winged blooms in tones ranging from deep blue-purple at the base to violet and lavender and, finally, white at the tip where unopened petals awaited. When growing near the base of old Ponderosa pines, they were an eye-catching contrast against the trees' furrowed, rusty-orange bark. Lupine also like the same open hillsides favored by arrowleaf balsamroot (sunflowers) and red Indian paintbrush, which created riots of vibrant color between more heavily forested sections.

I loved the mountain wildflowers so much that I decided to create a wildflower garden at my new house. Over several years, as the garden thrived, I came to love the columbine. As tall as lupine (which also grew in my home garden), columbine are slender and delicate where the lupine are muscular and bold. After several years, my garden columbines came in a variety of colors and combinations: blush, yellow, cream, magenta, watermelon, even the occasional purple. Delicate and lovely, they were often bicolored—magenta at the base with cream tips, for example. Each year was a surprise, with new colors and combinations emerging as the bees cross-pollinated. But what I loved most about the columbine blooms was their frivolous, pleated extravagance, each flower's five petals precisely folded, like waves in the silk fabric of an elaborate Victorian gown.

Hummingbirds and bumblebees became regular visitors to my garden. The bees collected pollen from the lupine, but seemed to prefer the columbine. They would crawl inside the hanging flower, disappearing briefly, emerging with yellow pollen thick in the "pollen baskets" on their legs before flying to the next flower.

I spent hours in that wildflower garden, watching, photographing, and videoing (often in slow motion) the bumblebees at work. It was one of the most soothing and awe-inspiring wildlife encounters I had been privileged to witness, and it was right beside my house.

Whenever the girls alerted me to something off-trail in the trees, I stopped and followed their gaze. While I couldn't always see what they were seeing, usually I was rewarded by the sight of wildlife I would've missed if I'd been by myself or running with people: a drumming male grouse on his drumming stump; elk; foxes; does with fawns; coyotes; hawks; ravens; and, on that one magical, memorable occasion, a wolf.

It never got old. Just as my dogs encountered new smells, tracks, sounds, and sights every time we ventured into the forest—even on trails we visited frequently—I was also entertained by the subtle changes in the environment as each season progressed. The next year, I'd see it all again, but just a little different, especially when it came to wildlife sightings. Another benefit: I was constantly learning, often with the help of bird and wildflower identification books or online searches once I got home.

In Idaho, I rarely ventured into the forest with another human. When I did, it was about socializing rather than observing nature. Chatting, focused on the give-and-take of our conversation, we were distracted from the details of the landscape we were moving through, hardly taking notice. While time spent this way with friends was (usually) enjoyable, it didn't recharge my batteries like the quiet peace of immersing myself in nature alone with my dogs.

Much like the easy friendships I made with trail-running friends early in my ultra-running life, running with the girls on wilderness forest trails allowed us to forge codependent and intimate bonds that would have been much less likely living in a city or suburb. We all had to exercise our big brains as we moved at a slow running pace, thinking independently and as a pack, working together to be safe so we could go out and do it all again the next day and the next.

To paraphrase the closing line of Mary Oliver's poem "How I Go Into the Woods," only those I love and deeply value spend time in the forest with me. Most are dogs.

My truth: People wear me out. Nature and dogs charge me up. It's that simple.

I often joked—in a serious way—that I preferred dogs to people. When I did interact with people, including friends, neighbors, colleagues, clients, I preferred doing so in ways that didn't unduly sap my energy, especially after the CSF leaks started. The emerging digital world was perfect for me. I could communicate with those I chose to or needed to, on my own schedule, from my rural home.

Growing up, I thought I was shy. That's how I heard myself described by adults, and eventually that label became part of my self-talk. Turns out, I wasn't shy. Rather, I was quiet, reserved, and uncomfortable with drawing attention to myself. I had no problem meeting and interacting with people of all ages, but I was happier on my own, or engaging in one-on-one time with select people.

As a child, I was regularly scolded by my mother for being "too sensitive." It frustrated her that my feelings were easily hurt; that I cried at sad stories, especially if animals were involved; that I felt personally attacked when people raised their voices or were mean to each other, a horrible jolt of bad energy running through my body like electricity, even if I wasn't in the same room. I felt physical and emotional pain vicariously.

Thanks to my mother's words and attitude, I grew up believing that being "too sensitive" was a bad thing, that I needed to toughen up and never cry in public or show my feelings. To do so was a sign of weakness, and being weak meant people would take advantage of me.

Luckily, my father's outlook was the opposite. He never chastised me for being aware, sensitive, and feeling. With him, I could cry and receive a hug. My father encouraged my sensitive nature toward animals, sharing his own love and empathy for them, encouraging me to develop the same.

As a young adult, I realized my intuition, empathy, and keen ability to observe were my secret superpowers. A knack for reading people and animals, their facial expressions and body language—all those non-verbal cues so critical to human and animal communication—turned out to be a good thing as I caught subtle cues others missed. Those superpowers got put to use in my personal relationships with people and animals as well as in my professional, legal role as a court-appointed *guardian ad litem* for children and incapacitated adults (a role often described as "the eyes and ears of the court"). I observed to understand rather than judge. Those superpowers served me well, even if I was sometimes slow to acknowledge what my gut was trying to tell me about my own life. For example, it took me nearly five decades to finally acknowledge and admit my mother's narcissism, to realize how wrong she was about me, and to set appropriate boundaries with her.

While I knew all these things about myself, I didn't have a label for them until I was in my early fifties. A trail-running friend, during a long run in deep, meaningful conversation, suggested I might be an introvert.

"But I'm not shy!" I proclaimed instantly. Like many, I linked the two terms and had a sense that introvert was a derogatory term, meaning someone not quite up to normal social tasks and interactions, someone socially awkward.

But, curiosity piqued, I started researching the traits that define an introvert, reading articles by researchers, psychologists, and therapists and nodding at each bullet-pointed trait on their lists.

How could I not have known this for so many decades?

My entire legal career involved working with families in crisis, consulting with the psychologists and family therapists who were diagnosing and treating them for various personality disorders, addictions, dysfunctional behaviors, and interpersonal dynamics. I'd attended countless seminars to learn more about various psychological diagnoses and how they manifested in peoples' lives and relationships.

Turns out, introversion isn't a disorder or a detrimental trait. It doesn't require intervention or treatment. In fact, most psychologists and therapists consider it a perfectly healthy way to negotiate life. Introversion never came up in all those seminars or in my conversations with experts.

I had been flying under the introvert radar all those years.

Once I learned about introversion, my life and approach to relationships made so much more sense. It was as if new and wonderfully bright colors had been added to my life's palette. I wasn't broken or shy or awkward. I was simply me: quiet, introspective, and creative. Good with people, in my own way.

I no longer dangled off my mother's barbed "too sensitive" hook. I no longer felt obligated to attend social functions just because I was invited; it was okay to prefer staying home with my dogs. I didn't feel lonely when I was alone. Or bored. Ever. I had a lively inner life.

I also had a wonderful network of friends who, if they weren't introverts themselves, learned to respect my introversion and not take it personally if I declined an invitation. Those friends accepted that I preferred an email, or even a text, to a phone call. When we got together, it was best if it was just two or three of us and we did something active, like walking or running.

True friends never dropped by unannounced.

A common misconception about introverts is that we're aloof or think we're "too good" to be around others. In reality, we simply prefer lots of alone time. And, when socializing, do better in quiet surroundings with one-on-one or small-group conversations that are meaningful or on topics of shared passion. Loud concerts shoulder-to-shoulder with thousands of people? Party small talk? All that was way too draining, requiring days for me to recharge. Don't get me wrong—in the moment, I usually enjoyed social engagements and loved spending time with my friends, even attending small events like summer outdoor concerts. But there was always a part of me that was simultaneously looking forward to getting home and being alone and quiet again, just me and my dogs.

No wonder I loved being in the peaceful quiet of nature with only my dogs for companionship, especially right after I had been around people. Having a chronic CSF leak only intensified my introversion, diminishing my tolerance for small talk, boisterous groups, and large events even further. My noise-free house and dogs were like powerful magnets drawing me to them, my refuge from the busy-ness of the larger world.

Finally, at the age of fifty, out of necessity and desire, I had created a life and lifestyle that accommodated and nurtured my introversion *and* my neurodisability. Being introverted was an orientation, not a lifestyle or choice. I embraced it and all the creativity, empathy, and insight that came with it. I doubt I would have adapted to the CSF leaks as well as I did if I hadn't been introverted.

As fate would have it, not long before the girls and I arrived in Idaho, wolves migrating out of Canada as well as Yellowstone National Park—where other Canadian gray wolves had been reintroduced in the mid-1990s—also began to settle in parts of Idaho, including the Salmon River Mountains.

Soon, we would share a home! I couldn't be happier. In fact, it was the realization of a life-long dream: to live among wolves, to see them in the wild, to hear their soul-stirring howls echoing through the mountains.

Those intrepid gray wolves were also reinventing themselves, overcoming adversity, starting fresh. They formed tight-knit packs for safety and social bonding, mostly independent of other wolves.

Starting in the late nineteenth century, White settlers, assisted by government employees in newly created national parks such as Yellowstone, exterminated gray wolves throughout the West. Wolves had coexisted with Indigenous peoples for centuries. Unable to learn from or tolerate such coexistence, settlers invoked Manifest Destiny and swept aside or destroyed Indigenous groups, wolves, and other "competitors" unlucky enough to get in their way as they moved across the continent, changing the wilderness to fit their needs and sense of safety.

Like the reintroduced wolves and those moving in naturally from Canada, I also was an outsider in Idaho, learning how to survive and thrive in a new and wild place, relying on my own resilience and adaptability.

Wolves had fascinated me since childhood. I fell in love with Alaskan Malamutes because of their resemblance to wolves, both in appearance as well as certain behaviors, including pack sensibility and vocalizations. *What would it be like for Maia and Meadow and me to potentially see wolves in the wild? To hear their howls?* I desperately wanted and needed that life-affirming possibility.

The intrepid wolves repopulating Idaho's Salmon River Mountains became my beacons, an integral part of my own renewal and recovery after the CSF-leak diagnosis. If they could beat the odds and thrive, maybe I could, too. I also couldn't ignore that wolves were great mountain runners. Fast and smooth, with incredible endurance.

All of that is why the wolf encounter the girls and I were privileged to have in July 2006 had such a profound impact on me. Gray wolves were my north star.

Unfortunately, in my new home, I was an outlier. Most locals feared wolves and didn't want them "in *our* mountains."

I realized that many people are hardwired to fear wolves, experiencing an instant, instinctual, physiological "fight or flight" reaction. Some transfer that fear to coyotes and dog breeds like Malamutes because they resemble wolves. Just as I can feel the hair on the back of my neck rise when confronted with a black bear in the forest, many people experience a strong fear reaction to wolves or any animal they initially mistake for a wolf. They can't help it.

But did dogs have the same fear reaction as people? It wasn't until Maia and Meadow showed me that they instantly knew the wolf we saw was a creature they should respect that I made the connection to the reaction they frequently received from other dogs.

In Seattle, when walking suburban sidewalks or visiting off-leash dog parks, the girls and I often encountered dogs that took one look at Maia and Meadow—friendly dogs who enjoyed greeting people and other dogs—and either retreated or rushed at them, snarling aggressively. Not all dogs, but a significant percentage. Owners of the latter would frequently say with genuine honesty, "I've never seen my dog do that before."

Before my magical wolf encounter, I figured they were embarrassed owners covering for their poorly socialized dogs. But after, I realized something else was happening. Just as the girls reacted to the wolf in a very specific way—a reaction unlike any they'd had toward another dog, which I think showed they knew the wolf wasn't a dog—other dogs reacted to them as if they were wolves, with fear or fear-aggression, depending on their temperament. It wasn't personal. It was instinct.

With that insight, I became more proactive in our interactions with other dogs when out and about in Idaho. This was especially true if we were running trails in the forest. If the strange dog showed any signs of fear or aggression, we moved away and avoided contact. I never tried to make an introduction if the other dog was wary or anxious, even if the girls were calm and even if the other dog's owner sought one. Owners were often clueless when their dogs were stressed. The risk of a negative interaction wasn't worth it.

Also, I stopped being surprised when some Idaho local drove up in his pickup, stopped beside us with the driver's window down and asked, in a slow drawl while nodding his trucker-capped head toward the girls, "Are those wolves?" I no longer thought (hoped?) they were joking.

I was surprised, though, when in 2007 a rancher living nearby—a man my age whom I considered a friend and neighbor, a guy who had met and petted the girls while helping me build their yard fence—stopped his pickup as he drove by us one spring afternoon. He pointed at Maia and said through his open window, "I shot a wolf that looked just like her last night. It was coming too close to my cattle," before driving off.

I didn't sleep that night. Had my neighbor given me a warning? Or a threat?

And thus began my use of bright yellow or orange vests for the girls. From then on, every time we walked or ran in the Payette, they wore what I called their Do Not Hunt Me vests.

STONES

In May 2013, I had an unusually vivid dream: I was on vacation someplace in the mountains, a place that felt like Glacier National Park. Wandering through an enormous timber-and-stone lodge, I came upon a low display case where you'd expect to see trinkets or clothing for sale. Instead, oddly, I saw the girls, curled up and napping. I tapped on the glass but they didn't stir. As I anxiously tried to find an employee to help me reach them, the scene shifted. Now I was standing on the lodge's second-story deck watching the girls romp and wrestle playfully, as they always had, on the resort's lawn below. I called out to them, but they didn't respond.

I awoke, puzzled, remembering every detail of the dream, something that rarely happened. Shaken, I hugged both girls.

That May, Maia was fourteen and Meadow, twelve. Maia had been diagnosed with lymphoma in January. She underwent chemotherapy in Washington and was in remission by the time we arrived in Idaho for the summer.[5] But old age had finally caught up with her, something I expected but dreaded. I wanted her last days to be in Idaho, where she could survey the subdivision from our yard and deck, watch the deer moving across our lot, smell all the smells on the summer breeze.

One morning, Maia told me she was done. Ready. She refused all food and water. With coaxing, she went outside in the yard to pee, then came back inside and snoozed on the cool concrete floor. I sat with her, holding her head on my thigh, stroking her face and ears. My throat constricted and tears leaked from my eyes. I felt such a profound sorrow at losing the

---

5   To ride out the 2008 recession, in December 2008 I accepted a full-time job in Washington state and moved there. Over the next few years, the dogs and I spent as much time as possible at our Idaho home.

dog who had given me so much wilderness knowledge and confidence.

Finn, the rescue Australian shepherd who'd joined us in the summer of 2008, stayed a few feet away, keeping an eye on us, while Meadow rested in another room.

That afternoon, June 6, 2013, Maia died at home with the help of our Idaho vet. Kneeling beside her, whispering in her ear and telling her how much I loved her, I stroked her soft fur for the last time.

I'd read that other dogs in the home should be given an opportunity to view and smell the body of the pet who had died, so I asked the vet for some time so they could do that. As it turned out, if some acknowledgement that Maia was gone occurred with Meadow and Finn, I didn't detect it. Each approached her body, took a quick sniff of her fur, and left the room.

The vet and I carried Maia's limp, heavy body to the vet's car; she'd be cremated at the vet's clinic and her ashes returned to me. I cried again as I watched the vet drive away from my house.

During Maia's final days, I thought a lot about how I wanted to handle her remains, how best to honor and celebrate her life. Maia was my heart dog, the one with whom I'd enjoyed the deepest and most rewarding bond. She was smart, playful, kind, a "follow the rules" girl who always did the right thing. Meadow, two years younger and goofier, bonded more to Maia than to me. Maia's keen sense of space, her awareness of her surroundings and nearby wildlife, gave me confidence to explore forests, in Washington but especially in wild Idaho. She taught me how to read "Malamute." Even Meadow relied on her body language as lead dog.

I knew from prior experience with Opus and my cat Prosser that burying a beloved pet didn't work for me. I moved, sold, or otherwise lost access to the land where the grave was located. With Maia, cremation was the best option. But once I received her ashes—in a nice, white cardboard box, sealed with a paw-print sticker—I couldn't decide what to do with them. Spreading them on the ground at the Idaho house didn't feel right, and since Malamutes—including Maia—aren't big swimmers, tossing them on a body of water was unthinkable.

As I pondered the best approach, Meadow was slowed by an as-yet-undiagnosed limp. All she could tolerate were short forest walks. Finn accompanied me on the long, early-morning trail runs that not only helped me deal with the grief of losing Maia but were catalysts to the creativity I needed to finish writing my first book that summer.

Just like after my father's death in 2009, trail running saved me, kept my emotions on an even keel and my creative juices flowing as I processed my feelings.

Soon after moving to Idaho in 2005, the girls and I started running/hiking a steep, three-mile trail in the Payette that took us to the Granite Mountain Forest Service fire lookout. The trail started in a big open meadow, then climbed steeply through trees for the first mile. For the second mile, it zig-zagged steeply up through large, open scree fields and more trees. The last mile was mostly above the tree line, a single-track dirt trail that climbed gently past ancient whitebark pines toward the summit at 8,200 feet.

In July and early August, we often found pockets of snow from the previous winter still clinging in shady spots. The girls enjoyed eating snow as well as cooling their feet in it. Every time we went to Granite, I took lots of photos. Not just of the stunning views of distant peaks and pristine Goose Lake far below, but also, of the abundant wildflowers, gnarled trees, quartz-lined boulders, the girls in the snow, and the cairns—piles of stones that marked the trail through the scree.

After our first trek to the summit in 2006, I noticed that hikers, and perhaps Forest Service contract employees who spent the summer manning the lookout, were adding new cairns. Some were quite elaborate and lovely in their construction.

I had always loved cairns. My first exposure was likely along a trail somewhere high in the Cascades of Washington, or maybe on the rocky shore of a river when I was a white-water kayaker. But beyond admiring their balanced elegance and elemental beauty, I didn't think much about any meaning behind them.

The word "cairn" is Gaelic, meaning "heap of stones." Over millennia and across continents, humans have constructed cairns for a variety of purposes: as burial monuments, wayfinders, astronomy aids, land boundaries, or battle memorials; during spiritual ceremonies; or to mark the location of buried food or objects.

Buddhist writers describe the construction of a cairn as a form of worship, a way to ask for good fortune or an effort to balance energies. In

Scotland, carrying a stone from the bottom of a hill to place on a cairn at the top is a long-held tradition. As an old Scots Gaelic blessing goes, "I'll put a stone on your stone."

Granite Mountain was just one of many places in the Payette National Forest that Maia, Meadow, and I explored and visited repeatedly during the first four years we lived in Idaho. While the Payette always felt like my back yard, close to home and accessible, I wouldn't have explored a tenth of the trails I did if I hadn't had the girls alongside me.

Finn joined us in July 2008, when the girls, nine and seven, were slowing down. Our trail runs had become shorter and less frequent. Sensing dark clouds on the horizon, I decided to get another dog, a running dog who wouldn't be mistaken for a wolf in the forest.

The recession hit that same summer. In December 2008, all three dogs and I left Idaho and returned to Washington, where I'd accepted a full-time position as a deputy prosecutor. My job was to establish paternity for children receiving public assistance. The work allowed me to pay the mortgage on my house in Idaho until I could return. It also sorely tested my ability to endure a forty-hour workweek with active CSF leaks, but I didn't have a choice. ("Don't sell your house," my father admonished when, in a weak moment, I asked him if I should. "You worked too hard for it." I'm glad I listened to him.) Two years of full-time work was all I could handle; in October 2011, I quit my job and returned to private practice so I could work part-time and better manage my symptoms. That choice also meant more time for dogs and trails.

While back in Washington, I took Maia and Meadow on long daily long walks through the neighborhoods of Bellevue and Kirkland where we lived. They got to meet tons of admirers on those walks, a reminder of just how bizarre it had been for them to be instantly feared in Idaho. Finn, just two years old, became my midweek road- and weekend trail-running companion. I enjoyed introducing Finn to the trails where I first learned to run long distances with the girls.

In the five years I'd been gone, those close-to-Seattle trails had exploded in popularity. Hiking, trail running, and ultra-distance trail racing had boomed as well. Trailhead parking lots filled by nine in the morning on weekends, and parking passes were now required. While Finn was well-behaved and responsive to my voice off-leash, even more than the girls, now I was frequently yelled at for allowing him to run free, something that had never happened with the girls.

During this time, the Idaho home was our vacation spot. In late May

2013, the dogs and I took up residence there for the summer. I was determined to finish the book I'd been working on for years. We were all relieved to leave the busyness of Seattle behind.

That summer, Finn and I ran Idaho mountain trails most mornings. Those runs allowed me to think about Maia, and about the book I was writing. I continued my practice of taking photos, and later, when I edited them, I realized that Finn often posed in the same wild, beautiful places I'd run with Maia and Meadow in previous years. One morning, as Finn and I ran on the dirt and rocks of a forest trail, surrounded by trees, wildflowers, and peaceful silence, an idea took root. I would leave some of Maia's cremains in these places we'd shared and loved. As I ran, the idea blossomed—like the beautiful lupine and sunflowers fringing the trail – into a plan.

I would build a small cairn in a few of our favorite places, spots where I had taken photos of the girls, and put some of Maia's cremains at the base of each. Her essential essence would be free to run with the breeze in the wild land she loved and I could visit and remember her each time I ran by the cairn in the future.

With Finn for company, I soon built cairns alongside two of our favorite trails. In both cases, I piled a few rocks atop a large base boulder several feet to the side of the trail, in open areas where the trail itself was obvious, choosing places with an abundance of spring wildflower blooms. I scooped some of Maia's ashes into a plastic baggie—emotionally difficult, at first—and put the baggie in my running pack. When I came to the cairn, I put some ashes on the base rock beneath the stones' protective arch. Standing back to look at my creations, I offered a blessing to Maia: "I love you. I miss you. Thank you." I took photos of the cairns and Finn standing near them. I wished Meadow could be with us, but she was twelve and her nagging limp wasn't improving.

On July 10, roughly a month after Maia died, I learned that Meadow had bone cancer in the leg she was favoring. I had thought (hoped) the cause was a trauma injury after Finn accidentally slammed into her right hind leg while they were playing in the yard in late May. Sadly, her yelps of pain that day were because the bone was already compromised, the marrow eaten away by cancer. Finn just happened to hit the exact spot.

The diagnosis was a shock. The vet's face told me what she was going to say before she spoke a word. She held up the x-ray, and I could see the cancerous bone. Both of us cried at the horrible news, even more horrible so soon after Maia's death.

Cancer explained why Meadow had slowed down so much since January, preferring to walk rather than trot. That slow-down had coincided with Maia's lymphoma diagnosis and I worried that had distracted me from Meadow's less-obvious condition.

After considering Meadow's age, recovery from the surgical option (removing the leg), and how much time surgery might buy her even if successful (maybe six months at best, assuming the cancer hadn't already metastasized into her heart, lungs, or other organs), I decided to allow her to live the rest of her life without added pain or the need to adjust to the loss of a leg. I just didn't know how long that would be.

Palliative care and strong pain meds gave us three more weeks together. I wanted more, of course, but not if Meadow was enduring intolerable pain. I spent time sitting in the yard with her, or in the house, stroking her thick, wooly fur. I used the harness I initially bought for Maia that allowed me to take some of the weight off her hind legs when she went outside. Both Meadow and Finn got lots of evening marrow bones and chews.

The pain meds made Meadow groggy, and she needed higher doses every few days to control the pain. Soon, she didn't move around much, sleeping most of the time. Finally, too heartbroken to do it myself without blubbering on the phone, I asked a neighbor to arrange for a vet to come to the house. While Meadow's message wasn't as clear as Maia's—she was still eating and drinking—her lack of interest in most things because of the narcotics, high doses of which she needed to control the pain, told me it was time.

On July 22, 2013, Meadow's last day, I took her and Finn outside in the yard just after sunrise. First, she stood on the deck and stared through the fence gate into the driveway and the trees beyond. I looked, thinking she'd seen a deer, but didn't notice any movement. Nor did Finn, who was sitting quietly behind her. A minute later, on her own, Meadow limped to the gate and sat at it, staring in the same direction. Finn went and sat next to her. They stayed that way for several minutes before returning to me and back into the house.

Then I remembered: Maia had done the exact same thing on her last day. Standing at the same gate, with the same stare, Meadow by her side. I had photos.

The vet arrived later that morning. Because Meadow was already heavily medicated, he simply injected the pentobarbital into a vein in her front leg. She didn't even notice the needle. I cradled her big, fluffy head in my lap until she took her last breath and her heart stopped beating, tears falling from my eyes into her wooly fur. Getting up a few minutes later, I let Finn come look at Meadow and sniff her. The vet then lifted Meadow's body and placed it in the back of my SUV, the same place she had eagerly jumped to for years because it meant we were heading out for another forest adventure. I drove Meadow to the other vet's clinic where, like Maia, she would be cremated.

I was devastated. At fourteen, Maia's passing was hard but not unexpected. But I'd been looking forward to another couple of years with Meadow, years she could be top dog, pampered, playing with Finn without Maia interfering. Now, losing both girls so close in time, all I felt was an enormous void, a gaping wound in my heart that I didn't think would ever heal.

I reflected on the strange dream I'd had, the dream where the girls were playing at a lodge but couldn't hear me calling. The day after that dream, I'd asked a neighbor to help me preserve Maia's paw print in plaster, knowing the time to say goodbye to her was coming. As we knelt next to Maia, I shared details of my dream with my neighbor. We continued working on the plaster prints; not just Maia's, but Meadow's and Finn's as well, since I had enough plaster for all three. At the time, I didn't realize that, subconsciously, in my dream, I knew Meadow's limp was more than a simple bruise; deep in my core, I knew Meadow would soon join Maia in a place beyond my reach. My neighbor instantly interpreted my dream that way, but knowing I was already anticipating Maia's death, didn't want to tell me.

That reminded me of a similar experience involving my father. The day my father died in August 2009, I was stuck in Seattle's famously horrid midweek freeway traffic, trying to reach a hospital fifty miles away. His wife had called me at work to say he was being transported there, a last-ditch effort to keep him alive. He was eighty-five, had been weakening for months, and was terribly thin and frail. Surrounded by vehicles bumper-to-bumper and side-to-side, moving at five MPH, stopping, moving slowly again, I was agitated; my mind raced and I was fearful of what awaited me. Suddenly, I felt a strong, warm wave of energy pass through my chest, just a couple of seconds in duration. I looked at the clock on my dashboard, then I cried. Bawled like a baby, barely able to see the car in front of me through the wash of tears. I'd never felt anything like it before, but I somehow knew without knowing that my father had died in that instant. The world tilted for me. I would never again hear his wise advice or feel the warmth of one of his bear hugs.

Those experiences taught me that when beings are deeply bonded, as I was with my father and with the girls, intuition, feelings, and vague sensory inputs—energy—permeate and shift through our normal physical and emotional boundaries. Love's communication continues, in surprising and ultimately comforting ways.

I turned to trail running in the forest with Finn to assuage my grief over the unexpected loss of Meadow. Now, I added Meadow's ashes to the two cairns I'd already built, then built three more beside our favorite trails. Mixing Meadow's ashes with Maia's before heading up mountains with Finn, I placed their combined ashes beneath the new cairns. My heart's pumping reminded me that I was alive, and as long as I was, I would have memories of the girls to sustain me.

On July 29, Finn and I were on the trail where, in 2007, the girls and I had met the wolf. I'd also run that trail with Maia and Meadow a few times after the wolf encounter. Each time, we stopped in the precise spot so I could relive it, could once again see in my mind's eye that gorgeous wolf, his long legs, his curious eyes, his gray-brown fur dappled by the morning sunlight filtered through tall trees.

In terms of beauty, it wasn't one of my favorite trails—little elevation change, no big views—but the burbling of Ruby Creek was enticing; when the phlox were in bloom near the trail, they added a spicy, clove-like scent to the air. But here, the girls and I had communed with the wild world in a way few are allowed.

I wanted to memorialize that incredible moment with a cairn and the girls' ashes. As Finn waited patiently, I gathered enough small stones and built a low cairn several feet off the trail, snugged among grasses and saplings under mature trees, hidden to all but me. Then I took several photos of the cairn, Finn with the cairn, and the sunlight through the trees.

"I love you, girls. I miss you. Thank you." I choked on my tears as I said the last words, thanking them in my mind for being a significant force in my life, for helping me through the roughest times—CSF leaks, giving up the idea of Mike as a life partner, my father's illness and death—while showing me the secrets and joys of the natural world. Showing me the wolf.

"Okay, Finn. Let's go back," I whispered. He and I ran along the trail toward the trailhead, my cheeks wet until the dry mountain air dried my tears.

I spent the rest of those August mornings running in the mountains with Finn, visiting cairns and taking photos. Once back home, I wrote well into the evening, often forgetting to eat dinner. I was writing about happy things: my father and his career as a Boeing test pilot and my childhood, growing up within the cocoon-like Boeing culture. Those memories, coupled with the forest running, helped me manage my grief. By Labor Day, I was ready to return to Washington and hand off the manuscript to an editor.

That autumn, back in my townhouse in a Seattle suburb and running trails with Finn, I left some of the girls' ashes in big cedar stumps near streams in three places on Tiger and Cougar Mountains where we ran the most. Mike was with me on those occasions, which was fitting since he had run with us until the girls and I moved to Idaho in 2005. He loved them as much as I did. With Finn trotting happily ahead, Mike and I retraced the trails where we learned to run with the girls as a pack ... where the girls showed me how to pay attention to our surroundings, giving me the courage to venture far without another human companion. We shared our favorite memories of running with the girls as we meandered along the dirt trails, shaded by trees and crowded by undergrowth, wild water burbling nearby.

In late September, when the huckleberry shrubs high in the Cascades displayed their flaming fall colors, I left some of the girls' ashes at the edge of a small lake high in the Alpine Lakes Wilderness, where Meadow first tasted huckleberries and had quickly learned to pick them off the bushes herself because I wasn't fast enough. And finally, I left some ashes in an old cedar stump at Camp Zanika on Lake Wenatchee, where I'd hosted Maian Meadows Dog Camp every summer since 2002, a hobby business I named after the girls because their joy in playing with other dogs had inspired it.

"I love you. I miss you. Thank you," I told them, the same words every time I left ashes or visited one of those places later. "I'll be back soon," I began to add, a hopeful note for myself.

Once the prep work was completed, I published my first book, *Growing Up Boeing: The Early Jet Age Through the Eyes of a Test Pilot's Daughter*, in February 2014. During the next two months, I gave several talks to various groups in the Seattle-area aviation community. Then, in May 2014, Finn and I returned to Idaho permanently.

It felt good, and right, but way too quiet without the girls.

Finn and I were frequent visitors to the Idaho cairns. Every spring, after the deep snows of a long winter melted away, we would make our first runs into higher elevations to see the cairns re-emerge. Sometimes they were intact, sometimes a stone or two had fallen and needed replacing.

"Girls! I've missed you!" I'd say upon seeing each of the cairns in the spring. After a few photos with Finn posing nearby, ready to continue our run, I'd whisper my mantra.

"I love you. I miss you. Thank you."

CONALL

In July 2014, not long after moving back to Idaho, I fostered Riggs, a young male dog, for Moonsong Malamute Rescue in Boise. He came to them because it was suspected that he had wolf DNA and shelters refused to take him. At the time, I was trying to decide if I should get another Malamute.

In 2011, wolves had been delisted as an endangered species in a few western states—including Idaho—and hunting them became legal there. The official "season" included a significant portion of the year. I worried about keeping a Malamute safe in the Payette, even if he was wearing an orange Do Not Hunt Me vest.

Riggs was delightful. And gorgeous. Finn liked him, too. I considered "failing" at fostering Riggs and adopting him, but he looked even more wolflike than any of my Malamutes. I decided he'd be safer as a city dog and was happy when he found a forever home with a woman in Boise.

But I couldn't stop thinking about bringing another Mal into my life. I knew I would always carry a level of anxiety when we ventured into the forest, fearing someone would mistake the dog for a wolf and shoot. I remembered the reaction of the post office worker when, on my way home from the magical wolf encounter, I tried to share my excitement. After a sharp intake of breath, fear written on her face, she said, "Did you have a gun?" But my intense desire for another Mal outweighed my fears.

Finn was a terrific trail-running dog, but he didn't offer wildlife alerts like the girls had, nor was he any good at knowing the way back to the car. A herding dog, he didn't have the hardwired skills to keep me safe in the wilderness.

Riggs had shown me that Finn would accept another male dog, so I started looking. In mid-December, I found a breeder in Colorado who had a litter born in early December; I could choose a male and welcome him into my home at the end of January.

I hoped this new boy would be as good a wilderness guide as the girls had been. As I waited for the Colorado puppies to reach eight weeks, I attended a "Santa Paws" photo fundraiser for the local animal shelter where I'd just become their executive director. There, I met a family with two Samoyeds, one of whom had a seeping, crusty wound on its chest, surrounded by a big, square shaved area.

"What happened?" I asked the father, trying to imagine what would cause such an injury.

"Thanksgiving weekend, we went to Last Chance Campground to go for a walk in the forest," the man said. "I parked and let the dogs out while my wife and kids were still getting ready. Next thing, I heard a rifle shot. Some guy came up and said, 'I thought they were wolves.'"

The father went on to explain that the bullet had gone cleanly through the dog with the wound and lodged in the body of the other dog, where it would remain for the rest of her life.

On January 30, 2015, I drove to the half-way point of Ogden, Utah, where I met Conall for the first time. (I'd chosen an Irish name that means "strong wolf.") An eight-week-old, eleven-pound ball of light gray fluff, he was not happy to be in a crate for the seven-hour drive to his new home, despite several stops to stretch his legs and pee. And Finn wasn't too thrilled about the noisy, complaining creature sharing the back of his SUV. But once we arrived home, the boys got acquainted properly and within days, were best friends. Both Finn and I fell hard for Conall.

Over the next several months, I took Conall out into the forest for walks with me and Finn, and he displayed the same natural-world savvy I'd come to rely upon with the girls. He paid attention to our surroundings. He alerted me to squirrels, deer, and cattle moving through the trees. He found bones hidden off the trail. In the yard, he often caught voles; he had, in fact, caught one his first full day home.

I exposed Conall to everything and every situation I could think of during those early months, including other dogs, people, horses, vehicles, mowers, and the deer moving across our lot. He took it all in with interest, curiosity, and confidence.

Every single time we ventured into the forest, though, Conall wore a Do Not Hunt Me vest. Finn, too. I hated that every photo I took of Conall in the forest included the vest, but that was the price of keeping him safe and I was willing to pay it.

By the age of eight months, Conall was already an accomplished—if often goofy—trail runner. Early on, we did short runs at an easy pace, and his enthusiasm and energy determined how far we went as he grew in size and athleticism. Also early on, Conall showed an amazing affinity for climbing huge boulders, including one that gave him a view from twenty feet above the trail. He was fearless.

At home, Finn house-trained Conall by showing him how to use the dog door. In the forest, Finn demonstrated staying on the trail and coming when I called. Conall mimicked Finn's every move. It was almost too easy.

In Conall, I saw Maia's keen senses and awareness of surroundings mixed with Meadow's gentleness and good humor.

In Conall, I got both the girls, and then some.

I was now ready to fully embrace my inner nature child. Through each season, the boys and I spent time in the Payette, exploring, learning, and getting to know intimately our slice of the natural world while running trails together, free and wild. With this pair, I could go for some truly long runs.

Sadly, though, I didn't think Conall would be as lucky as Maia and Meadow and see a wolf.

SEASONS

Summer

Brundage Mountain Resort was a fifteen-minute drive from home, a drive that took us 2,000 feet higher in elevation. Brundage, which had operated as a downhill ski resort since 1961, had a small-town vibe beloved by McCall locals and tourists alike. Plus, the snow was awesome, deep and dry. (My friends and I had skied in waist-deep powder when we visited McCall during Winter Carnival in the mid-1980s.)

Brundage, on Payette National Forest land managed by the Forest Service, operated under a long-term lease. Between ski seasons, locals hiked and rode mountain bikes on its trails. In 1991, Brundage began offering lift-assisted mountain biking and, with Forest Service approval, undertook a years-long expansion of the trail system.

It was those hiking and mountain biking trails that my dogs and I came to love, our go-to place to run when I didn't want to drive deeper into the Payette. The girls had helped me start exploring the area in 2005, and they (and later, Finn) spent lots of time running there with me every year.

Elk Trail was six miles of meandering single track, considered an easy descent for bikers and perfect for running both uphill and down. Other trails offered plenty of options for greater elevation change and different terrain. Hidden Valley was the most difficult, a steep, black-diamond climb/descent that included a large rock scree field near the summit.

In the summer of 2015, Finn and I introduced Conall to the trails on Brundage. Like Mount Rainier in Washington state, Brundage was a riot of colorful wildflowers in summer: lupine, Indian paintbrush (including a pink variety I never saw elsewhere in the Payette), yellow columbine, pinkish-white phlox, dark purple larkspur. It was always a delight to run those colorful trails in summer and catch phlox's spicy scent in the air.

Brundage was also home to lots of white-tailed deer and, sometimes, elk. I had to watch Finn closely; if the deer or elk moved or ran, Finn would chase. If they stood still, he didn't notice them. Thankfully, Conall, like the girls before him, observed rather than chased ungulates.

On June 18, 2020, Conall was my sole companion during a morning run at Brundage. Finn was twelve, and while still spry for an old guy, the run I planned was longer than I wanted him to attempt. It was a beautiful morning. Deep blue skies carried wisps of cirrus clouds moving slowly on a high breeze. It was early, well before the resort opened the lifts for mountain biking, so it didn't feel like we had to rush.

Starting from the resort parking area at 6,000 feet, Conall and I ran up a lesser-used service road/mountain bike trail to a creek crossing where I'd built one of the girls' cairns in 2014. From there, we ran another four miles up Elk Trail, a steady but runnable climb. Once near the summit at 7,500 feet, the views opened up.

To the south, Payette Lake and Little Payette Lake sparkled deep blue in the morning light. McCall hugged the south end of Payette Lake, with Long Valley spreading beyond. To the west, I could see snow on peaks in the Wallowa Mountains, across the Snake River in Oregon. To the north, the higher peaks surrounding us in the Payette, including Granite Mountain, also held some winter snow, white accents on their emerald green-blue shoulders.

Brundage is covered in firs, pines, and the endangered whitebark pine, a slow-growing tree that can live up to a thousand years. One of the summit's most distinctive features is the thick and twisted silver-gray skeletons of dead whitebark pines, stark against the blue sky.

As Conall and I started back down Elk Trail, we reached a dead whitebark trunk lying beside the trail, thick branch stubs protruding from its enormous body. Conall loved jumping up on that trunk, walking along it like a gymnast on a balance beam. He often faced west, taking in the expansive view. I stood up-slope from him and took photos, Meadows Valley below and the snow-capped Seven Devils and Wallowa Mountains far beyond.

Photos taken, Conall and I continued down Elk Trail at an easy pace. I felt good. Strong. The air was cool, and early wildflowers, like dainty yellow avalanche lilies, were just appearing. Conall enjoyed the patches of snow lingering in the wooded shady sections and even found an animal bone to play with.

As we neared the base of the mountain, we ran again on the service road through a flat stretch of recently thinned tall pines mixed with firs, edged with newly emerging plants and older huckleberry shrubs. The sun broke through here and there, like theater spotlights on the ground.

Conall suddenly stopped and turned slightly, staring into the trees.

Taking another step, he put his front paws on a mound of dirt for a slightly higher view. Stopping just behind him, I followed his gaze.

To my surprise, a white-tailed deer was about fifty feet away, busily munching plants around the base of some trees. She didn't seem aware of us.

Deer were common at Brundage, and Conall often alerted me to them in just this way: stopping and watching. Usually, seeing or hearing us, the deer would run off. Not this time, and that was strange.

Also strange was Conall's keen focus on the deer: he seemed transfixed. So much so that I trusted him to not move while I took a photo. I then switched to video just in time to capture the doe looking up and around, sensing something.

Conall and I were so still that the doe didn't see us until, needing better footing, I stepped on a twig that cracked under my foot. The doe turned her head in our direction, sniffed the air, and listened. Conall and I remained still and so did she. She still didn't seem to see us, but she knew something was nearby. Then, a tiny fawn emerged from under her belly where it had been nursing. No wonder the doe was reluctant to move. As the doe and her fawn started slowly moving away, a second fawn appeared beside them. Twins!

White-tailed fawns are born in May or early June. These two, moving on thin legs impossibly long for their tiny bodies, still had the white spots on their reddish-brown coats that helped them blend into their environment. Their speed and agility were impressive as they bounded away through the trees, the doe protectively behind them.

"Thank you, Conall," I whispered, then turned off my camera.

Back home, I played the short video of Conall, the doe, and her twin fawns over and over. I wanted to freeze-frame in that happy, life-affirming tableau in a forest I considered sacred.

Autumn

Near me, the Payette was primarily evergreens—firs and pines—with a few aspen and birch here and there. In autumn, the latter's yellow foliage highlighted the mountain slopes, the dying leaves clacking gently in the wind before falling to the ground. There, they decayed to a mottled yellow and black, all the better to showcase the silvery, sun-lit droplets of water that collected on them.

Soon after the aspen and birch leaves were done, the western larch, a deciduous conifer, provided a second wave of brilliant yellow accents to the predominantly green forest. In Idaho, western larch trees are commonly referred to as tamaracks. I first noticed them in October, when just a handful made themselves obvious; then many more came out of hiding, collectively assembling for their last, showy hurrah of the season.

I thought of the tamaracks as stealth trees, hiding all spring and summer among the firs and pines until late fall, when their needles slowly turned lime green, then a brilliant yellow before dropping and littering the ground with a soft ochre carpet.

Before moving to Idaho, my only exposure to larch trees came on autumn hikes along the high eastern slopes of Washington's Cascades. There, the alpine larches were stunning if you caught them at the peak of their yellow phase. They were much shorter than the western larches I saw in the mountains of Idaho, but just as pleasing to the eye.

In Idaho, yellow tamarack trees were a sure sign that snow would soon follow.

After the larch needles dropped, the landscape was mostly shades of brown and dark green hunkered down for winter. Even the bright-red rose hips began to blacken and drop. The undergrowth was devoid of leaves or died back until spring. The forest felt open, and I could see through the tree trunks for some distance.

By November, the livestock ranchers grazed on national forest land all summer were finally gone, trucked away to winter pastures lower down, or to slaughter. Their absence allowed me to relax when we were out. All of my Malamutes did an excellent job of alerting me to cattle, their body language allowing me to prepare. This mattered because, if we startled the cattle into running, it would bring out the dogs' prey drive, Finn's especially. Cattle took the path of least resistance in those circumstances, staying on the dirt roads rather than disappearing through the trees, which made it easier for dogs to chase them. Far better if I saw them first.

Also by November, most of the song birds had departed for warmer territory, leaving magpies, blue jays, red-tailed hawks, and ravens to periodically break the forest's silence with their calls.

Free-flowing water was scarce in late autumn. The few creeks near my house that flowed year-round, fed by a nearby reservoir, were often ice-covered by late November. Nights were consistently cold, usually below freezing, and the sun's arc was lower; many places in the forest remained shaded all day, holding on to any early snow. The dogs didn't need as much water in autumn, not like during the warm summer months, but still, I planned outings with a creek or alpine lake along the way whenever possible.

I had always loved fall and the cooler days it brought. I enjoyed the bright leaf and needle colors, and, at higher elevations, the welcome show of late-blooming pearly everlastings; their tiny white flowers reminded me of sprigs of baby's breath. And cooler temperatures meant that long runs were more comfortable for me and the dogs.

After moving to Idaho, though, autumn became the season I learned to dread.

I still looked forward to the crisp mornings, which seemed to give all of us more energy. Near my house, the tall field grass changed hues—from spring's bright green to summer's mature green, to autumn's burnt orange and yellow, and finally to the dry beige of ripe wheat glowing in a sunset's last rays of light. It was a feast for the eyes. And because I loved snow, I also enjoyed the early hints of its arrival autumn provided, dustings that quickly melted and the sparkling frost that covered the plants.

But in rural Idaho, as in many rural areas across the country, autumn is also hunting season. Beginning in mid-August, hunters stalked the Payette National Forest. August through September was bow season, October through November brought rifles. And in the Payette, people could "target shoot" whenever and wherever they liked, year-round, disturbing all living creatures with the harsh sound of firearms, leaving behind spent shotgun shells and lead bullets, not to mention empty beer cans that littered the Forest Service roads.

At first, I was angry. With every shot, my body tensed, my jaw clenched. But anger didn't change anything; it only made me feel worse. Nor was I willing to live my life in fear of hunters. I wouldn't let them push me out of a place I loved, a forest I had as much right to use as they did, even during hunting season.

So I swallowed my anger, but it festered inside me each autumn. My stomach knotted as I thought of the thousands of deer, elk, bear, moose, cougar, coyotes, foxes, and wolves killed in Idaho's forested public lands every year in the name of sport.

However, out of necessity and safety, I changed. I adapted, just as I imagined the wolves and other wildlife adapted. Dawn and dusk were when hunters were most likely to find their targets on the move, so we waited until much later in the morning before venturing out. We wore bright colors during hunting season. For the dogs, orange vests with neon-pink flagging strips attached to their collars for added visibility from the front. I wore bright yellow and orange running shirts or jackets, with pink flagging tied to the back of my running pack. I talked to the dogs more as we ran or walked, loudly blew snot, and made as much noise as possible so that any hunters lurking in the trees would hear us coming.

When I arrived in 2005, only locals hunted in the Payette near my house. When I saw their trucks parked on a Forest Service road, I'd go somewhere else, far away. Local hunters got their deer or elk (or both) and left the forest for the rest of the season. By 2015, though, hunting tourists were everywhere, taking advantage of every single day of a given "game" season.

After 2011, wolves could be legally hunted between September and March. That's when the forest began to feel really dangerous, and my anxiety about Conall being shot ramped up even higher. When running or walking in the forest, the boys and I often heard rifle fire in the distance. We would listen carefully, I would judge distance, and if it was not too close, we'd continue. Many times, though, I reluctantly told the boys, "Let's go back" because the gunshots sounded dangerously near.

I'll never understand it. The urge to kill, I mean. I know the hunters' justifications, including that hunting provides meat to feed their families, or meat that's healthier than anything store-bought. But we're long past frontier times when hunting kept a family fed. Today's hunters spend phenomenal amounts of money on camo clothing, high-powered rifles with scopes, late-model pickups, and trailers to haul the UTVs that get them into more remote areas without them having to actually walk or hike. They could buy enough meat to feed their families for years with those investments. There's plenty of meat available at the grocery store or a local butcher's, meat raised by ranchers and farmers on land near and far who could use the income, meat that goes to waste if not purchased by its expiration date.

But wolves? They're considered trophy animals. They aren't eaten. There's no reason to hunt them except hatred and fear. Some hunters want their pelts, or to mount their taxidermized body on a wall. Most just want a photo of themselves posing with the dead wolf to post on social media. It's barbaric and senseless.

And today? With climate change hastening habitat loss and species extinctions? Wildfires raging across the western US and much of Canada? Killing for sport and a trophy is, to me, an example of amoral humans piling on, adding to the devastation we've already wrought and continue to make worse. Unsporting. Unethical. Hunting is simply not necessary for all but a tiny minority. A sentient animal living its best and only wild life is taken for ... entertainment?

When wolves returned to Idaho, I listened as hunters projected onto them their own worst traits: killing for sport, viciousness, wasting wildlife, taking all the elk, decimating herds of cattle and sheep. I had a hard time wrapping my mind around the level of hatred and misinformation, the inability to see the irony in their statements.

All these disturbing trends, sights, and sounds, sparked intrusive emotions and worries in me, robbed me of what would otherwise have been enjoyable time running with my dogs in the national forest in autumn.

If there was any upside to autumn's hunting season, it was that Conall often found deer or elk bones the coyotes, foxes, ravens, and skunks left behind after consuming meat left by the hunters. I was glad that at least other forest wildlife got sustenance from what the hunters abandoned. Conall's nose told him where such "forest treasure" was stashed, or sometimes, the noisy cawing of a few ravens fighting over remains drew his attention, just as ravens have alerted wolves to carcasses for millennia.

During a forest run, when Conall made a sudden departure from the trail and moved a few yards into the trees, he'd sniff and look around, then return with a bone, or bones. More than once, he found most of a spinal column or a rib cage, but usually it was a single leg bone with hoof.

Tail wagging, Conall always brought his finds to me to show them off. He reminded me of Meadow, equally adept at finding forest treasure. She enjoyed carrying bones she found for a mile or two before finally dropping them. Finn wasn't interested in forest bones; he was far more intrigued by things that moved (squirrel!) that he could herd.

When Conall found a good bone, he wanted to stop and gnaw on it, and it took much coaxing to get him to leave it behind so we could continue on. He always—always—remembered exactly where he'd left a bone. The next time we passed that way, even if it was a week or three later, he'd go right to the spot he'd left his treasure (unless a coyote had moved it) and proudly show it to me again. It became an ongoing game for us, me pulling out my phone, Conall posing for a photo with his reclaimed treasure.

Winter

Shhh. Listen. Can you hear them? Snowflakes are gently falling through the air. Billions of them, landing on tree branches, boulders, the ground ... flake on flake on flake. The sound is barely perceptible; stand utterly still and calm your breathing to hear it. Try. Because it's there, this faint whisper of a sound. Look up at the sky. Watch the snowflakes fall toward you, touching your face, tickling your eyelashes, surrounding you on their gravity-ruled glide to the ground. Delicate, soft, enveloping, welcoming.

Snowflakes land on my nose, on the bill of my cap, collect on the dogs' fur like white cloaks. The snow, the air, the near-silence embrace us in a sense of utter, complete peace. I hesitate to move, knowing my footsteps crunching through the snow and my breathing, laboring with the effort of running or hiking, will break the spell.

Snow sloughs off tree limbs, heavy clumps landing with a muffled thump. It sounds like distant drums, nature's winter heartbeat.

In this forest I love, I'm practicing what Australian Aboriginal peoples refer to as *dadirri*: reflective and respectful listening.

The scent of animal tracks left on the snow's surface tease the boys' noses, but mine? With everything shrouded in a thick blanket of snow, there's little for me to smell in the forest. There are no wildflowers or newly emerging pine needles; no dirt or mud; no musky scent of cattle, deer, or elk grazing nearby. But there is the smell of snow on Malamute fur.

I first discovered that unique, heady scent when the girls and I moved to Idaho. I remember running up into the forest on the groomed snowmobile road one snowy morning with the girls. After a few miles, we stopped so I could remove ice balls from the fur between their toes. That done, I gave first Maia, then Meadow, a hug. My face against their furry necks, I inhaled deeply. *Malamute essence.*

I fell in love with that smell, a mix of iron, earth, copper, and damp. It's the same smell their fur has when dry, but enhanced by snowflakes collecting on their coats that amplify an elemental aspect of their essence. So distinctive, like petrichor, the smell of rain on warm, dry ground. You know it when you smell it, and it sparks deep emotional feelings. That snowy Malamute fur smell was yet another way I imagined my Mals were like wolves.

Winter running in the forest with Conall, smelling the same earthy scent on his snowy coat, always brought happy memories of the girls. A link to the past.

Early mornings in January meant temperatures near zero—the sort of cold in which breath becomes fog and nose hairs freeze and tickle. The rising sun sets the snow aglitter with multitudes of miniature prisms.

It took time to dress for those cold winter-morning runs. So many pieces of clothing and equipment were needed. I've worn many of the same clothes since the 1990s; tears would flow if I ever lost or could no longer wear my three-quarter-zip with pit-zips running jacket. As soon as I pulled out running clothing, the boys grew eager, knowing what was coming. We'd pile into the car, whether it was a quarter-mile drive up the hill to the snowmobile parking lot (to avoid having to run past a cranky neighborhood dog), or two miles down into the valley to run on a plowed road.

Even wearing all those layers, I needed to move to get warm and keep moving to stay that way. The first few steps were chilly. The boys would race off ahead, excited, as my muscles slowly heated up and I was able to pick up my pace.

Sometimes we ran up into the forest on the main Forest Service road, which was groomed every week or two for snowmobiles. If we got out early on a morning after the groomer had come through and before snowmobiles tore it up, the corduroy snow was an ideal surface for all of us. Those tended to be our longest and fastest winter runs: three to four miles steady uphill, then an exhilarating downhill return.

Early on in Idaho, if the girls and I started up the groomed road at daybreak, we were usually finished and back in the parking lot before the snowmobilers showed up. But by 2017, more snowmobilers were coming out, and they were coming out earlier to secure a spot in the small parking lot. The boys and I could usually run up to our turnaround point while the forest was still quiet. On our return, though, the roar of engines and thick, smelly exhaust broke the forest's serenity. Adding insult to injury, the newer snowmobiles ran on narrower treads, which quickly tore up the groomed surface. As the snowmobilers crossed over each others' tracks, it became uneven and choppy, a mess to try to run on.

When the groomed route was chewed up, the boys and I took an even steeper, illegal snowmobile trail straight up through the forest, following what was a wildlife-trail-turned-cattle-trail in summer. Often, that narrow and illegal side trail, compacted by a few old-style snowmobiles, provided better footing than the heavily used groomed road. Conall loved this trail because he often uncovered "forest treasure," animal bones left by autumn's hunters and spread by forest carnivores and scavengers.

After a mile of steep climbing and about four hundred feet in elevation up the side trail, we reached an ungroomed Forest Service road that ran level across the flank of the mountain, intersecting with the groomed road about two-tenths of a mile to the south. The same riders who came up the illegal trail often ran on the road, heading north and packing the snow well enough for us to run on.

I knew that road well because we ran and walked there almost year-round. One of its appeals was that we were unlikely to encounter another human. On level terrain, we could run more easily (okay, I could) even in fresh snow, at a slow jogging pace that allowed the dogs to find snowshoe hare tracks. On clear mornings, I often took photos of the boys and of Meadows Valley below, framed in the trees. A beautiful spot, ignored by most snowmobilers, this was our private winter wonderland.

As winter settled in and the snowpack deepened, most wildlife hunkered down, remaining still, listening, observing, resting, hibernating. Their only traces were nocturnal tracks in fresh snow that teased the dogs' noses. On occasion, the scolding chatter of a red squirrel feeling we'd come too close broke the silence, especially in late winter when the sun's higher angle and warming daytime temperatures hinted of spring. *I get it, squirrel; I'd be irritated, too.* I offered a silent apology as we ran by.

Whenever the boys and I stood at the upper end of the side trail, ready to start our steep downhill descent to the parking lot, Conall would get a gleam in his eye, then start running down the trail at full speed, the snow absorbing his weight, until he was out of sight. "Conall, wait!" I'd shout, laughing, as Finn and I followed as fast as we could. That short, steep stretch of snow-covered trail brought out the puppy in Conall and the child in me. Every time we flew down it, I laughed out loud, high on snow-running in deepest winter, enveloped by the forest.

As winter was beginning its slow transition to spring in 2016, Conall's reaction to finding forest treasure was noticeably different one morning, and for good reason. He wasn't even two yet, but his senses were already as keen as his ability to interpret what he saw and smelled. It was fascinating to watch his natural abilities grow and refine, to imagine how similar he must be to wolf pups exploring and interpreting their world.

The previous day, just before sundown, the boys were in the yard and I was inside at the computer. Both suddenly became loudly vocal about something in the field above the house. Through my window, I followed their gazes. Movement caught my eye: two medium-sized, dark-furred (nearly black) canines moving through the snow and trees of the uphill neighbor's lot toward their cabin. The neighbors, who only used the cabin sporadically, weren't there at the time.

The canines were far enough away and the fading light was so low that I couldn't identify them before they disappeared from sight.

At first, seeing just one, I thought maybe it was a new dog in the neighborhood, perhaps a German Shepherd puppy. But then I saw the second, nearly identical in size and color. Their fur was too dark to be a fox or coyote, although they were about the size of a full-grown coyote. Surely, I would have heard if neighbors had recently acquired two young dogs. Maybe they belonged to visitors? Another neighbor rented their house on Airbnb and I never knew who was staying there.

I briefly wondered if they were wolf pups. Was an adult somewhere just out of sight? It would explain the boys' strong reaction. They typically didn't bark so exuberantly at neighborhood dogs, although Conall, looking for a play session, would gently woof at any dog he saw. No, the boys were clearly upset at what they perceived as interlopers, their barks more like those reserved for a coyote crossing the field. They may have also caught a scent on the air that was beyond my detection. I, too, was convinced we'd seen something out of the ordinary.

Darkness fell, the boys came inside, and eventually we all went to bed, excitement forgotten.

For our walk the next morning, I chose a Forest Service road that went two miles south beyond the nearby snowmobile parking lot, along the forest boundary. Most of winter's snow had melted off at this lower elevation, which provided easy access.

It was the remaining snow that convinced me that we'd indeed seen young wolves.

First, we came upon a large animal bone, and then, a bit farther along the road, a second one. Both had been recently gnawed on, and each was surrounded by lots of paw prints, including some that were quite large. The overnight temperature had been well below freezing, so the remaining snow was hard and crusty; it not only supported our weight, it also preserved the prints, keeping them from enlarging due to melting.

Paw prints in the snow and mud in the forest were common. Usually left by my dogs, neighbors' dogs, coyotes, or foxes, I saw them all the time. These prints included different sizes, some of which were big, really big. Conall has big feet, but his prints were small in comparison.

Hopeful, I took photos and once home again, I googled wolf prints versus cougar prints, just to be sure.

Wolf.

The canines we saw the night before must have been wolf pups, nine or ten months old. Litters typically arrive in May or early June. By March of the following year, they'd be big enough to do some exploring on their own.

My other evidence: Conall took no interest in either of the bones. Instead, his tail dropped as he sniffed the prints in the snow around the bones, scanning the forest anxiously as though making sure we weren't being watched. It was as if Conall knew the bones belonged to others—wolves—and he'd better not steal their stash.

Wolves in the forest near my subdivision would explain why I hadn't heard the usual nightly chorus of coyote yips during the previous month. Wolves and coyotes compete for territory and wolves always win.

I worried, though. These wolves were too close to humans and their homes. If seen by certain neighbors, or others accessing the forest just beyond, they might be shot without hesitation and for no reason other than ignorance and fear. Why were they moving through my subdivision at all? They typically avoided humans. I knew that people leaving garbage cans outside their homes frequently brought bears close, generally with disastrous results for the bear.

I hoped the wolf pups and their pack would move higher up, away from those who would harm them. I wanted—needed—them to thrive in the Payette. As predators, they helped keep the forest wildlife balance healthy.

And for me? Seeing or hearing wolves in the Payette was priceless, an affirmation that grit and determination ultimately overcome obstacles and opposition. Wolves were why I lived at the edge of the Payette, why I chose to live in Idaho. When I spent time in the forest with my dogs, I always hoped for another sighting. I longed to hear another midnight chorus of howls echoing through the forested mountains down to my yard.

Spring

Spring arrives late in the Salmon River Mountains. Even by the end of April, when the lawn around my house had emerged in emerald green, the trails a few hundred feet higher in elevation were still a mix of snow and newly exposed dirt and rocks. Two thousand feet higher, they were completely buried in snow.

I loved this aspect of spring in the Payette. I could extend the joys of watching spring emerge by simply venturing to higher elevation trails and Forest Service roads every few weeks. The higher we went, the fresher and livelier the plants, wildflowers, trees, song birds, and wildlife appeared as they emerged. It made spring last from late April to early August.

Spring's first single-track dirt trail run was always a delight. Any snow that remained was soft and not too deep; it was easy to run through, and as a bonus, cooled the dogs' toes. There was a short window of time in May, maybe a week, when the boys and I went to Brundage Ski Resort after ski season ended. The runs still had plenty of snow, especially near the summit, and the resort's grooming left the snow on the main runs compact and runnable. On bluebird mornings, just after sunup and with no clouds in the big open sky, we ran three miles up the service road (mostly bare after being plowed all winter) to reach the summit and its 360-degree views of the surrounding mountains, McCall, New Meadows, Payette Lake. We were the only ones on the mountain at that hour.

Then we'd take off down a ski run. The boys went full speed ahead of me, leaping playfully, letting gravity have its way with them. I was more cautious. As I leaned back to control my speed, my quads quickly started complaining from all the braking. Those ski runs were *steep*, dropping from 7,500 to 6,000 feet in a mile, straight down, no curves. Even the boys sometimes zig-zagged across the steepest faces for traction. Within a week, though, the sun would soften the snow too much to support our weight without postholing, and this unique running fun was over until the next spring.

That transition period of slow snowmelt to dirt (what locals called "mud season") primed me to start looking for spring's first wildflowers alongside the trails: yellow avalanche (glacier) lilies and white trillium were the earliest. Throughout May, as spring finally took hold in the forest, the dogs and I visited various trails and roads in the Payette, depending on whether we were looking for remaining snow or wildflowers.

Just a mile from my house was a south-facing open hillside at about

4,500 feet in elevation, on the Payette's boundary with a rancher's property. From up there, I could look over Meadows Valley to the south, across Goose Creek Canyon toward McCall, and east across several drainages to the mountains lining the east shoulder of Long Valley. The girls and I had discovered this beautiful spot our first summer after moving into our new house while searching for ripe huckleberries.

In May, that hillside was home to three major wildflower blooms: the bright yellow arrowleaf balsamroot with its large spear-like green leaves and bonny, multi-petaled flowers; the medium height orange Indian paintbrush; and showy purple-lavender lupine with their palmlike leaves spreading wide at their bases. The thick greenery, bursting with vibrant color above, completely obscured the dry, rocky soil underneath. Dainty dark-purple larkspur, blooming close to the ground, sometimes hid under their sheltering leaves.

This area became special to me as a place where, with the girls (and later the boys), I celebrated the arrival of spring wildflowers every year. I gave it a name: Sound of Music Hillside. When the flowers were at peak bloom, it reminded me of my first visit to Mt. Rainier's Grand Park, with its abundant wildflowers. When I was there, I felt like Maria in the opening scene of *Sound of Music*, surrounded by mountain peaks, twirling joyfully in a field of wildflowers, on top of the world.

Over the years, I took many photos of the wildflowers, the girls, and later the boys on Sound of Music Hillside.

After the girls passed, I built a small cairn of rounded rocks there, placing it at the base of an old, wise Ponderosa pine. It was one of the first cairns the boys and I visited each spring.

Different forest trails offered different wildflowers. I enjoyed learning this unique forest "map" over the years. On one open west-facing and rocky hillside in Bear Basin, near McCall, early spring brought delicate lavender grass-widow flowers, drooping toward the ground on their thin stalks. Sometimes I would find them encased in ice after a rain and subfreezing overnight temperatures. I rarely saw them elsewhere. At the base of Brundage, mountain bluebells with their clusters of tiny bell-shaped purple-and-blue flowers, and periwinkle-blue Jacob's ladder flowers with pale yellow centers were some of the first to bloom.

On walks along Forest Service roads near my house in May and June, at elevations between 4,000-5,000 feet, I might see bright yellow arnica (another sunflower); clusters of tiny ground-level amethyst-colored violets; tall blue or purple penstemon; light pink dog rose flowers with big yellow centers, the bloom-laden shrubs adding a welcome, fresh scent to the air; low-growing butter-colored monkeyflower; tiny bell-shaped, whitish-pink huckleberry flowers promising delicious blue-purple fruit in July; purple clematis on vines tangled around shrubs; and in a few spots, carpets of white daisies as tall as the dogs, growing right on a decommissioned Forest Service road, nodding in the breeze.

Running or walking, the dogs explored and followed scents. Conall found forest treasure. I stopped to take wildflower photos. For the low-growing ones, I had to kneel down, which always brought Finn and Conall close, curious about what I was looking at. One or more of their paws and legs often wound up in the frame. I started collecting those dog "photobombs" and sharing them on my blog, Wild Sensibility.

Pines and firs put an inch of new needles on the ends of their branches each spring. Bright green against the older, darker needles, these displays of growth would otherwise go unnoticed from a distance. Tamaracks grew a whole set of new needles. Aspens brought out their roundish lime-green leaves, a beautiful contrast against the bright white-with-black-eye-spots bark. Their gentle leaf-shaking sound on the spring breeze always calmed my mind and heart.

The forest in spring was bursting with youthful plant energy: growing, spreading, and blooming, covering the ground, creating a short understory beneath the tall pines and firs that offered cover for wildlife.

Spring also brought the sound of birds, small and large, a welcome sound after a quiet winter. By May, I'd hear Canada geese honking while flying in V formation on their northward migration. One year, I watched an enormous flock of honking snow geese going north, a murmuration of white moving in a pattern only they understood.

Eventually, I'd hear the distinctive call of Sandhill cranes, some flying in small groups to breeding grounds farther north, others arriving for the summer, raising their colts (an archaic term for chicks) in valley pastures. Sandhills have a primitive-sounding call, a rattling sort of bugle that can be heard for more than two miles. Those that stayed in the valley often bugled at sundown, a lovely salute to the end of the day.

I also heard from the great horned owls, *hoo-hoo-whooing* usually at night or at sunrise in competition with the early-rising songbirds. Sometimes just one, other times, a pair calling and answering. Once, I saw two flying side by side, swooping right in front of me and Finn across the Forest Service road we were walking on. I watched in awe as they glided downslope through the sunlit pines and firs, their four-foot wingspans deftly avoiding trees and branches while staying together.

At the house, spring meant the return of the tree swallow pair who claimed the nest box on my fence rail as their home. Sunlight made their blue-and-gray wing feathers iridescent, and their short, white chest feathers fluffed when they preened; they looked like portly butlers. But oh, could they fly. The fighter pilots of the bird world, they playfully flew together, catching bugs in the air at dusk. I also watched them mate, feeling voyeuristic at first. The female perched on the fence railing and the male flew up and fluttered behind her before moving closer, hovering right behind her for a second or two, wings beating furiously. He'd then back away, still hovering, and move toward her again. He repeated this maneuver several times until the female decided they were done or the male got tired.

And there were the house wrens who annually made use of a small-diameter hole in the side of my garage wall (where a propane pipe once ran) for their nest. Tiny dull-brown birds, the mated pair chirped and flitted about the columbine and lupine in my wildflower garden. By the end of June, their fledglings would appear. One year, Conall found one just inside the dog yard, on the lawn. He picked it up in his mouth, then dropped it when I asked him to. I set it down on the other side of the fence, near my front door, several feet from the nest. It didn't move. It didn't seem afraid, just stared at me as I checked on it and took closeup photos. Its feathers were damp with Conall drool, and it had a tiny mohawk on the top of its head. A day later, I saw the same fledgling on the fence railing on the other side of the house, still sporting the mohawk.

One June, I found two house wren fledglings standing on the concrete walkway near the front door. Knowing they were safe from the boys, I ran for my phone; I was amazed that they didn't move when I returned and crouched low and close. One of the parents, however, was quite concerned, chirping loudly at me, or them, from the lupine nearby. When I checked an hour later, a third sibling had joined them. They all made it up to the fence railing nearest the nest. I kept the dogs on the other side of the house, just to be safe.

Every spring day brought a new display growth and next generations: plants bursting with leaves and bright flowers; bees and butterflies arriving to gather pollen and nectar; birds returning from migration, tending their chicks, helping their fledglings learn to fly; white-tailed deer fawns and elk calves carefully walking on wobbly legs while following their mothers across my lot and into the forest; wolf pups, coyote pups, and fox kits emerging from dens, tottering on their stubby legs, exploring their forest domains under the watchful eye of a parent or older sibling.

Most of all, I loved spring because the forest remained devoid of most human noise. People (mostly tourists) didn't arrive with their wildlife-disturbing trucks and camper trailers, side-by-sides, ATVs, and dirt bikes until July, when the snow and cold nights were mostly gone. Until then, the dogs and I ran and walked in the forest as much and as far as our legs would carry us, moving quietly and reverently, higher and higher in elevation, rejoicing in nature's annual renewal.

Spring always restored my sense of hope.

Meadow and Maia on Ruby Meadows Trail, June 8, 2007, a year after the wolf encounter.

Opus at Snow Lake, Cascades, 1988.

On Mt. Rainier's Wonderland Trail, August 1998.

With Maia, age eleven weeks, 1999.

The girls in 2001: Meadow, four months, Maia, two years.

*Sunrise over distance Andean peaks,
seen through tent opening, June 1, 2001.*

With Meadow and Maia, trail sweeping the Cascade Crest 100 course, August 24, 2003.

Sunset from the Idaho lot.

Meadow and Maia in Squirrel Creek, August 19, 2007.

Meadow and Maia on Sound of Music Hillside before the wildflower bloom, May 2007.

Meadow and Maia near mid-lake boulders, Hard Creek Lake, June 15, 2007.

Meadow and Maia on East Fork Lake Fork Trail in wildfire smoke, July 16, 2007.

Following the girls down Grass Mountain Lakes Trail, July 20, 2007.

Maia and Meadow running up the groomed snowmobile trail, January 16, 2008.

Meadow taking in the view from Granite Mountain Trail, July 17, 2008.

Maia on ridge above Grass Mountain Lakes, July 31, 2008.

Maia and Meadow among the lupine and Indian paintbrush on Sound of Music Hillside, June 1, 2007. Photo: Sheree Sonfield

Meadow with her red teddy bear on her last morning, July 22, 2013.

Girls' cairn in Ruby Meadows, July 29, 2013.

Conall and Finn on Hidden Valley Trail, girls' cairn on flat boulder, August 18, 2020.

Conall near the girls' Goose Creek cairn, May 28, 2021.

Fostered Malamute Riggs and Finn playing in the yard, July 25, 2014.

Conall bouldering, May 2017.

Finn and Conall on the groomed snowmobile trail, February 28, 2020.

Conall ready to follow Finn down the illegal snowmobile trail, February 24, 2020.

Running with Finn and Conall on a snowshoe trail in Bear Basin, March 23, 2021.

Conall among wildflowers on Sound of Music Hillside, May 17, 2016.

Conall and Finn on Sound of Music Hillside, May 17, 2016.

Meadow among the wildflowers on Sound of Music Hillside, May 27, 2008.

Phlox alongside Hidden Valley Trail, Brundage, June 21, 2021

Conall posing on whitebark pine trunk, June 18, 2020.

Indian paintbrush and lupine on Hidden Valley Trail, Brundage, July 20, 2020.

Magenta Indian paintbrush on Brundage, July 27, 2020.

Yellow columbine on Brundage, July 27, 2020.

Columbine and lupine in home wildflower garden, June 10, 2021.

Finn and Conall at Loon Lake, September 27, 2018.

Fall colors on Brundage, September 28, 2020.

With Conall and Finn at Upper Hazard Lake, October 1, 2018.

Aspen in fall colors, Hidden Valley, Brundage, October 4, 2020.

Finn and Conall harvesting rose hips, October 8, 2018.

Conall on Granite Mountain Trail, October 15, 2019.

Bright yellow tamaracks line a Forest Service road in the Payette, October 21, 2018.

Pearlie everlastings blooming in autumn at Hard Creek Lake.

White Ford Explorer, barely visible, passing the end of Campbell Road, February 27, 2019.

A peaceful Campbell Road walk with Finn and Conall, March 4, 2019.

Conall and Finn among spring wildflowers, May 13, 2021.

House wren fledgling with mohawk courtesy of Conall, July 3, 2018.

Conall admiring the view from Lakeview Vista Trail at Brundage, October 30, 2020.

Conall alerting to a doe with twin fawns, June 18, 2020.

Finn watching the raven pair fly overhead near sunset, February 24, 2021.

A raven flying off with one of Conall's voles, January 11, 2021.

Finn and Conall watch construction of girls' Vermont cairn with day lily bloom, July 22, 2022.

Vermont wildflowers at sunset, August 10, 2021.

Vermont trails are different. Conall on Owl's Head Trail, August 24, 2023.

Chann enjoying his first winter in Vermont's snow, November 29, 2023.

WOLVES

Summer: Tufts of downy white fur, remnants of winter's insulating undercoat, cling to the breeding female wolf's sides and belly as she moves silently through the pine and fir trees of the Payette National Forest. Most had come off in spring, white flags of fluff that stuck to the shrubs and plants she skimmed against as she traveled, providing nesting material for songbirds and ravens. Other clumps fell to the ground as she paused to rake her sides, armpits, neck, and shoulders with a hind foot, scratching the itch that goes with this annual shedding.

She has a section of fawn carcass in her mouth and her distended belly reveals where the rest of it went. Trotting with purpose in the cool morning breeze, she lifts her nose, sifting the air for scent. Her eyes constantly scan the terrain, her ears flick toward any sound. By sight, smell, experience, and internal compass, she knows the shortest and safest way to her pack's rendezvous site, an open area near a stand of trees with wildflowers and huckleberry shrubs in the understory.

Her four pups are growing fast and need many calories. Because they're not old enough to hunt on their own, the female and her mate must bring food to them. This is their third litter together, so they're seasoned parents.

Arriving at the rendezvous site, the female's mate and son from last year's litter greet her, sniffing the carcass she drops to the ground. As the males eat, the pups rush their mother in excitement, licking her muzzle to trigger her to regurgitate a portion of the meat she'd eaten earlier. Hungry, the pups leap on the food she provides. Later, the pups play with each other and the adults, honing the running and pouncing skills they'll later use when they learn to hunt.

The breeding male will head out later to hunt on his own, grazing on ripe huckleberries along the way, taking advantage of the short season. He, too, can carry food for the pups in his belly—as much as twenty pounds—while transporting a carcass in his mouth. Their yearling son brings food to the rendezvous site as well when he's not watching the *pups. In this way, the pack meets the caloric demands of four weaned and rapidly growing wolf pups.*

Over the years that I read and collected research articles about wolves, it was clear much had been learned and many old theories discarded. The intense study of Yellowstone's wolves and their impact on the park's flora and fauna since their reintroduction in 1995 opened a lot of eyes and shifted some long-held beliefs.

Of necessity, all of the information gleaned from researching the wolves in Yellowstone was based on obtaining verifiable data, including GPS tracking, pack sizes and numbers, biological measurements and samples taken while an animal was sedated for tagging and/or GPS collaring, necropsies, and verified observations of numbers and types of prey taken.

Based on this information, researchers came up with theories and interpretations of pack composition, breeding and hunting success, and impact on the greater YNP ecosystem. When I read those theories, they often made sense, like the trophic cascade effect: Wolves prey on elk and deer, causing them to move more frequently and thus eat fewer aspen and willow saplings along waterways. Less concentrated grazing allows river- and streambanks to stabilize, literally returning the landscape to its more balanced, pre-wolf-extirpation state.

I found little if any research regarding the social lives of wolves, but that information gap was filled by retired NPS ranger Rick McIntyre and park employee, naturalist and wildlife advocate Rick Lamplugh.

McIntyre spent four decades observing wolves (twenty-five of them in Yellowstone) and was involved in their reintroduction to the park. Able to identify individuals within the packs he had watched so closely over the years, he noted their personality traits, such as empathy, playfulness, and compassion toward other pack members. As for Lamplugh, in the early 2000s, he spent three winters in the Lamar Valley, observing the wolves on his own time.

Both men, who have written books documenting their field observations, helped educate the public, debunking old myths and battling misinformation. They also drew direct social and behavioral lines between wolves and humans, and wolves and our canine companions.

Autumn: *The breeding male's all-black coat is beginning to thicken. His new undercoat will provide protection against the coming winter's harsh mountain cold and snow. There's a sharp chill in the night air, and the scent of an early snowfall that dusted higher-elevation peaks flows on the wind down through the pines and firs, into his territory. He's lean after a summer of hard work feeding his growing pups.*

After surveying the pack's territory on this late-November night, the wolf returns to their current rendezvous site with a snowshoe hare in his mouth. He's greeted enthusiastically by his mate, who chose him because of his black coat, a visual sign of his immunity to the canine distemper virus. He's also greeted by their yearling son, who has yet to leave his parents, and this year's two surviving offspring. The pups, six months old, resemble adults yet are still playful as they explore their world, tormenting their older sibling with nips to his ears and tail. Sometimes they go with their pack on hunts; too small to help, they're old enough to learn.

The adult wolves know this time of year is especially dangerous. There are more humans in the forest, some on foot, others noisy on fast-moving vehicles. Often, just after dawn or before dusk, the quiet is shattered by the sharp reports of rifle fire, a warning for the wolves to stay hidden or flee. The pups learn to avoid humans and their scents by observing their parents' reactions and movements.

The hungry pups quickly devour the hare. The breeding male rests on a large, flat lichen-and-moss-covered boulder, surrounded by huckleberry shrubs with a few of autumn's orange and red leaves clinging to their branches. Dog rose bushes still hold a few ripe rose hips, vitamin-rich snacks. His mate is nearby, keeping watch. Having eaten, the pups play-fight each other, leaping and pouncing, chasing and wrestling, playing hide-and-seek and tag, sometimes bumping into the male. He reprimands them quickly but gently.

Later that night, the wolf, his mate, and the yearling will go out to hunt together, leaving the pups alone at the homesite. The pack has eaten less in recent days because of the influx of humans into their territory. With five mouths to feed, satisfying hunger requires them to take risks. Deer and elk are at their healthiest after a summer of abundant food and now, even the fawns and calves are fast. The wolves will need all their combined skill and speed to have a successful nighttime hunt.

Before Farley Mowat's observational studies of Canadian wolves in 1946 and the study of Yellowstone wolves in the 1990s, wolf research was primarily carried out by scientists with a Western European mindset, weaned on centuries-old fairy tales that depicted wolves as dangerous, vicious, and evil. Barry Lopez, in his book *Of Wolves and Men*, delves deep into how wolves have been depicted through history, especially in Europe.

> It is curious to find the wolf as a character in children's literature, for all wolves in literature are the creations of adult minds, that is, of adult fears, adult fantasies, adult allegories, and adult perversions. So the tendency to look on animal stories as simplistic is misleading. The wolf of Aesopian fable has changed little in twenty-five hundred years, but he is not just an unchanging symbol of bad behavior. He stands in the child's mind for something very real. It is Aesop's wolf, not Science's wolf—a base, not very intelligent creature, of ravenous appetite, gullible, impudent, and morally corrupt—that generations of schoolchildren are most familiar with. . . . Some children weaned on fable never inquired deeper into the animals than the stories led them, and so went through life believing the wolf evil, the fox sly, the bee industrious, and the ass foolish.

Lopez goes on to draw a distinction between early medieval fable and later fairy tales and folklore, which often painted a much darker picture of wolves.

> In fables—short, didactic, usually plotless aphorisms—the wolf's poor nature is ascribed to his having been born a wolf and it is possible to feel some sympathy for his predicament. Wolves are not hated in fables, the emotions elicited from the reader are not strong, the wolf is not hell-driven and malicious. He is not a complex beast at all. The wolf of fairy tale and folktale is a much fuller character, capable of diabolical evil and also, occasionally, of warmth and unflinching devotion.

After examining fairy tales like *Little Red Riding Hood*, *The Three Little Pigs*, and *The Seven Little Goats*, Lopez notes that each story is violent. "And the violence done to the wolf is socially acceptable." He adds, "Our historically ambivalent vision of the wolf is, again, very evident. An odd thought that remains with all these stories is that as adults it is often only these violent tales of hedonistic, ravenous wolves that we most easily recall. Why that should be I do not know. Perhaps these were the stories our parents and teachers emphasized. In any case it seems disconcertingly clear that this is the wolf we are preoccupied with."

Before the Yellowstone wolves, most studies involved captive wolves kept in small groups and tight spaces. They were often aggressive toward each other, fitting the dark pictures painted by folktales. Scientists assumed that wild wolf packs operated similarly, and those assumptions were readily adopted. This led to the alpha/beta theory of wolf behavior, where dominance by the alpha male keeps the rest of the pack in line. Unfortunately, that theory was later extrapolated by dog trainers, who encouraged owners to train their dogs with the use of dominance, even pain.

For decades, scientists with such blinders couldn't believe ancient humans and wolves ever cooperated or bonded, or lived in close proximity. Yet they did. The recent work of archaeozoologists and paleogeneticists suggests that the domestic dog was derived originally from Pleistocene wolves sometime between 40,000 and 15,000 years ago, during the Last Glacial Maximum (aka, ice age). If true, wolves were the first animals to be domesticated by humans, at least four- to five thousand years before livestock species such as sheep and goats.

Such discoveries almost immediately led to the "garbage pit" theory: Wolves needed food and found it where they found humans, eventually forming tenuous relationships based solely on the wolf's hunger. That eventually led to selection and breeding that resulted in dogs. My first reaction when reading that? What an astounding lack of imagination.

The idea that wolves required humans and their leftovers to survive made no sense to me. Wolves are incredibly adaptable, at times thriving across the entire northern half of the planet, in the arctic as well as scrublands and deserts. They are excellent hunters, usually able to kill enough wildlife to maintain their pack without wasting or overindulging, caching any excess for later. They didn't then, nor do they now, need food from humans. Nor do they seek our garbage (like black bears often do). Finally, it's hard to imagine that early humans had much waste food or lived in large enough settled groups to create consistent garbage pits for other animals to raid.

Plus, the garbage pit theory doesn't explain archeological evidence from burial sites. Wolves, ancient dogs, even a fox have been discovered deliberately and carefully buried with humans in ways suggesting that they were highly valued companions.

Winter: By late December, snow blankets the ground in the wolves' mountain territory. More will fall in the coming months. Winters are long and hard for most wildlife. Birds migrate to warmer climes, bears hibernate, and ungulates struggle to find food. Wolves, though, are in their element.

The pups continue to grow, reaching nearly full size. They go on hunts, still learning from their parents, sometimes helping. After a successful hunt, they feed on the carcass when their parents finish with it. Their older brother has left the group. Infected by Toxoplasma gondii, a protozoan parasite from drinking contaminated water during the summer, his risk tolerance increased, prompting him to leave the pack in early December. In search of a mate and his own territory, he forages by day and howls at night to attract a lone female.

The remaining pack of four sleeps out in the open, the pups having outgrown dens long ago. To stay warm when temperatures dip below zero and wind stirs the pine branches above them, the wolves curl into balls, tails over snout, catching their warm breath and keeping their feet warm. Their fur, with its insulating winter layer under water-repelling long guard hairs, prevents the snow that collects on their backs from penetrating to their skin. In the coldest weather, they sleep close together, out of the wind, sharing their warmth with one another.

In late January, the breeding male and female show more-than-usual affection toward each other, part of their annual mating ritual. They sleep closer together, nuzzle, walk side-by-side or follow closely, even wrestle playfully. The female marks territory more frequently. When she's ready to breed, she lets her mate know by prancing around him, rubbing his body with hers, nuzzling him, and placing her chin on his back affectionately. As it was the previous year, their breeding is successful.

With a thick blanket of snow on the forest floor, ungulates have fewer food sources. They become weak and slow from lack of calories and the effort to stay warm. Their hooves, so good on dirt and rock, make movement through deep snow challenging. In winter, the wolves have an advantage. Their large paws spread out like snowshoes, allowing them to run in pursuit of floundering, tiring prey.

This winter, the wolf pair was successful in taking old and sick deer and elk, enough to cache some for spring. Hunting is always dangerous for the wolves. In addition to kicks that bruised their bodies, a deer's kick to the mouth had broken one of the male's upper canines and knocked out two upper incisors and one lower. Still, they have enough to eat, as do their pups.

As snow melts off the lower portions of the mountain, the wolf pair finds a new den site, digging under a jumble of large boulders that form a *sort of cave. The abundance of food found this winter helps the breeding female through her two months of pregnancy.*

After forty years living and running in the wilderness with Malamutes, I can easily imagine many scenarios in which early humans and wolves cooperated, playing out in multiple locations over millennia, a slow yet steady progression from wild wolf to habituated wolf to domesticated dog as indoor pet.

For example, perhaps early humans recognized how beneficial wolves could be—following their well-worn paths through forests and fields as both sought food for their packs and clans, alerting to potential food (wildlife) and dangers from predators that the humans couldn't hear or smell (e.g., bears, tigers), and protecting humans and their young offspring as well as their own pups from other predators. Wolves' knowledge of the landscape and predatory skills likely helped small groups of migrating humans thrive by adopting their hunting locations and techniques as they ventured into new territory with new wildlife (e.g., crossing Beringia from eastern Asia to North America).

Intuitively speaking, it also seems possible that this early cooperation would evolve into relationships of mutual compassion and support. Just as my Malamutes and I "read" each other and communicate through eye contact and body language, conveying messages of curiosity, joy, fear, anger, pain, interest, compassion, and empathy, it's easy to imagine similar abilities enhancing the bonds between ancient humans and wolves. Humans and canids are social animals who evolved to rely heavily on reading and interpreting body language, especially eye contact.

I can also imagine early humans recognizing some social benefits. Connections with wolves, especially wolf pups, might have relieved loneliness or even provided entertainment. I can imagine wolves, curious and watchful, interacting with humans who didn't fear them or chase them off. The bonding hormone oxytocin would have flowed in human and wolf brains alike, providing positive feedback, encouraging ongoing close interactions.

These interactions and relationships would have occurred across thousands of years, during a time when wolves had less reason to fear humans and humans were more accepting of wolves' presence because they had no domestic livestock to protect. Without direct competition for food, each species likely gave the other space and respect. Those wolves exhibiting an affinity for close contact with humans were probably encouraged and nurtured, reinforcing that trait and passing it to their offspring.

Today's wolves in Europe, Asia, and North America are survivors of centuries of relentless persecution by humans who—for several reasons—demonize them, mythologizing them as evil. Modern-day wolves' perception of humans must be quite different than that of their ancient ancestors, since avoidance is what has kept them alive. But it wasn't necessarily always that way.

Spring: *With winter's snow gone at lower elevations, migrating birds begin returning to the forest, filling the air with their mating songs and territorial calls. Finding food once again becomes challenging for the wolf pack. Deer and elk can run more easily and they grow stronger and faster with more food, making it harder for the wolves to catch them. To eat, the pack scavenges carcasses from winter, including some they cached when luck and skill meant food was plentiful.*

The breeding pair, helped by their yearlings—a male and a female—hunt smaller animals to help fill the spring hunger gap. Her hind leg broken in early winter, the female yearling is slower than her brother. After weeks of not putting weight on it, there's now a calcified mass where the bone healed. She limps slightly but can run and hunt again. Beavers, voles, and squirrels fill their stomachs when they aren't able to take a deer or elk. The yearlings are now adept at finding and hunting game and feeding themselves.

In early April, the breeding female retreats into the den to give birth. Her mate and their two yearlings keep watch from nearby, bringing her food as she nurses and cares for her six tiny, deaf, and blind pups. The pups will depend on her milk for at least three weeks, then start eating the regurgitated meat brought to the den by her and the rest of the pack. Every pack member plays a role in feeding, nurturing, and teaching the pups.

At two weeks, the pups open their eyes, which at this point are blue. They begin to waddle and squirm in the den. At three weeks, they start poking their heads out, carefully exploring the world in which they'll grow and eventually create packs of their own. They stay close together, tumbling over tree roots, rocks, and each other as they gain strength, balance, and agility. With summer approaching, the pups spend more time outside the den. Usually, they're carefully watched by at least one pack member while the others are away hunting, but this is a small pack. Sometimes the pups are left alone for several hours while the adults forage. They must find enough food to quell their own hunger and also feed the pups. The food they bring back to the den gives the pups a better chance of surviving their first six months.

Today, humans and dogs are tight. Working and companion dogs are common, and have been for hundreds of years. The benefits that flow both ways in these relationships are now well-documented. It doesn't require a huge leap of faith to consider that early humans and wolves bonded in a similar, symbiotic fashion, with many of the same benefits.

The pervasive and important role wolves have played in Indigenous cultures across North America, passed down in stories through generations, is testament to the strong bonds between ancient peoples and wolves, even after domestic dogs became their favored companions.

Letters from US tribal leaders and Canadian First Nation leaders to US Secretary of the Interior Deb Haaland written in 2021 affectingly described the wolf's place in the Indigenous world:

> In most Native cultures, the wolf is considered a medicine being associated with courage, strength, loyalty, and success at hunting. Like bears, wolves are considered closely related to humans by many North American tribes, and the origin stories of some Northwest Coastal tribes tell of their first ancestors being transformed from wolves into men. In Shoshone mythology, the wolf plays the role of the noble Creator god, while in Anishinabe mythology a wolf character is the brother and true best friend of the culture hero. Among the Pueblo tribes, wolves are considered one of the six directional guardians, associated with the east and the color white, and associated with protection, ascribing to them both healing and hunting powers. Wolves are also one of the most common clan animals in Native American cultures. Tribes with Wolf Clans include the Creek, Cherokee, Chickasaw, Chippewa; Algonquian tribes like the Shawnee and Menominee; Iroquois tribes; Plains tribes like the Caddo and Osage; the Pueblo tribes of New Mexico; and Northwest Coastal tribes.

> The gray wolf is an extremely important species with tremendous cultural significance to many of our Nations with ties to Tribes across the Medicine Line (Canada-US border). It is the wolf who has brought us much of our knowledge and understanding of Mother Earth. As a symbol of survival and spiritual reciprocity, the wolf has influenced many of our Nations' societal structures, imparted the communal responsibility to sustain life, and provided us with guidance for environmental stewardship—showing us the critical importance of ensuring balance, health, and structure in ecosystems and the environment.

I believe those early human-wolf bonds, whenever and wherever they occurred, were a heady blend of mutual attraction, compassion, empathy, companionship, and pragmatic food-finding and protection. Reinforcing those affinities and traits over generations would have opened the door to habituation, and eventually to the development of basal dog breeds.

Humans being humans, ancient peoples undoubtedly encouraged breeding of the wolves they liked best, at some point mixing wolves with early dog species. Eventually, with that influence, wolves led to Malamutes and other basal breeds. Those basal breeds became the foundation lines modern humans used to begin modifying dogs to fit various needs and whims, from work to fancy, giving us the two hundred (and counting) breeds recognized by the American Kennel Club today. And we're still tweaking; the AKC has added twenty-two new breeds in the past decade.

While all dog breeds have gray wolf DNA, some retain more markers for appearance, traits, and behavior. Modern humans were initially more interested in working dogs, creating herding, guardian, and retriever breeds. Later, there was demand for fancy "designer" and lap dogs, like pugs and Pekingese. With each tweak to create specialized dogs suited to highly specific work and/or lifestyles, we lost touch with some amazing and valuable wolfish traits: their social and environmental smarts, their stamina and agility, their ability to think independently while navigating the natural world.

Over forty-plus years of living with and running countless miles and hours through the wilderness with my Malamutes, I've had ample time to ponder the many ways Malamutes are like wolves.

It's easy for me to imagine ancient wolves and humans interacting as I do with my Malamutes in the wilderness.

I appreciate that Indigenous peoples of North America revere and embrace wolves as integral parts of the natural world.

The rest of us have much to learn from them.

EMPATHY

When I first moved to Idaho in 2005, the girls were six and four years old. Suddenly, there were few (if any) babies to greet. Nearby towns were small, the winters long and harsh, and our summers spent in the forest by ourselves. If strangers saw us, they either moved to the other side of the road or cautiously asked, "Are those wolves?" I was deeply saddened by that attitude.

In 2009, during the recession, the girls and I—with newly adopted Finn—returned temporarily to the Seattle area. Being back in western Washington was such a relief, to once again be among people who thought the girls were beautiful and wanted to meet and pet them rather than fearing them based solely on their appearance. No one in Washington asked me if they were wolves. The girls got to meet babies again.

At the time, we lived in a townhouse a couple of blocks from a nice park on the shores of Lake Washington. On walks to the park, we passed a nursing home. First, I met the director, who often stood outside on his breaks. He thoroughly enjoyed getting to know the girls. Then, we met two of the home's long-term residents: a man with Parkinson's, who used an electric wheelchair to get around, and his "lady friend," who used a walker.

Their infirmities made it challenging for them to engage directly with the girls; there was almost no petting. But the girls were instantly drawn to both, and any time they spied either or both outside the nursing home or at the park, they eagerly dragged me toward them for a greeting. Always gentle and respectful, they seemed to understand that while these two humans weren't very exciting to be around—no pets, no treats, few words—they needed and wanted the attention and love the girls offered.

One autumn, we were on one of our late-afternoon walks through the surrounding neighborhood. Now twelve and ten, Maia and Meadow were mellowing but still enjoyed daily walks of three-plus miles. Our route followed residential streets with wide, meandering sidewalks and little traffic. We didn't often run into people on this route; those interactions tended to happen at the park.

This time, though, I saw an older woman approaching us on the sidewalk. Dressed against the chill in a fuzzy hat, long winter coat, and gloves, she hunched her shoulders and moved slowly, carefully placing her steps. Worried that she might not like dogs or might be startled by us, I checked to see if it was safe to cross the street to give the woman space. Then, tugging on the leash, I encouraged the girls to come with me, but they planted their feet and wouldn't budge.

"Come on, girls, this way," I urged as I tugged again, but they didn't move. They stood stock still, both of them looking at the slowly approaching woman. By this time, the woman was standing on the sidewalk just ten feet away. She didn't say a word, but her eyes locked on mine and sent me an entreaty: *Can I pet your dogs?*

I let the girls pull me gently toward her. When they got close, I saw her almost imperceptible smile. They lifted their big heads simultaneously toward her gloved hand, which shook as she held it out for them to sniff. Tails wagging gently, eyes focused on the woman, they remained calm as she placed her hand gently atop Maia's head, then Meadow's. I watched, heart swelling, as they did their Malamute thing of making people love them and sending it right back—what I often referred to as being Malamute ambassadors.

I didn't want to break the spell with words. Smiling, standing quietly behind the girls, I watched the elderly woman as she continued to stroke the girls' heads, murmuring something I couldn't quite hear.

After a minute she looked up at me. As a tear ran down her cheek, she whispered, "I miss my dog so much. You are so lucky." Then she stepped carefully past us and continued on her way.

I watched her go, my throat tight, thinking how lonely it must be to have to live without a beloved dog.

As the girls and I finished our walk, I remembered another time they'd shown similar gentleness and concern for an elderly woman. They were young, maybe four and two. We were running around Green Lake and that day, had been on the outer dirt path adjacent to the road circling most of the park. As we approached a five-way intersection, I watched in horror as an elderly woman in a crosswalk was hit by a car. The driver saw her at the last minute and braked, but still made contact, knocking her to the pavement. She quickly scrambled up and stumbled, startled, toward where the girls and I were standing on the path. The car's driver, aghast, asked the woman through his window if she was okay. She didn't answer; fear written on her face, she was intent on getting off the road.

We went into the street to meet and assist the elderly woman through the rest of the crosswalk and into the park. Focusing on her, I took her elbow to steady her across the curb and over to a spot under a tree not far from the road. I helped her sit down on the grass, held her hand, and talked to her, trying to find out how badly she was hurt. The girls were beside me but I was hardly aware of them. The woman seemed okay, mostly startled. Other witnesses quickly arrived, and someone said they'd called 911. Within minutes, I heard a siren. When the firetruck and EMTs arrived, we stepped away to so they could assess the woman's condition.

The girls didn't once pull on the leash or make me tug it to keep them near me. They didn't interfere when I helped the woman up and onto the grass. They just stayed beside me. When the woman was seated, they didn't try to greet and lick her as they would have anyone else sitting on the ground, but instead, sat next to me and waited.

I'd never seen them so quietly patient, especially in a place that for them was always full of fun and activity and happy meetings with strangers.

After the woman was loaded into an ambulance, the fireman who was first on the scene came over to thank me for watching over the woman until they arrived. "You have amazing dogs," he said. "They were so calm the entire time, despite sirens, people moving all about. Just amazing."

The girls' most startling and enlightening display of empathy, however, involved Meadow and an adult woman in emotional distress.

In 2006, soon after moving to Idaho, I took a position as executive director of a domestic violence crisis center. It was a tiny nonprofit funded entirely by state grants, and I was its only employee. A small house in the county seat, right behind the sheriff's office, had been donated for use as an office.

Taking stock of my new place of employment, I found the bedroom/office closet stuffed full of teddy bears of all sizes and colors, donated by concerned local women. The sheriff's office had taken as many as they could use to comfort children who had to be removed from their homes; my organization took the rest. I set a few teddy bears out in the greeting area (the home's living room) and in the second bedroom, where victims watched a court-sponsored video about how to acquire a domestic-violence protection order. The thirty-minute video was required viewing for anyone seeking a protection order. Part of my court-ordered job was to verify that victims had viewed it and to answer any questions they might have.

Because this "office" was forty miles from my home, I often took the girls to work with me. The house had a small, fenced back yard, so if anyone coming to see me in my official capacity as ED of the crisis center wasn't comfortable with dogs, the girls could stay outside.

One afternoon, a woman was referred to me to view the protection-order video. Over the phone she told me she loved dogs, so I kept the girls in the house when she arrived. They greeted her warmly and she seemed comforted to have them near, sinking her fingers into their thick fur, stroking them to calm her nerves.

After a brief chat in the greeting area, I showed her to the back bedroom to view the video, leaving the girls in the greeting area. The video room was small, most of the space taken up by a couch and equipment. She and I settled on the couch and I started the video. Within a couple of minutes, the woman was overcome with emotion, crying and reaching for the box of tissues we kept on hand.

Meadow suddenly appeared in the doorway with a bright-red teddy bear in her mouth. She looked at me, then slowly approached the woman and gently dropped the teddy bear in her lap.

The woman, still crying, cooed at Meadow as she stroked the fur around her ears. "Thank you," she whispered. After accepting a few pats, Meadow walked out of the room.

After the woman left, I gave Meadow a big hug. *So. It's not just babies,* I thought, so proud of my girl. Then I retrieved that red teddy bear, which I later brought home with me. I still have it, a reminder of Meadow's extraordinary act of empathy.

To my delight, but not surprise, Conall carried on the Malamute tradition of empathy toward babies, children, the elderly, and the vulnerable. The first example Conall offered came in 2016 when he was just over a year old. At the time, I was executive director of the regional animal shelter. Every January, McCall hosted a ten-day event called Winter Carnival. In addition to ice sculptures, a monster dog pull contest, snowshoe golf, and other fun distractions, the premier event was the Mardi Gras Parade. This march of floats and groups took place on the event's first Saturday morning. Regardless of weather, thousands of tourists and residents lined the main street through town to watch. Beaded necklaces and penny candy were tossed from the floats into the crowds.

The animal shelter encouraged those who had adopted dogs to march as a group, and shelter volunteers brought available shelter dogs wearing "Adopt Me" vests. Conall and I joined them.

As we started moving along the parade route, Conall kept tugging on his leash, pulling me toward the side where spectators watched from behind a rope barrier. After resisting for a few minutes, I finally let him go where he wanted. He made a beeline for a baby in a stroller positioned right below the rope; the baby was dressed for the cold, bundled in a snowsuit with mittens, hat, and hood. Before I knew what was happening, Conall gave the baby's chubby face a lick. The baby giggled and the parent behind the stroller laughed (thank goodness), while those standing nearby hooted and cheered.

For the rest of the march through town, we stuck to one side of the parade route so Conall could greet every small child he saw, whether the child was standing or in a stroller. The spectators loved it and I can't remember ever smiling so big for so long.

One summer morning two years later, when Conall was three, I took him for a stroll in downtown McCall. I did this periodically to keep his social skills sharp. We meandered through a lakeside park; it was early, so there weren't too many people out and about. But whenever Conall spied a child, he pulled me toward them and greetings were conducted to the joy of all.

Then Conall focused on a lone woman—eyes downcast, shoulders hunched—walking on one of the paths above the beach, near the parking area. As soon as the woman saw Conall, she smiled, relaxed, and slowed. I let Conall lead me to her and once near, he lifted his head toward her outstretched hands for a greeting. He allowed the woman to sink her fingers deep into the soft, thick fur around his ears and neck. Wordlessly, she crouched down to face Conall nose-to-nose, eye-to-eye, and rubbed his head and neck in slow, rhythmic circles. Then she touched her forehead to his and inhaled deeply.

"This is Conall," I said quietly, a little afraid of breaking the magic of whatever was being communicated between them. The woman looked up and smiled at me, then focused on Conall again, murmuring his name as she cradled his cheeks. Slowly, Conall turned his body so the woman could massage his hips. I sensed that this was his way of reducing the emotional tension of such intense eye contact while still giving the woman the tactile sensations she needed.

The woman began to cry, tears tracing lines down her cheeks before splashing onto the path. She clearly just wanted time with Conall, without conversation, so I stood there quietly, holding his leash, letting him move however he wished.

After a couple of minutes of rubbing Conall's hips and flanks, the woman looked up at me. "I had to say goodbye to my precious dog last week. It's why I'm here in McCall, by myself. I had to get away. The house was too quiet."

Conall never fidgeted, like he did when meeting most strangers. Amazed at what I was witnessing, wanting to always remember it, I asked the woman if I could take her photo with Conall. She nodded.

The woman stood, hugged Conall one last time, and thanked me. "I so needed this today," she said before she turned to continue her walk through the park.

I didn't teach my dogs any of this empathy. How could I? I don't have children of my own. Babies are not part of my home life or even my social circle, so my dogs didn't learn to be gentle around babies from me. We weren't typically around the elderly or people who are emotionally stressed. Though I'm sensitive and empathic, and had spent my legal career helping those in distress, representing children, the elderly, and incapacitated adults, I rarely recognized sad, grieving strangers in need from a distance like my dogs did. They always knew. They pulled me directly toward those people without hesitation.

The fact that all of my Malamutes have exhibited this trait of empathy tells me it's buried deep in their ancient DNA. It seems logical, at least to me, that it comes from their wolf ancestors, perhaps the same wolves that lived and cooperated with ancient humans.

Indeed, Rick McIntyre, the retired national park ranger who spent decades in Yellowstone, watching the wolves he helped reintroduce the park and their progeny, observed empathy among many of them. For example, in his first book, *The Rise of Wolf 8,* McIntyre described how Wolf 8 arrived as a pup during the first wave of reintroduced wolves in 1995. At age 18 months, Wolf 8 joined a pack after its breeding male had been illegally killed; the remaining pack consisted of the breeding female and her eight six-month-old pups. Wolf 8 became the lead male, raising the pups as if they were his own.

Later, one of the pups—Wolf 21—was a yearling when he watched

Wolf 8 defeat a larger breeding male, but spared his life. The next year, Wolf 21 joined a different pack where the breeding male had just died. Like his role model, Wolf 21 willingly helped raise the five pups of that pack.

In a later book, *The Reign of Wolf 21,* McIntyre brings years of observations to his focus on Wolf 21. He describes how Wolf 21 never lost a fight with another male, but always let them live, as he'd observed Wolf 8 do when he was a yearling. Wolf 21 was gentle with pups, also like Wolf 8, playing with them, pretending to let them win in games of chase and wrestle. McIntyre once watched a sickly lone pup on a hill, shunned by the other pups; Wolf 21 went up to the pup to simply keep him company.

Empathy. Genetic. Learned.

SHATTERED

Black-and-white magpies and an occasional red-tailed hawk shared the sky overhead, swooping and calling. Soon, red-winged blackbirds would herald the arrival of spring, the males perching on telephone lines, singing loudly for a mate. Otherwise, Meadows Valley was, as usual, calm and quiet at three in the afternoon on February 27, 2019, a winter Wednesday. Most human sounds were muffled by the blanket of snow, the solitude broken only by the occasional rumble of an eighteen-wheeler on the state highway a mile to the west.

I parked at one end of the one-mile stretch of road the boys and I favored for quick walks. We rarely encountered vehicles here, so they could be off-leash. I was bundled for the cold, including a balaclava under my hat to cover my cheeks and chin, and two layers of gloves. The sky was a mass of pewter-colored clouds, the ground and road covered with snow. Brown fence posts and telephone poles stood out starkly against the white and gray.

When I opened the back passenger door, the boys exploded out of it. I kept my eyes on them as they moved along Campbell Road, following their noses. Conall got the zoomies, racing atop the snow berms lining both sides of the road, a winter's worth of plowed snow filling the ditches and reaching as high as the tops of the fence posts. The boys were always excited to walk here; they often wrestled and chased each other over the first quarter-mile of our walk, letting off steam. Especially on days when we didn't go running or x/c skiing, walking for an hour on this stretch of country road satisfied their need to move, explore, and think, keeping me entertained while also allowing time to reflect.

We walked here several times a week, usually in late afternoon, year-round. Yet even on this road, well out of the forest, I always made sure Conall wore his bright orange vest. Coyotes, deemed vermin in Idaho and unworthy of any legal protections, could be killed anywhere, any time, by any method. I lived in constant fear that Conall would be mistaken for a wolf or coyote and shot. Finn, an Aussie who didn't look anything like a coyote or wolf, could have gone without his orange vest, but I felt two orange vests in proximity made it abundantly clear to all that Conall was a dog, not a wolf or coyote.

We walked past the single house on this stretch and were less than a quarter-mile from the southern end of Campbell Road, where it intersected Farrell Road. Suddenly, Conall, about twenty feet ahead of me, stopped. His fluffy white tail, normally curled over his back, dropped. That put me on alert. Conall was looking intently over the four-foot-high snow berm at something on Farrell Road, maybe fifty yards to the southeast. Having learned to implicitly trust Conall's senses, just as I had Maia's, and knowing that a tail drop meant either danger or uncertainty, I stopped walking when I reached Conall's side and followed his stare.

I saw what he saw: a vehicle. Given that the snow on the road muffled tire sounds, I wasn't surprised that I hadn't heard it approaching, although Conall had. I noticed this vehicle wasn't moving, although its headlights—bright, small-diameter LEDs—were on, pointing toward me and the boys rather than straight along Farrell Road.

Strange. Had it slid off the road into the snow berm? No; I quickly realized if that were true, I wouldn't be able to see headlights because they'd be buried. And the driver's side door was wide open. So strange. I couldn't see anyone standing on the road…

Ping! Crackle, crackle, crackle….

My body froze but my mind raced. I tried to wrap my mind around what I just heard. I was pretty sure what it meant, but didn't want to believe it because it was my worst nightmare: *Did someone just shoot at Conall, mistaking him for a coyote or wolf? Or at me??*

Head down and tail tucked, Conall instantly got small, turning and diving between my legs, clearly terrified. Through my thick winter pants, I could feel his body shaking. Finn, concerned about Conall's behavior but not otherwise alarmed, stood still on the road a few feet ahead of us. Shorter, Finn couldn't see over the top of the berm.

Quickly deciding that what I'd heard was indeed a rifle and bullet, my primary focus became ensuring Conall's safety. As he moved nervously around my legs, urging me to retreat, I held on to his orange vest while struggling to unbuckle the leash and coupler fastened around my waist. Finn stayed close, aware something was up but not sure what. Deciding that Finn was not likely a target, I didn't connect him to Conall with the coupler. Instead, I relied on Finn's innate Aussie obedience to stay near as I contemplated my next move. All the while, I kept an eye on the vehicle.

No more than a minute or two passed as I got Conall secured, although it seemed much longer. The vehicle—driver's door now closed and facing the correct direction on Farrell Road—started to creep slowly westward. Now that I could see the vehicle better, I was confused: It looked like a county sheriff's patrol car. But no, in our county, the sheriff's SUVs are a dark steel or dark green, not white. And the vehicle was clean, no mud splatter on its sides, which was odd given sloppy winter driving conditions recently. All those details quickly registered in my mind, things to remember, years of legal training coming into play.

Turning to look across the big open pasture to the west of us—the ground covered in nearly three feet of snow—I tried to see if I could detect what the person in the SUV might have been shooting at. Nothing. Even Conall, with his keen eyes and nose, scanned the pasture and saw nothing. I looked back toward the SUV, still rolling slowly along Farrell.

Furious, I felt a flood of adrenaline flash through me. It may always be open season for coyotes, but it was illegal to hunt or shoot from a vehicle, or to shoot across a road. I wanted the license plate. I wanted that person cited. I pulled out my cell phone and took several photos. I expected the SUV to stop once the boys and I were clearly in view, but it didn't. It just kept rolling slowly westward.

Then, surprisingly, it stopped maybe thirty feet past the intersection. With Conall on-leash, Finn by my side, and fury in my blood, I started walking quickly toward the SUV to get a clearer view of it and, I hoped, the driver. When I got about ten yards from the intersection, afraid the SUV would drive away, I stopped and took more photos even though the snow berm obscured part of the vehicle. Walking again, moving even closer, ready for a confrontation with the idiot driver/shooter, I watched as the SUV started rolling along Farrell again, slowly, either still oblivious to our presence or not caring. Because the SUV's windows were tinted, all I could see was the shape and height of the driver's head. There were no passengers.

"Hey!" I yelled loudly, startling my already stressed-out dogs. The driver's head swiveled in my direction, clearly hearing me, but the SUV kept going. "Hey!!" I screamed one more time, as loud as I could, but it was obvious the driver wasn't interested in me and kept moving toward the west end of Farrell, where the road curves ninety degrees and heads south toward the town of New Meadows. By the time I reached Farrell Road, the SUV was too far away for me to read the license plate, but I took several photos anyway.

In the time it took someone to squeeze a trigger, my years-long sense of peace and safety in a place I walked regularly with the boys was shattered.

I knew it wasn't smart to approach someone who'd been *shooting* from a vehicle, but I was so intensely angry in that moment that I didn't care. I wanted to confront them. This emotion was amplified by a days-long bad headaches and loud tinnitus caused by a significant CSF leak. When I was in this mode, my anger switched on easily and quickly, something that would never have happened with a normal CSF level. It sometimes scared me; I hardly recognized myself when this happened.

The boys and I walked back toward Campbell Road to return home. Conall and Finn were relieved, picking up their pace, eager to reach the car. I let Conall off-leash again, but he stuck close to me, and his tail stayed down, a sign of how badly he'd been shaken. He stopped frequently to look behind us, even climbing the snow berm once to look back toward where we last saw the SUV. He didn't relax until we were near our car.

On the short drive home, I mentally replayed the incident. I'd been around the sound of rifle fire at various times in my life, especially after moving to Idaho and living so near a national forest. But this sound was different, new to me, more of a high-pitched ping than the bang of a hunting rifle or the booming blast of a shotgun.

The unforgettable sound of the bullet flying by was also new. I'd read that high-powered rifles were becoming more common with hunters in Idaho, and wondered if that's what I'd heard.

Once home, I called a neighbor, a retired colonel in the Army National Guard, and asked him what the bullet from a high-powered rifle sounded like. Before answering, he asked me to describe what I'd heard. "It sounded like the crackle of electricity, right next to my ear," I told him. After a long pause, my neighbor said, "Yes. If you heard that, you were almost hit by a bullet from a high-powered rifle. Way too close. That crackling comes from the bullet traveling faster than the speed of sound."

Later that day, I called the county sheriff's office to report what happened. I also mentioned that I'd recently noticed coyote carcasses laid out on the snow berms in my subdivision, something I'd never seen before, which was disconcerting. One carcass was up in the snowmobile parking area, two others in the lower part of my subdivision on Wallace Lane.

A few days later, driving toward town in the early morning, I saw four dead coyotes laid out in a tight row, each close to the next, atop the same berm on Wallace Lane. Wallace Lane provided access to our subdivision but it was also a primary access to the Payette National Forest. The snowmobile parking lot, where I noticed the first dead coyote displayed, was where Wallace Lane ended and the national forest began.

This obscenity of dead coyotes on public display happening so fast on the heels of our horrifying close call with a high-powered rifle bullet was too much. My low-CSF-fueled temper flared again. I wanted justice for those coyotes, and myself.

I took photos of the four coyotes and emailed them to the county sheriff's deputy who'd taken my complaint after the close-call shooting. By the time I returned home two hours later, all four carcasses were gone. The only trace left behind was the blood-tinged snow.

That afternoon, I called the county sheriff's office. I wanted to try to understand what was happening. According to the deputy who took my complaint about the February 27th shooting, it was highly unusual for someone to display coyotes they'd shot. Usually, he said, they just left them in whatever field they were in. To transport them by car, risking getting blood in their vehicle, just to dump them elsewhere, was out of the ordinary. The deputy also shared that shooting coyotes moving across snow-covered fields from valley roads was a form of sport for certain locals. He and the other deputies were trying to stop it.

Someone was killing coyotes at a high rate and displaying them openly along my road. *My* road. Leading to my home. Defiling my sacred space, stealing my hard-earned sense of peace and security. Was it the same person who nearly killed me and Conall?

I was both pissed and unnerved, knowing that Conall could easily be mistaken for a wolf or coyote by someone bent on killing anything resembling either. I was still unsure if the shooting incident was someone mistaking Conall for a coyote (in an orange vest), or, more likely, someone shooting at a coyote in a field beyond us without seeing us walking on the road, right into their line of fire. Both scenarios kept me awake at night, full of anticipatory dread.

The afternoon of March 2, a different sheriff's deputy dropped by my house to check in with me about the close call on Campbell Road. He hadn't seen the gruesome photos of the four coyotes on the berm on Wallace Lane, so I queued them up on my computer and showed him. I also showed him the photos I took of the SUV. He wasn't sure if the State Patrol could enhance the photos to read the license plate, but said he'd send them along and ask them to try.

It was all so strange and creepy. I was thankful the sheriff's office was taking it seriously, but I wasn't sleeping much. My world suddenly felt very dangerous.

As winter waned and snow in the valley melted, I remained wary. On March 12, another coyote carcass, this one quite bloody, was displayed on the snow berm at the same spot on Wallace Lane. Whenever I drove to McCall or into New Meadows, I noticed every white Ford Explorer in the area. I was shocked how many there were. I'd almost given up finding the shooter's SUV until one day in July, when I decided to visit the New Meadows Cemetery to take photos. In addition to interesting old headstones, the cemetery has amazing views of the valley to the north and Granite Mountain.

On the way to the cemetery, I drove past a ranch house. I knew the owner because she'd often fostered kittens for the local animal shelter when I was its executive director. She and her adult daughter had sheep, goats, and a few horses on the pastures they owned. Each spring, I enjoyed watching their lambs and kids cavorting in a small pasture.

A few months earlier, for a local online magazine I'd created, I interviewed the daughter about the goat cheese she made and sold locally. I asked her, "Do you ever have issues with coyotes?" A smug look came over her face as she answered, "No, the coyotes don't bother us." I didn't pursue it, but left the interview bothered both by the answer and her expression. I wondered how that could be, given they didn't have any guardian-type dogs.

The family's vehicles were parked in front of their detached shed. One was a white Ford Explorer SUV.

Suddenly all the dead coyotes made sense to me, as much as something so senseless can. Late February/early March was lambing season, and goat kids are often born then as well.

I'd noticed a young woman with short, bleached-blonde hair living with the family that spring. She was about the same age as the daughter. My guess? In February, she was on a mission to protect the kids and lambs from coyotes by killing as many of the latter as she could. But that didn't explain why they were displayed so gruesomely on Wallace Lane. Was she trying to scare, or impress, someone who lived in my subdivision?

I'd also heard a rumor that a young woman who lived on the dead-end road that intersected Wallace Lane where the dead coyotes were laid out had lost her cat over the winter. It didn't come home one night. She assumed a coyote got it. Were the carcasses proof of revenge on coyotes for allegedly taking the cat?

The deputy with whom I'd filed the shooting incident report made a visit to my house that evening. He was up to speed on all the coyote carcasses as well as the inability to identify the vehicle using the photos I'd taken. He agreed that my theory made sense. What did I want him to do? We still had no direct evidence of who did the shooting or even who was driving the SUV that day.

"I just want them to stop," I told him, slumped in my office chair, exhausted by the whole ordeal. "I want them to stop shooting in the valley from their car. To stop killing coyotes. Stop being an irresponsible idiot, endangering people and pets," I said. "If you talk to them and get that assurance, I'll let it drop." The deputy said he would.

True to his word, the next morning on my way into McCall, I saw the deputy's green Explorer SUV at that family's house, parked behind their white Explorer. I would have loved to have been a fly on the wall for that conversation. The only follow-up I got was that the deputy had talked to them and felt certain the shooting and displays of dead coyotes wouldn't happen again. He didn't tell me if anyone admitted to being the shooter, but I didn't see that young blonde woman around their house again for a long time.

Nor did I see any more coyote carcasses displayed anywhere near my house, that year or the next. I'm sure, though, that many coyotes were still being shot out of hatred or for "sport"; locals bragged about it on various Facebook pages.

I knew wolves in the forest suffered the same fate as coyotes in the valley. The only difference? The wanton killings by those who hated and feared them were remote and out of sight.

To my utter dismay and horror, Conall was never the same after the incident on Campbell Road. He had been traumatized by that single, senseless gunshot. From then on, any time he heard gunfire, whether while at home (target shooters at the forest boundary a quarter-mile away) or while we were running or walking in the forest, he became scared and nervous. If we were home, he'd immediately come inside and huddle next to me, his body shaking for a good half-hour after it stopped.

Previously, he and I could sit outside on the deck and watch a storm with lightning and loud thunderclaps pass over, or the New Year's or Fourth of July fireworks displays across the valley. Same for gunshots coming from the forest; he'd listen, but didn't flee inside or shake with fear. After the close call in February, he was a different dog. Terrified of gunshots and fireworks and uncomfortable with thunder. And if he heard a high-powered rifle? It almost undid him. He knew the difference now, just as I did, between that vicious weapon and all the others.

Suddenly I realized: all of the animals in the forest, but especially the deer, elk, coyotes, and wolves—those animals targeted by hunters who often miss—must also feel terror, every time they hear a rifle shot.

Thereafter, Conall and I never let down our guard, either at home or in the forest. We were always on alert for the sound of gunfire. I did my best to shield and comfort him, but there was only so much I could do. Thankfully, Finn wasn't traumatized by the shooting incident or the sound of gunfire in general. But by 2019, he was twelve and losing his hearing; perhaps he just didn't hear most of it. Lucky Finn, because by then, we were starting to hear people target shooting with automatic-fire weapons just up the road.

NATURALISM

"Dad, what's going on? Why is that loon following our boat so closely?" I asked.

"It's trying to steal any fish I reel in," Dad replied.

Some of my fondest memories of my father are when we were in nature together. That day with the hungry loon, we were drifting in a small aluminum boat on a remote lake in the interior of British Columbia, talking while Dad fished. He was retired, I was in my forties. He loved fishing and I loved tagging along to enjoy nature and time with him. During these outings, we had fabulous discussions about life and the natural world while sitting around an evening campfire, listening to loons calling.

Earlier in the day, we'd watched two bald eagles harass another bird. The eagles screeched, swooped, and turned directly over our heads as they flew threateningly toward the equally large bird perched in a tall evergreen. Dad, a pilot, admired their aerobatic skill. Eventually, the other bird flew off and the eagles returned to their tree, calmly sitting on a high branch.

"Wow. What was all that about, Dad?"

"They were kicking their kid out of the house," Dad said, smiling. He explained that the third bird was a juvenile that didn't yet have white head or tail feathers. "Adult pairs often have to chase their young out of the nest to start life on their own," Dad continued. "They've grown too big and the parents are tired of feeding them." We couldn't believe our luck, to be quietly drifting on a pristine lake, directly below the drama, observing it like a documentary closeup.

A bit later, Dad started the trolling motor and continued fishing. That's when I noticed the loon following us. Each time it surfaced just behind the boat after a long dive, silvery water beaded and rolled off the feathers of its shiny black head and white-spotted back. When Dad reeled in a small fish, I watched the loon swim just under the surface, following the fish closely, trying to snatch it. Dad reeled fast, not wanting the loon to accidentally get hooked. After he unhooked the fish and tossed it back into the lake, I wondered if the loon was finally successful in getting a meal.

That trip, I felt the same closeness to nature and my father I remembered feeling as a child, when he and I watched wildlife documentaries on television. Dad always added details and answered my questions, which is no doubt what initiated our life-long bond over animals and the natural world.

My father taught me everything he knew about the natural world, unfettered by a Christian sense of control and conquest or Manifest Destiny (man = good, nature = scary and requires human taming). He taught me respect and love for all animals and plants. He taught how to move carefully through a landscape, to never litter. He taught me that cruelty, control, and waste were bad. He showed me how animals—dogs, cats, horses, gerbils, even a harbor seal named Butch—would reward my respect with trust and mutual connection. He showed me how to quietly observe, with wonder, awe, and—above all else—intellectual curiosity. He encouraged me to learn the environmental sciences—among them, physics, anatomy, physiology, biology, meteorology, chemistry—to help me understand the why and how of everything I observed.

After parking in a tiny gravel lot, no other vehicles in sight, I let the boys out of the car. It was September 2020. At this high-elevation trailhead, the air was crisp and cold, the sky azure. Both boys wore their orange Do Not Hunt Me vests and I had on a bright-pink, long-sleeved shirt under a purple cyclist's nylon vest. It was hunting season. I wanted to be visible.

First order of business after a long drive: Move away from the lot for a pee. Then I donned my running pack, pulled on my gloves and cap, locked the car doors, secured the key in a zippered pocket, and said, "Okay, boys, let's go!" Conall excitedly jumped into the lead, Finn right behind him, me struggling to keep up. Frost covered the ground and plants alongside the trail.

"Easy, boys. Stay close!" I called out, because within a few yards we would pass the edge of Hazard Lake Campground. It was around eight-thirty in the morning and I didn't want to disturb anyone. To my delight, the campground was empty. Hazard Lake is nestled among pines and firs at 7,050 feet, so by autumn, temperatures drop well below freezing at night, discouraging campers.

Once I realized we did indeed have this amazing wilderness playground to ourselves, I let the boys run ahead. They trotted down the trail, always keeping me in sight, never leaving too big a gap between us. Because the terrain here was mostly open, we rarely saw wildlife; any animals nearby would certainly hear us coming and disappear. The boys stayed on the trail when we ran, and usually the only wildlife they "chased" were chipmunks, who darted up nearby trees.[6]

We ran south along the narrow, dirt, single-track trail cut into the open meadows by both foot and dirt-bike traffic. Sometimes the deep and narrow dirt-bike ruts required those on foot to move to the grass alongside the trail, thus creating a second trail. Thankfully, the section of this trail open to dirt bikes was so remote and short it didn't get a lot of use.

Early in the run, we were greeted by a string of three open meadows. To their east stood tall, jagged peaks that cast long shadows across the terrain. The rising sun breached them within minutes of our start, spilling streams of bright sunlight across the landscape. I stopped to take several photos of the sunrise that was turning the ground ahead of us from a cold shade of blue to warm shades of green and gold. On the west side, there were gentle, grass-covered slopes; enormous gray boulders; a few fall wildflowers; and silvered tree trunks among the blackened, snags, evidence of the 1994 Corral Fire.

I loved running through these burned areas in the Payette, although it took getting used to after years of running in western Washington's lush evergreen forests. I learned to gauge how long it had been since the fire based on the size and variety of plants regenerating the soil: grasses, wildflowers, shrubs, and young trees. Some burned areas seemed more like meadows than forests because the new trees were still short, which gave a sense of openness. Many established trails through burned areas required regular maintenance to keep them clear. Easily toppled by strong winds and winter snow, dead trees often fell directly across a trail,

---

6   Once, running with Finn on this same trail, two hikers heading back to the campground warned me there was a squirrel in the trail ahead. "Is it alive?" I asked, puzzled, since the trail at that point wasn't near any trees. "No, it's dead. Just thought you'd want to know because of your dog," one man replied. "Oh, thanks, but if it isn't moving, it doesn't exist to him," I laughed. Indeed, when we reached the dead squirrel in the trail, Finn trotted right over it, never breaking stride.

requiring either a clamber or a detour until they were removed. During my time in Idaho, the Forest Service's budget began focusing more on fire suppression; money for trail maintenance (let alone trail-building) fell sharply. Volunteer groups of trail users—hikers, runners, horse riders, mountain and dirt bikers—often filled the void, clearing miles of trails each summer and helping build new ones.

Our trail gained a gentle four hundred feet over the first two-and-a-half miles, bringing us to Upper Hazard Lake at 7,450 feet. As was our routine on this route, I urged the boys to leave the trail and drink from the lake. The sun, which had just risen above Bruin Mountain, highlighted most of Upper Hazard's surface with a glistening brightness. At nearly 8,700 feet, Bruin is the highest of the peaks that form a cirque on the east and south sides of Upper Hazard Lake. A slight breeze rippled the lake's surface, sunlight sparkling on the tips of small waves like precious gems. Conall played on logs near the shore while Finn waded. In early summer, this end of the lake is full of white marsh marigolds and delicate pink shooting stars, sometimes blooming within yards of snow yet to melt.

Taking it all in, watching the boys, I felt blissful. Content.

"Come on boys, let's go!" I called after a few moments, and we rejoined the trail. Continuing south, we briefly ran near the shore of Upper Hazard Lake, where I noted the handful of vacant campsites. As the trail veered steeply up and away from the lake, we scrambled up a short, near-vertical section—I had to use my hands to keep from slipping back down on the dry soil and pebbles—past huge boulders and mature trees toward a large, open saddle that offered views of Upper Hazard Lake and the peaks surrounding it. The saddle, enormous slabs of granite, offered a gentle pathway, and I led the boys off-trail to run across it, gaining yet another good view of Upper Hazard Lake overlooking a section of unburned forest thick with healthy, mature trees.

Returning to the trail, we started dropping down through another burned area with large boulders here and there, young trees, and lush meadows. Soon we arrived at Hard Creek Lake at 7,424 feet. On this end, the ground near the lake was often saturated, small streams of summer snowmelt from those surrounding peaks meandering across the meadows and around the boulders to reach the lake's inlet side. This bounty of moisture and sunlight in early summer guaranteed an abundance of wildflowers in July and August.

Wildflowers were just one of many reasons the stretch of trail between Upper Hazard and Hard Creek Lakes was one of my favorites in the Payette. At that elevation, the vistas are wide and long, the mountain peaks high and near, the air clear, and the changing seasons obvious. In September, grasses in the meadows and along the edges of the lakes were starting to turn gold and most of the wildflowers had gone to seed. Pearlie everlastings were the exception, their abundant clusters of tiny white flowers that look like the tips of cotton swabs until they open to reveal their yellow centers waving atop two-to-three-foot stalks.

The trail hugged the southern shore of Hard Creek Lake through sections of grassy meadow littered with more burned tree trunks and huckleberry shrubs. In July (spring, at this elevation), this area is bog-like, ensuring wet dog feet and muddy running shoes. Nearing the west end of the lake, the trail climbed abruptly through mature trees growing on a steep, boulder-strewn bank, watched over by yet another high peak to the south.

Hard Creek Lake was a special place to me. Unless I brought them with me, I rarely saw another human here. Remote and truly wild, it was where I experienced nature without artificial noise or interruptions. Just me and my dogs.

Midway along the south side of Hard Creek Lake, more enormous, smooth boulders jutted from the shoreline several feet into the shallow lake. The water, so clear, betrayed the boulders' size and extent under the surface. The boulders marked our turnaround point for the day's run: a place to rest, and to let the boys drink and play in the wild water. Just like Maia and Meadow before them, Finn and Conall loved running over those boulders, jumping off into the shallow water, splashing around, then chasing one another over and around them. I enjoyed watching their game, taking photos and videos of them having so much fun. Finn went swimming, something he loved and didn't get enough opportunities to do. Conall, who never swam, waded and delighted in playfully preventing Finn from climbing out of the lake back onto the boulders.

I remembered being here one summer with Maia and Meadow, probably in 2007. It was the second time the girls and I had run to Hard Creek Lake, approaching from the west rather than the Hazard Lakes trailhead.

As we began the west end's short but steep drop through boulder-strewn, tree-filled hillside to the lake shore, Maia stopped suddenly. As usual, I was right behind her, with Meadow bringing up the rear. I saw that she was staring at the shoreline, mid-lake. Her tail was down and her body language told me she was concerned. About what, though? Hikers? Campers? Following her gaze, I searched the shore area, but mature trees obscured much of the view. Other than the large boulders that jutted out into the lake midway down the shoreline, I saw nothing unusual.

"It's okay, Maia. Just rocks. Let's go," I said, and urged both girls to keep moving.

The trail quickly dropped us to lake level. My focus was on the placement of my feet on the narrow trail and the wildflowers blooming alongside. About a quarter of the way along the shoreline, Maia again stopped abruptly, focused on something ahead. I nearly bumped into her. Meadow, as curious as I was about the source of Maia's concern, tried to see around both of us. Once again following Maia's gaze, I realized she was looking at the same boulder as previously. Then I saw the "boulder" start to move.

Moose! HUGE! With a full set of antlers!

My heart pounded in my chest. *It's as large as a Volkswagen Beetle,* I thought, awed and a little afraid. The girls and I stood completely still. *What do I do if he sees us and charges? The girls can run, but me? Hide behind a tree or boulder?* I thought of putting the girls on-leash but quickly realized that would only increase the chances of one or all of us getting hurt if the moose charged. My brain went into survival mode, planning our escape, just in case. I held my breath. The girls seemed to, as well. None of us moved.

To my immense relief, the bull moose waded deeper into the lake until everything but his eyes, nose, and antlers was submerged. Watching him slowly swim across the tiny lake, I marveled at the small waves that rolled away from his body in a V. When he emerged at the other side, I saw his mate, waiting patiently, munching grass.

"Maia, you're amazing," I said, stroking the fur behind her ears as I praised her for preventing us from getting any closer to the moose. I should have listened to her the first time she stopped. Such a close call was a reminder to always trust Maia implicitly. If she said turn around, we should.

And that's what we did that morning.

"Alright boys, let's go home," I said reluctantly, basking in the sun as I sat on one of the large boulders. We'd been out for nearly an hour and it was time to finish our seven-and-a-half-mile outing and head back to the car. We weren't on a schedule, but none of us enjoyed overheating and the sun was rising higher in the sky, quickly warming the air.

On the way back, we settled into an easy pace. As I kept my eyes on the boys, the trail, and the scenery alongside the trail, I let my mind roam. I don't remember what sparked the thought, but that day, religion came to mind.

I'm not religious. Never have been. Neither was my father. My mother was, sort of, but not enough to keep dragging her four children to church after I was about five, or to attend church on her own. In college, as a history major, I enjoyed studying how world religions shaped peoples and cultures, but my takeaway was that religion did far more harm than good. Religions were so varied across the globe and over time. How, I wondered, could anyone believe they, and only they, had the "correct" religion or belief system?

Maybe I was reading Barry Lopez's *Of Wolves and Men* at that time. In it, he delved into the impact of myth and religion in shaping European and American cultural views and opinions of wolves over the centuries.

I'm an atheist, I thought to myself as the boys and I approached Upper Hazard Lake again. For decades, I'd had trouble admitting that. I mean, at eighteen, I married a Catholic in a Lutheran church of my choice. Even then, I knew I was faking, that my lack of belief in any god made me an outlier, an oddball. I remembered a time in my twenties when, if someone asked what my religion was, I'd answer "None. I'm agnostic." That answer avoided the need to explain, and the social shame attached to being an atheist.

When I was in college in the late 1970s, the born-again Christian movement was strong. I was genuinely intrigued by the converts I met; interested in their journey, I wondered *why* they believed in what seemed to me a system based on fairy tales. My interest then was more as a curious social scientist than someone searching for religious answers of my own.

As I got older, when asked about my faith or religion, I joked that I didn't inherit the religion gene. Another light answer meant to avoid questions about or require justification for my lack of belief. Being areligious in America was a lonely place.

Never, though, was I pulled away from my sense that reality, nature, and the universe, were all there was. That was enough, and perfectly fine with me. I never needed a fear of hell and damnation to do the right thing on a daily basis. Morality and religion are not synonymous.

These thoughts swirled through my mind as I ran along the trail, watching Conall show off by climbing boulders or walking along a fat downed tree trunk. (I took nearly a hundred photos that day.)

So, what am I? I asked myself. How should I describe my worldview? That I just don't have any need for a "god" or religion, or any concept of an afterlife? That I'm perfectly content knowing this is it, my one and best shot at life, and then it's done? That I never lose sleep over my lack of faith in some higher power? Sometimes I heard people refer to their spirituality, but even that word felt wrong to me, with connotations of religion or a too-inward focus. My energy, my happiness, my contentedness came from my relationships with dogs, wildlife, and the natural world around me.

When the boys and I arrived back at the trailhead, they jumped into the back of the SUV and I poured water into their bowl. Peeling off my running pack, I got behind the wheel, pulled a restorative diet Dr. Pepper from my small cooler, and turned on the MP3 player. It was now a little before ten in the morning. The earlier frost was gone and the air, still crisp with the coming autumn, was quickly warming. Perfect timing. Perfect run. Perfect morning.

As I pulled out of the trailhead parking area and pointed the car toward home, the boys settled for a nap. Driving, half-listening to music, I kept thinking about religion and non-religion. There must be a term that describes someone like me who prefers the natural world to any spiritual one.

Back home, after showering, eating, and napping, I started doing some research. Eventually, I stumbled upon an excerpt of an interview with Sean Carroll, a theoretical physicist. I had never heard of him, but I liked how he explained the concept of naturalism, how it's different from atheism.

> Atheism is a reaction against theism. It is purely a rejection of an idea. It's not a positive substantive idea about how the world is. Naturalism is a counterpart to theism. Theism says there's the physical world and god. Naturalism says there's only the natural world. There are no spirits, no deities, or anything else. . . . I'm saying that despite appearances to

the contrary in our everyday life, this world we live in is governed by laws that don't have goals or purpose that are not sustained by anything outside the world. It is just stuff obeying the laws of physics over and over again. . . . Naturalism says that we were not put here for any purpose. But that doesn't mean there isn't such thing as purpose. It just means that purpose isn't imposed from outside. We human beings have the creative ability to give our lives purposes and meanings. Just as we have the ability to determine what is right or wrong, beautiful or ugly. That point of view is not only allowed, it is challenging and breathtaking in its scope.[7]

Reading that was an "aha!" moment; it crystallized why it never felt quite right to proclaim myself as agnostic, or later an atheist.

I am a naturalist. So, it seemed, was my father.

The word "naturalist," a noun meaning student of plants and animals, comes from the French *naturaliste*. A definition from the 1580s: One who studies natural, rather than spiritual, things. In the late fourteenth century, the Middle English word *naturien* meant natural philosopher or scientist.

Energized by both the run and the insight, over the next two months I took the boys out for more beautiful autumn trail runs in the Payette. Fall's dry, cool weather was perfect for us as long as I chose routes where the boys had wild water to drink and we were well away from hunters. We ran in the forest right above my house, at Brundage, Bear Basin, Goose Creek, and to Hazard/Hard Creek Lakes again. At Brundage and Goose Creek, we visited the girls' cairns.

"Hi girls. I love you. I miss you. Thank you. We'll be back soon!"

---

7   Sean Carroll, from a May 2016 interview with Wired about his book *The Big Picture: On the Origins of Life, Meaning and the Universe Itself.*

MASCULINITY

On a Friday morning near the end of October 2020, I took Conall for a trail run at Brundage. It was the final weekend of rifle-hunting season and I purposefully started later than I preferred—just one of many precautions I took during hunting season to reduce the chances we would encounter hunters or hear gunshots. Brundage was, I thought, a place of maximum safety, one place I felt relatively safe from hunters because of limited access and steep terrain. Plus, there were always resort employees about, getting ready for ski season and making lots of noise.

The base of Brundage is privately owned by the resort, but the ski slopes and trails are public, on leased Forest Service land. But, because the Payette is open to hunting, even at Brundage I was always cautious. At least three times in previous years, I had encountered hunters sitting right on hiking trails high on the mountain, surrounded by litter, rifles at the ready. (The following spring after the snow melted, I'd haul out that litter.)

When we arrived at the parking area, I saw the usual assortment of employee vehicles near the lodge but no trucks or campers (typical signs of hunters) at the back of the parking lot. Encouraged, Conall and I headed up the Forest Service access road to the summit, purposefully avoiding our usual hiking/biking trails in order to be more visible. This road is gated at the bottom and the top, so only resort vehicles have access.

As we started our run, Conall searched for employees to greet, but didn't see any. Staying a few yards ahead of me, he matched his pace to mine. A mile up, the road steadily climbing, Conall suddenly stopped. I could tell he saw something ahead, but the rise of the road prevented me from seeing what he did. When I caught up, I saw two people dressed head-to-toe in camo, kneeling on the downhill edge of the road, watching us. Then I saw the rifle of the one closest to us, resting on the ground next to him.

Realizing they were hunters, I told Conall, "It's okay" and we continued toward them. It wasn't okay, though. It's illegal to hunt from a road or shoot across one, upslope in this instance, where resort employees could be doing trail- or ski lift maintenance. I had a flashback to the high-powered rifle incident in February 2019. But I didn't want Conall to be nervous, so I repeated, "It's okay." Conall cautiously went to greet the hunters as I watched closely, a few feet behind him. To a friendly dog like Conall, anyone sitting on the ground was begging for a greeting.

Neither moved or said a word as Conall approached, and he pulled back when he saw they weren't receptive. He's not a pushy dog.

That's odd, I thought. *They didn't even stand up or say hello to me.* Most hunters at least said hello when they saw me and my dogs on a trail. These two were frozen, except when the man moved his rifle slightly closer to his leg, as though he were afraid. Neither put a hand out, either to pet or push Conall away.

I got a hinky feeling.

As I passed in front of them, walking, I said in a conversational tone of voice, "You shouldn't be hunting from the road." It was at this point, when I was close, that I realized the other hunter was a young female. They remained silent and motionless as they watched us pass. Because I spoke to the hunters, Conall wanted to go back for another hello—he's not used to being ignored by strangers—but I called him to me. The hunters were giving off a strange vibe and I didn't trust them.

The encounter was so off that after getting about fifty feet up the road, I decided to take their photo, just in case they did something stupid. The girl saw me take the photo and said something to the man, who gave me a fierce stare.

Conall and I continued up the access road. Within two or three minutes, a resort vehicle came up from below and passed by us. They would have passed the hunters as well, further illustrating how dangerous it was for them to be taking up a shooting position on the road.

Once at the summit, still troubled by the encounter, I decided to risk running a new single-track trail, Lakeview Vista. It traverses the back side of the mountain not far below the summit and was a longer route than I intended. But it'd allow more time for the hunters we'd encountered to leave. I didn't want to see them again.

We took our time. I got lots of photos, enjoying the fall colors and views of Payette Lake, Little Payette Lake, the town of McCall far below, and the tall peaks embracing the edges of Long Valley south of McCall.

When we eventually returned down the access road to the parking area, I was relieved to see that the hunters were gone.

At the base of Brundage, just before entering the parking lot, Conall greeted an employee working on the resort's day-care building. The staff, especially the trail crews, loved Conall because he was so gentle and happy to say hello. And fluffy. People always remarked on his fluffiness.

From there, we walked into the big gravel parking lot. My SUV was parked close to the day-care building. Not far from my vehicle I saw a large, black, late-model pickup. Conall went right up to the truck and its people, which was unusual, even for him. I didn't recognize the guy standing at the front of the truck talking on his cell phone. He ignored Conall. Then a tall, portly man wearing a trucker-style camouflage cap—beer gut, bad complexion, and scraggly gray goatee—came around from the far side of the truck.

The guy started yelling at me as he kneed Conall out of his way.

"Do you know it's a felony to interfere with a hunter? A felony! Do you even know what a felony is?" he yelled while approaching me with big, purposeful strides.

Conall immediately came to my side. He knew this was not normal behavior and it made him nervous. I now understood why Conall eagerly approached the truck, though: He'd recognized the man on the phone as one of the hunters we'd seen earlier on the road.

I don't often feel threatened, but when I do, a strange calm comes over me. My brain focuses, sifts options.

"Actually, I do know what a felony is," I responded calmly. "I'm an attorney."

"Oh sure, an attorney," the man (who I mentally nicknamed Big Guy) snorted, dripping sarcasm. He paced in front of me, neck veins bulging, spittle in his goatee. "You interfered with a father and his daughter hunting."

Worried for Conall's safety, I opened the passenger door of my SUV and he jumped in. Big Guy continued pacing near me, invading my space, ranting, trying to intimidate me. But why? What "felony" did he think I committed? He never said. Nothing about the scene made sense.

"Are you from California?" Big Guy continued his bombardment of vitriol, getting louder, face more red. "You don't look like you're from here. Out there jogging with your dog. Skank!"

Big Guy shoved his cell phone right in my face, taking video, upping the intimidation factor. I turned my back to him and shut the SUV's back side door, relieved that Conall was safely inside. *This is surreal,* I thought. I'd read of people doing this—creating a confrontation and videotaping it with their phones to post on social media or YouTube.

"I should call law enforcement," Big Guy said to my back. "Please do," I responded over my shoulder as I opened the driver's-side door. "Let's get Randy Martinez up here," I added. Randy was the Idaho Fish and Game enforcement officer for the area.

"Oh yeah, Randy Martinez, like you know. . ." Big Guy sputtered. I had called his bluff and I could tell it made him uncomfortable. A crack in his toxic masculinity armor.

It was now clear to me they weren't local but wouldn't admit it. But what was truly strange about the entire interaction was that the two I encountered on the road seemed to be taking a back-seat role. The man, still talking on his phone, stayed near the black truck, but his daughter picked up on Big Guy's intimidation tactics, videotaping with her pink cell phone, making sure they included my car in the scene.

It was way past time to disengage. But their efforts to get video of my car made me reconsider. I took a photo of their truck's license plate. That's when I knew for certain they weren't local. Idaho plates are issued by county of residence.

"Get her license plate," the girl said to Big Guy after I took my photo. He did. He hadn't thought to do it before I photographed theirs.

"You need to leave. *Now*," Big Guy ordered, coming toward me menacingly, invading my personal space again, pushing his big gut into my chest.

These people have weapons, I thought. *And they're none too smart.* Refusing to engage in any further conversation, I got in my car and shut the door. But I worried that if I drove away, they'd follow me. Instead, I drove closer to the resort's main lodge, parked again, rolled down the back windows so Conall had air, locked the doors, and headed up the stairs to the administration offices.

"Oh yeah, sure, go get help. . ." I heard Big Guy say in the distance.

After a quick explanation to the first staff person I saw, I sought and received intervention from the resort CEO, someone I'd met when I created a dog-friendly trail race at the resort to benefit the local animal shelter. With a couple of male employees by his side, the CEO approached Big Guy and the other two in the parking lot. I watched from the main lodge; I couldn't hear the conversation, but it appeared the CEO and staff managed to de-escalate things.

After ten minutes or so, the CEO returned to where I waited. "They've calmed down," he told me. "I would have made them leave," he added, "but they were waiting for someone so I let them stay. I'll make sure they don't follow you." The CEO offered no additional information about *why* the hunters were so upset.

I didn't sleep that night. Over the next several days, I was filled with anxiety. Would Big Guy and friends somehow find me through my vehicle license plate and seek revenge? I'd seen news clips of men like him "patrolling" Black Lives Matter demonstrations with their rifles and AR-15s, seeking to provoke fights. Would he or his buddies try to harm me or my dogs? Would we be safe at home? In the forest? After verifying that Idaho doesn't disclose names or addresses based on license plates, I felt some relief. But at night, I tossed and turned, my brain refusing to settle as the ugly scene replayed on endless loop.

What caused such an over-the-top reaction from those hunters? Me taking their photo? Is that what they meant by "interfering" with their hunt?

For the first time since moving to Idaho I was afraid to venture into the forest, something I had been doing daily for years. It wasn't the wildlife I was afraid of. It was this new breed of angry male with weapons. I realized that, had the encounter happened at a remote trailhead without others nearby to intervene, it could have gone very differently. I knew from experience and years of practicing law that most bullies like Big Guy are all bluster and no action, but I didn't like testing that theory in the highly charged political climate of late October 2020, just before the election. Times had changed, for the worse. For four years, the Trump administration emboldened those who used to be all talk and no action into taking real and dangerous action. Confederate and Thin Blue Line flags were now far more common in my part of Idaho.

It was several days before I felt able to take the boys for a trail run in the forest. The entire time we were out, though, I worried that I'd return to find my vehicle disabled, no cell phone coverage to seek help, Big Guy and friends lurking nearby. Hardly the relaxing experience I was seeking and was used to having.

Slowly, after a week or so, I began to relax. A little. I couldn't forget the incident, but the tension and anxiety lessened each day. Knowing that hunting season would be ending soon helped.

Two weeks after the incident, I made my weekly trash run to the local transfer station. The guy in charge, Fred, was thirty-something, friendly, and outgoing. I knew Fred because I'd interviewed him a couple of years earlier for my local online newspaper. A truly nice guy, Fred was a local born and raised, a little rough-looking but civic-minded, with a proverbial heart of gold. I tossed my bag of garbage into the container and was getting back in the car when I saw Fred exit his tractor and approach.

"What happened at Brundage?" he asked as he got close enough for me to hear, a look of concern mixed with compassion on his face.

It took a few seconds for me to realize that he was asking about the incident with the hunters. Fred explained he had seen a video one of them posted to a Facebook hunting page, but only because someone else in town had also seen it and mentioned it. Fred didn't know the person who posted, but he recognized me in the video.

Fred told me he commented on the post. "I wrote something like, wait a minute, I know that lady. She's nice. This doesn't sound right." Shaking his head in disgust, Fred said, "Locals know better than to hunt at Brundage where there are hikers and mountain bikers about." Then he did a little research on the poster and discovered he was a recent transplant from out of state.

But here's the kicker: Fred shared that the poster claimed Conall had attacked the two hunters on the service road.

I laughed out loud. I couldn't help it. The allegation was so absurd. "All Conall did that day was try to give them kisses," I told Fred. "He's the sweetest, friendliest dog on the planet."

Driving home, thinking about what Fred disclosed, everything about the incident started to make a weird sort of sense.

I wasn't surprised that one of them posted a video of the parking lot encounter. Big Guy, I imagine, since he was the one shoving his phone in my face. That's what angry bullies do now. Social media makes it easy to feel powerful and vindictive. Somehow, being publicly mean to others, trying to humiliate them, makes some people feel good about themselves.

But the claim that Conall attacked them?

That really pissed me off.

Big Guy might as well have put a huge bullseye on Conall, a dog already a target of wolf-haters in this forest because he resembles one.

Over time, I'd heard various versions of wolf "facts" from many locals, or read them in letters to the editor of McCall's weekly newspaper and the *Idaho Statesman*, the daily out of Boise. I attended an informational community meeting about wolves held at the McCall field office of Idaho Fish and Game. One attendee said, "I have a buddy who works for Fish and Game. He said they were surveying elk herds in an airplane and watched a pack of wolves surround an entire herd of elk and kill them all for fun."

Rather than call the man a liar, the fish and game representative responded, "We don't do aerial surveys." The allegation—killing animals valued by hunters, for fun or sport—was a common trope against wolves, and he knew better than to engage in an argument with the man. That meeting gave me a greater appreciation for the challenges any wildlife advocate had when talking to people who had their minds made up about wolves.

As wolves thrived in Idaho's forests and mountains, their numbers increased and locals clambered for their numbers to be tightly controlled (if they couldn't outright kill them all). So, starting in 2009, when the feds turned over "management" of wolves to the state, Idaho began allowing a set number of wolves to be legally killed per year. The goal was to sustain a minimum of thirty breeding pairs.

By 2011, having continued to thrive, wolves were delisted from protection in Idaho and Montana. After legal wrangles over Wyoming's stated wish to eliminate them all over again, they were delisted there in 2017, with guarantees of minimum numbers maintained. A newly sanctioned slaughter ("management" by each state's Fish and Game departments) started. In Idaho, hunters could purchase a wolf tag for five dollars and kill as many as they wanted over a long wolf-hunting season. Only if wolf numbers dropped below a certain small number would the hunts be restricted.

How would the state game managers know if or when that number was reached? I couldn't believe that killers so intent on eliminating their competition (which is how most hunters saw wolves, as competitors for the elk and deer they loved killing every autumn) would be honest in reporting exactly how many they eliminated. And I'd heard from friends in the Forest Service about the latest "sport" among some of the locals: drive the remote Forest Service roads, spot a wolf, shoot it, then drive away. "Shoot, shovel, and shut up," they called it. The same fate as the coyotes in Meadows Valley.

I finally understanding the root cause of what transpired that awful morning at Brundage: Those two hunters were *afraid*. The way they remained kneeling on the side of the access road, so still and quiet, even as Conall, wearing a bright orange Do Not Hunt Me vest, slowly approached them? I didn't recognize it in the moment, but they were petrified of Conall. Not because Conall did anything threatening or unusual; he exhibited the same friendly behavior as he did with all people, as he'd done with the staff working on the day-care building just before the ugly encounter with the hunters in the parking lot.

No, Conall's offense was that—to them—he looked like a wolf. My offense? Being a strong, confident woman, running free in the national forest with him during hunting season.

Fear and embarrassment emasculated the father in front of his teen daughter. Since he couldn't legally shoot Conall, I, a woman, had to pay for that. Their actions in the parking lot—the anger, the attempts to intimidate me—were, sadly, predictable given the social and political climate of the moment.

This western-states version of white male entitlement and toxic masculinity had been playing out for decades, an attempt to cover fear and cowardice. Hunting had become a sanctioned, even promoted, outlet for proving one's masculinity. Angry people got to shoot and kill innocent, sentient animals, boosting weak egos to help feel competent and in control of their world.

In *Of Wolves and Men*, Barry Lopez offered another perspective. He didn't believe men killed wolves thoughtlessly. Hunters had their reasons, he argued. They believed they were doing something good, that wolves were bad and deserved to die.

> It is a convention of popular sociology that modern man leads a frustratingly inadequate life in which hunting becomes both overcompensation for a sense of impotence and an attempt to reroot oneself in the natural world. As man has matured, the traditional reason for hunting—to obtain food—has disappeared, along with the sacred relationship with the hunted. The modern hunter pays lip service to ethics of the warrior hunter—respect for the animal, a taboo against waste, pride taken in highly developed skills like tracking—but his actions betray him. What has most emphatically not disappeared, oddly, is the almost spiritual sense of identification that comes over the hunter in the presence of a wolf.
>
> Here is an animal capable of killing a man, an animal of legendary endurance and spirit, an animal that embodies marvelous integration with its environment. This is exactly what the frustrated modern hunter would like: the noble qualities imagined; a sense of fitting into the world. The hunter wants to be the wolf.

Like Lopez, I can understand hunters wanting to embody the traits wolves possess. I also agree with Lopez when he notes it demeans hunters to kill wolves, simply because they fall short of those ideals.

After 2015, I noticed a small increase in hunters in the Payette. By 2018, I started seeing hounds used to harass and hunt bears. But after the pandemic started in early 2020? By late summer/autumn of 2020, hunting tourists were like fleas: annoying and everywhere. More hounds, too, their incessant baying disrupting the peace of the forest. At the height of the pandemic, the outdoors, especially federal land, was one of the few unrestricted spaces. In August and September 2020, huge wildfires scorched wide swaths of public forests in California, Oregon, and Washington, closing significant hunting areas in those states. Many of their hunters came to Idaho, which welcomed them with open arms.

That hunting season, the Facebook page for the Payette National Forest was filled with posts about small wildfires started by unattended "warming fires" made by hunters. The level of foolishness exhibited by forest visitors rose exponentially. Conflicts between locals and tourists were occurring and increasing, yet Forest Service personnel seemed unwilling to confront hot-heads. Really, I didn't blame them; as I had so recently learned, interacting with entitled people who *think* they know what they're doing, but don't, can get real ugly, real fast. Unfortunately, lack of enforcement simply emboldens such people, putting more wind in their sails (or, perhaps a more apropos phrase, more ammo in their weapons).

I could no longer avoid hunters based on my knowledge of where locals hunted. Suddenly, there were out-of-state vehicles and campers everywhere in the Payette. Idaho's Department of Fish and Game encouraged the influx because out-of-state hunters paid far more for tags, generating more income. During a pandemic, that fee income was significant when so much was shut down.

I saw lots of shiny-new pickups and people outfitted head-to-toe in brand-new camo clothing. All of it screamed "Inexperienced!" I couldn't rely on these tourist hunters to know that a trail my dogs and I loved to run on transected an area they were stalking for deer or elk from a Forest Service road above or below. Too many times, I drove to a trailhead only to drive away after seeing a pickup with out-of-state plates parked nearby. Not worth the risk.

Ultimately, frustrated, I adopted the Stoic approach: I couldn't control others. I could only control my reaction to them and their actions.

After the ugly encounter with the hunters at Brundage, I thought a lot about what *was* within my control.

The prevailing trend—more killing, more shooting, more vehicle noise, more people in the Payette—left me depressed, anxious for my dogs, and worried for wildlife. I felt worn down and didn't see those trends self-correcting in the short term, let alone reversing to when I'd arrived in 2005. Pushes by environmentalists and wildlife advocates to relist wolves met with federal resistance, and western states were passing "game" management regulations that sanctioned their slaughter.

What I was observing in Idaho, socially and politically, felt like déjà vu, so similar to the late 1980s through 1990s when the Aryan Nation thrived in northern Idaho. Beyond my vote (which, in such a red state, was always an exercise in pure optimism), I had no power to change the negative trends swirling around me. At the age of sixty-four, I didn't have a lot of time to wait for things to improve, even though I hoped that the current gun-crazy, White Nationalist, right-wing conservative Christian movements flocking to Idaho would eventually go the way of the Aryan Nation.

Bottom line: I didn't want to keep living with such heavy concerns. I longed to once again feel safe in the forest, a landscape that had healed my internal wounds and helped make my life joyful and worthwhile. I just couldn't imagine regaining that sense of safety in Idaho any time soon.

I began imagining living in a new rural setting where there weren't any wolves so no one would mistake Conall for one and shoot him. I imagined how relaxed I would feel when out on trails with Conall. I envisioned myself writing and publishing a book about my time in Idaho, about dogs and wolves, without fear of reprisals from wolf-hating neighbors or offended hunters.

But if I left, I would also be leaving the chance, no matter how small, to once again be privileged to see or hear a wolf in the wild.

WOLF-BIRDS

Throughout human history, the raven has been a powerful symbol and a popular subject of mythology and folklore.

In flight, the raven's feathers produce a sound that's been likened to the rustle of silk. Acrobatic fliers, they often execute rolls and somersaults. They're bigger than crows, and their voice is deeper, a distinct *prruk-prruk-prruk*. One of the most intelligent birds, they can solve puzzles and mimic the calls of other birds, and even human speech.

In some Western cultures, ravens have long been considered omens of death and evil, in part because of their all-black plumage and their habit of eating carrion. In Sweden, ravens are known as the ghosts of murdered people, and in Germany, as the souls of the damned.

But in many Indigenous cultures (e.g., Tlingit and Haida, Indigenous peoples of the Pacific Northwest), Raven is both a trickster (a character in a story exhibiting high intellect or secret knowledge and using it to ignore conventional rules of behavior) and a creator deity or god responsible for the creation of the earth and/or universe.

In December 2020, with winter finally arriving and a few inches of snow on the ground, I observed the two ravens who considered my subdivision their territory flying close to my house, then landing in the field several feet beyond the yard fence. They walked around on the snow-covered ground, occasionally pecking at something I couldn't see.

From inside, I watched, puzzled. Finally, I figured out what they were doing: The ravens had discovered our bone yard.

About once a week, as a treat, I gave the boys marrow bones, beef femurs cut by the store butcher into two- or three-inch sections. The boys loved them, as had Maia and Meadow. It took them about twenty to thirty minutes to lick out all the marrow, leaving the bone hollowed and clean. Too hard to gnaw, the bones were then abandoned. After they finished, I'd hurl the "clean" bones over the fence into the field. Food for insects, I figured.

Most of the year, I couldn't see the bones, hidden as they were in the tall field grass or disappearing under the snow. Only during mud season—that short time in spring after all the snow has melted but before the new field grass appears—and late fall after the grass died back did I see them. Over fifteen years, that amounted to a lot! Thus, my nickname for that section of the field: the bone yard.

Conall began alerting me to the ravens in the bone yard with a quiet woof from inside the house. Finn, on the other hand, was irritated by this new raven behavior. When he saw them through a window, he'd crash through the dog door, barking as he rushed the fence, which caused the ravens to fly away. I hated that. I wanted the ravens to consider me and my house a safe place, but Finn did not like ravens.

Maybe Conall's ancient wolf DNA was responsible for his more casual reaction to the ravens, telling him they were friends, not foes. Yet the more Finn reacted to ravens—or more precisely, overreacted—the more inclined Conall was to join him at the fence, albeit more quietly and with less urgency.

If Finn was inside with me and Conall was alone in the yard, the ravens went about their business without harassment or worry. And if Conall challenged their presence by woofing quietly, they ignored him.

In the yard, Conall was an excellent vole catcher. Since I didn't like the damage they did to bulbs and plant roots in my yard, I praised him lavishly when he caught one. (I told the voles to please go live their best lives in my five acres of open field, but they didn't always listen.) During his first year, Conall brought several into the house to show me, seeking praise and validation for his hunting skills. Often, they were still alive. If I tried to rescue the vole, he'd quickly crunch down, then swallow it. Natural instincts are not always pretty to observe.

It was fascinating to watch him find voles. A sound would catch his attention from a few feet away. Ears perked forward and moving like furry satellite dishes homing in on signals from underground that only he could hear, he'd cock his head and turn it slightly side to side to better pick up the sound while staring at a spot on the grass- or snow-covered ground. His tail would drop and his legs were still, but primed. Suddenly, he'd rise up on his hind legs and pounce and land with a loud thump, all his weight on his front legs, paws close together. Then he'd start digging, fast and furious, stopping briefly to sniff the dirt or snow, then digging some more. Finally, he'd plunge his head into the hole he'd created and pull back with a vole in his mouth.

Over time, Conall continued to find voles in the yard, but he finally quit eating them. Killing them instantly with a pinch of his teeth, he'd leave them in the yard for me to find when I was pitching dog poop over the fence into the field. I pitched the voles over the fence as well, hoping they ended up feeding some other animal—fox, coyote, turkey vulture, red-tailed hawk, insects.

I hadn't thought about ravens being part of that calculus.

For whatever reason—a population explosion in voles or prime conditions of snow on the ground or both—Conall found more than the usual number of voles that December.

One day, I tossed the two voles Conall had dispatched into the field. Because the snow's surface had frozen solid over several cold, clear days, the voles remained on top where I could see them.

A day later, he caught another vole. It was early afternoon and I was inside. Through the window I saw the dead vole between Conall's front paws as he rested atop the crusty snow in the yard. I called him inside to get ready for a walk in the valley. From that same window I watched one of the ravens fly low over the field and then right over the yard where the newly dead vole lay.

When we returned from our walk, the vole was gone. The two voles I'd tossed onto the snow in the field the day before were also gone.

Because we were out for just an hour or so during daylight hours, the only creature I could imagine accessing the yard to take the vole was a raven. Possibly a red-tailed hawk, but I hadn't seen any close to the house.

I was betting on the raven.

It was exciting to think I might be able to "teach" this raven pair that Conall and I could provide food for them in the depths of winter. I was also excited by the idea of a relationship with these ravens, of adding a layer of understanding in my naturalist quest to truly know the ecosystem in which I lived.

Few mammals have symbiotic relationships with other animals. One notable exception is the raven and the wolf. Indeed, ravens are sometimes called wolf-birds because of this observable bond. Their complex relationship, thousands of years old, benefits both.

After the reintroduction of wolves to Yellowstone National Park, biologists noted that ravens (and aspen groves, but that's another story) were the biggest winners; wolf kills provided them with many a meal. Ravens stay close to wolves to grab their leftovers, but also to tease them. They seem to play with the wolves by diving at them to get a reaction, even pecking their tails to get the wolves to chase them. Wolf pups often reward the ravens' efforts. The ravens' play style isn't all that different from that of wolf pups (and Malamute pups), who nip each other's tails and legs to start a game of chase.

Over time, ravens and wolves learned to trust and rely upon each other. I think the ravens, as intelligent as they are, learned wolf behavior—play style, in particular—and figured out how to engage with them in a way that nurtured and promoted their symbiotic relationship.

In the wild, wolves and ravens have similar life expectancies, which may facilitate bonding between specific families of ravens and packs of wolves over generations as parents demonstrate to their offspring how to interact with, and trust, the other species.

I suspect there's much more to the wolf-raven story than we know, or may ever know. For now, though, I like the idea that wolves and ravens help each other and enjoy each other's company. Two highly intelligent and social species, hanging out together, sometimes just for fun.

Every time a raven followed me and my Malamutes while we moved through the forest, I wondered, *Do you think I've got a wolf with me?* Or were the ravens simply being playful? I witnessed that "following" behavior many times over the years. The raven—usually just one—never acted aggressively. Rather, it followed, swooped low but not too close overhead, landing in a tree and watching us pass, then following and swooping again, several times, until finally—either bored by our lack of reaction or reaching the edge of its territory—it left. I interpreted this behavior as curious and playful.

All of my Malamutes reacted calmly to ravens, whether they were flying high above the house, lower over our trail, or following us closely. They simply watched the ravens with mild curiosity. Finn, however, developed a hate for them after a series of low flybys by a single raven at Brundage during a trail run; chasing and barking at the raven, he'd tripped and fallen. After that, I think he blamed ravens for embarrassing him.

I tried convincing him that they were no threat, to no avail. I also advised him that ravens are known to remember the faces of humans they like or dislike, so they probably also remembered individual dogs.

"Don't be so snotty toward them, Finn," I admonished. "They might exact raven revenge someday."

The raven pair taking the dogs' marrow bones from the field or a dead vole caught by Conall from the yard or field seemed to me an example of a three-way symbiotic relationship—human, dog, raven. Though I'm pretty sure I was the least necessary part of the equation, since it appeared the ravens were willing to risk coming into the yard for a vole if they knew the boys and I weren't home. But I hoped the raven pair watched me toss the voles and marrow bones over the fence and into the field and appreciated my efforts. I wanted to develop their trust.

I started paying closer attention to when and where I saw the ravens. Over time, I was convinced they watched to see when my vehicle headed down my driveway, knowing from experience that the dogs were almost always with me and the field and yard were safe for their exploration. I also liked imagining the pair flying up over the forest to watch us running trails, or over the valley when we went for a walk, verifying they had time to visit the yard without being disturbed by Finn.

By January 2021, the vole population explosion was obvious. I saw evidence of voles in and on the snow in the yard: tunnels through the snow and turds on the snow's surface. Voles don't like to expose themselves to predators from above; being on top of the snow, their dark fur a stark contrast against the white ground, was risky.

I also noticed that Conall's nemesis, the fox, was quite successful at finding voles in the field. He'd come through regularly for a snack, pouncing and digging just like Conall.

Whatever the reason for the abundance of voles and their risky behavior, Conall enjoyed finding them. He had never caught so many—at least one most days, sometimes two or three.

The ravens benefited from Conall's skill. Realizing there was a steady source of food in the yard, they became more bold. In addition to their regular fly-overs of the house and yard, checking for meals as though reading the chalkboard outside a sidewalk restaurant for the daily special, one enjoyed its vole meal while perched on my fence rail. It, or its mate, spent some time on the snow in the yard, just below the railing, leaving tracks.

By late February 2021, after several days of new snow and nearly three feet of accumulation in the yard, the clouds parted and the sun reappeared. February was my favorite winter month in the Payette, a time when the sky couldn't seem more deeply blue. Overnight temperatures often dropped close to zero, making the snow-covered ground sparkle in moonlight and morning sunlight like an earth-bound galaxy of tiny stars.

One clear morning, I noticed a set of raven tracks on top of the snow in the field just below the yard fence where I had tossed the boys' marrow bones the previous afternoon. The bones were too long for them to clean out all the marrow, so some had been left in the middle.

Even from the yard, I knew the tracks had been made by ravens; they were isolated in the middle of the field. Four-legged animals leave long, meandering tracks across the entire field, showing where they arrived, hung out, and departed.

An hour later, I heard the boys crash through the dog door into the yard. Finn was barking furiously, the distinctive bark he reserved for the ravens. Running to a window, I saw both ravens on the snow in the field, just before they flew off.

One landed on the peak of the neighbor's garage and its mate landed on the higher peak of the house, where they often hung out, high perches that allowed them to keep their keen eyes on this part of their territory. That neighbor always went south for the winter, and the local foxes, coyotes, and ravens turned his house and property into their winter safe spaces. Nice wildlife viewing for me and the boys.[8]

Late that afternoon, as I attended to my daily dog-bomb-clearance chore in the yard and the winter sun was descending toward the horizon,

---

8 Later that spring, after the sun melted the snow off my neighbor's roof, I noticed several strange white dots on the dark asphalt shingles. Marrow bones.

the raven pair put on their show: a series of large, soaring circles over the neighborhood and my house before heading to the trees at the edge of the forest to roost for the night. Finn was not happy, but I surely was. *Oh, to fly like that, with your life-long mate,* the romantic in me mused wistfully.

I was grateful to have ravens visiting regularly, entertaining me and irritating Finn (which also entertained while simultaneously annoying me). In the depths of winter, there was less wildlife to observe, especially the winter of 2020/2021, when the snow was so deep. I hadn't seen any white-tailed deer crossing my lot in weeks.

I did, however, see a fox for the first time in a while. Actually, Conall saw it first and alerted me with his concerned woofing. I thought the coyote, who had been a regular visitor most of that winter, had chased the fox off. But the coyote had been absent (maybe the victim of a shooting), so apparently the fox felt safe returning. The snow finally consolidated enough that, light as she was, the fox could trot easily across its surface without punching through. Heavier animals, like deer (and me and my dogs) punched through regularly, which made travel arduous.

Even as the sun was setting that evening and the ravens were secure in their forest roost, Finn kept watching the sky, making sure we were safe. That was his job, herding away the ravens, protecting me and Conall.

Baby steps. By March 2021, I learned that's what it took to get the ravens to trust me. That was fine with me; I was having fun learning about them, endeavoring to build a relationship. I had grown inordinately fond of the raven pair, finding them mysterious, intelligent, and entertaining. A new and welcome part of my natural-world family. Focusing on them helped me ruminate less on the political nightmare into which our country had descended after the 2020 presidential election.

Even when neither Conall nor I had any food to offer the ravens, they regularly flew low over my house, morning and evening, calling, checking, observing. A constant, reassuring presence.

When I sat at the computer in front of a north-facing window looking out across the field to the forest where the ravens roosted, I watched for their flybys. Providing the voles those past months changed their routine. They started flying from the forest straight at my window, low over my house, just after sunrise every morning. I was certain they saw me, watching them through the window. I even started waving to them.

March 22, 2021, was one of those late-winter days best spent indoors. It was 33 degrees F and snowing—big, wet, fast-falling flakes at daybreak. The winter's snowpack was slowly melting but much remained on the ground in my yard, field, and the forest.

Working at my computer, I heard Finn bark loudly outside, his raven bark. But he wasn't barking from the usual north side of the yard. Getting up to investigate, I found both Finn and Conall facing the driveway to the south, looking intently through the fence wire.

Thinking maybe a package had been delivered, I stepped outside and checked the garage door where UPS drivers left my packages, but didn't see anything.

Both dogs kept looking intently in the direction of the driveway.

My next thought was maybe a neighborhood dog had wandered by or some deer were huddled under trees on the adjacent lot, but I didn't see any movement. Then, out of the corner of my eye, I saw a raven flying toward the downhill neighbor's house with something white in its mouth.

The raven landed on the peak of the neighbor's roof, its favored perch. It was too far away for me to see what exactly it held in its beak.

I looked at my driveway again and noticed bits of white stuff that hadn't been there the day before.

The previous afternoon, warmer temperatures having melted the snow off my small deck, I swept up the dog fur that had stuck to the snow when the boys snoozed there. The melted snow revealed months of shed fur, mostly Conall's fine, soft, white undercoat. I collected most of it in a bag, but some had blown away on the breeze, across the snow-covered yard, through the fence, and onto the driveway, finally getting stuck on the gravel exposed by plowing.

The raven apparently thought the soft fur would make a wonderful lining for its nest.

STEPS

The best advice any novice ultrarunner can receive: "One foot in front of the other." Break a seemingly impossible task (one hundred miles of trail!) into manageable, doable sections. When your body is tired and everything aches, when your mind is telling you to quit, when your finish-time prediction becomes unattainable and you're so nauseous your stomach won't accept food, just keep putting one foot in front of the other. Relentless forward motion, no matter how slow, gets you closer to your goal. Eventually, you start to feel better. Eventually, you arrive. Eventually, you succeed.

Few trails are straight. There are ups and downs, twists and turns, rocks and roots. Trail running is never easy; it requires focus and dedication. It teaches awareness; risk assessment; and, most of all, humility. The reward? Pride and confidence after a successful big effort.

I've learned that any big change in life is the same. Challenging, often nauseating, even emotionally painful. But it always leads to growth if you simply keep moving, however slowly, one foot in front of the other, toward your goal.

Life in Idaho became increasingly challenging. Adding to the concerns I couldn't keep ignoring—more tourists, hunters, and gunfire in the state's abundant national forests—were the more-frequent wildfires and their pervasive smoke.

The Payette's trees were suffering, assaulted by (among other pests) Douglas fir tussock moths, mountain pine beetles, bark beetles, and spruce budworms. Climate change was making all of these afflictions worse.

Historically, lightning and human-caused fires in the Payette were common. Many were small and put out quickly. Others raged for weeks and consumed thousands of acres, spewing huge columns of smoke for the wind to spread wide and far. But by the second decade of the twenty-first century, Idaho wildfires, and the smoke they produced, were no longer primarily a "dirty August" phenomenon. Instead, they burned from May through October or November, when snow finally extinguished them. And not just in Idaho. All the western states were experiencing longer, more severe wildfire seasons and all the smoke that goes with them. (Inhaled wildfire smoke is more damaging to lung tissue than smoke from cigarettes.)

So, I asked myself, is the devil I know better than the devil I don't? I could sell my home and move, a *huge* sacrifice, leaving behind my beloved forest and trails only to find myself in similarly offensive surroundings in terms of hunting and the treatment of wildlife.

I would miss the cozy, environmentally friendly house I worked so hard to design and build. I got depressed just thinking about it. Not to mention Dad's recession-era advice, which also echoed in my mind: "Don't sell it. You've worked too hard for it and love it too much."

Ultimately, I convinced myself that my father, who always wanted me and my dogs to be and feel safe, would urge me to leave Idaho. It had changed too much.

One sudden realization almost kept me in place, however: I'd also be leaving all the cairns I'd built in the Payette to honor the girls' memory. Then I recalled the heap of stones on the workbench in my garage. In the years after the girls died, when I saw an interesting rock alongside a forest service road or trail, I'd bring it home, intending to build a cairn in my yard—which I'd somehow never gotten around to doing. Now, I realized those stones would easily fit in a box.

I had all winter to think about it and do some research. That was within my control. Just considering the option empowered me and helped me sleep better.

My criteria included trees and nearby forest for my emotional well-being; access to dog-friendly, off-leash trails for exercise; a rural setting with open spaces and few close neighbors; and peaceful quiet to calm me when CSF leaks made me irritable and moody. And because my dogs and I really love snow, I also wanted a robust winter season.

The list of locations I found both attractive and affordable was short, and ultimately focused on Vermont, which is known for its progressive politics. Friends described it as a mix of hippies, loggers, and farmers. For a tiny state, Vermont boasts lots of mountains, forests, trails, state parks, and open spaces. On the downside, it has only one federal forest—Green Mountain National Forest—and no national parks. Hunting and trapping laws are similar to Idaho's.

But... almost every rural area in every state has holdovers of outdated, unscientific fish and wildlife practices and management. So far, wolves hadn't reestablished territory in Vermont, so presumably Conall wouldn't be instantly feared or vilified. He was less likely to be shot there, I figured, unless mistaken for a coyote. Most importantly, based on proposed legislation and polling, I sensed Vermonters' increasing support for ending trapping and hound-hunting, giving me hope that those practices would soon be illegal. In Idaho, I couldn't see that happening in my lifetime.

When 2021 dawned with the January 6 insurrection, my mind was made up. Watching the news coverage, I kept seeing Big Guy—pot belly and gray goatee, camo jacket and hat—in the hordes invading the Capitol Rotunda.

I knew I had to leave Idaho. As much as I'd miss the forest, the ravens, I had to go. Reaching out to the agent who helped me find my Idaho lot, we agreed that we'd list my house for sale in the spring. In the meantime, I started surfing online Vermont real estate listings.

Within a couple of months of the unexpectedly quick sale of my home, I found a place I thought would work. After seeing it only in photos and a video walkthrough with my Vermont real estate agent, I signed the purchase agreement. I started planning how to ship my household goods across the country.

In July 2021, after a six-day cross-country drive, Conall, Finn, and I arrived at our new home. When my belongings arrived two weeks later, I stored the box of Idaho stones in a shed, then forgot about them.

Vermont and I got off to a rough start.

In August 2021, thirteen-year-old Finn developed Old Dog Syndrome, a canine version of vertigo. For a few days, he couldn't walk; his sense of balance gone, he fell repeatedly. Meadow had suffered an episode like this when she was ten, so I knew it wasn't fatal and likely short-lived, with only palliative care needed. But I had to stay nearby to help him. After a couple of weeks, Finn was able to resume walks, but only slow, short ones; he would never run again. I had known that would happen eventually, given his age, but this abrupt end to his running life saddened me.

Consequently, Conall and I made five-to-six-mile runs close to home so I wouldn't be away from Finn too long. That first summer and fall, as we explored a few trails, I quickly discovered how Vermont's differed from those I was used to in western Washington and Idaho's mountains. Instead of dirt with occasional rocks and roots, these mountain and forest trails were rocks and roots with occasional stretches of dirt.

Tripping while trail running always led to a worsened or new CSF leak, followed by weeks of intense headaches, increased tinnitus, shitty mood, and zero motivation, so I moved cautiously. I walked most sections and swore when I slipped on the rain-slicked rocks and ledges, twisting my spine and nearly falling anyway. It wasn't fun. To improve the odds and maintain at least minimal running endurance, Conall and I took to running on roads, rail trails, and through kind neighbors' three hundred acres of fields and woods. I sorely missed Idaho's trails.

Though I welcomed winter's snow for its better footing, staying warm was another matter. That first winter, unable to find someone to install a heat pump, my sole source of heat was a wood-burning stove that required around-the-clock attention. Several times a day, I carried heavy cord wood up a flight of stairs and bent low to stuff it in the stove. Compounding the stress of trying to reestablish my living space, this chore meant that my spine never had a chance to heal. The headaches were bad, the tinnitus was loud, and my mood got even darker.

As winter deepened and the boys and I snowshoed on the neighbors' acres, I began having pain in my left hip area and down the front of my leg; at night, firing nerves made sleep nearly impossible. By April 2022, I couldn't move without intense pain. Even walking was almost too much to bear at times. I tried to take Conall for a two- to three-mile run every other morning, but pain reduced my gait to a shuffle. Miserable, not sleeping, isolated, I despaired that I'd made a huge, irreversible mistake.

Spring transitioned into summer. In May, a heat pump and solar panels were installed. By July 2022, the grass in the neighbors' fields had grown tall and green. Purple clover, yellow and orange hawkweed, and white bedstraw added splashes of color. I enjoyed finding and learning the names of Northeastern wildflowers. Walking there one morning with the boys, I remembered the stones. I could build a new cairn in my yard! Selecting a large, flat boulder that rises slightly above the grass, I stacked the stones in a pleasing shape. Placing some of the girls' cremains under the arch, I finished it off with a large, orange day-lily bloom, a legacy from my father.

In the 1990s, Dad dug up some day lilies at the family homestead in Kansas and planted them in his yard in Washington. When I moved to Idaho, he gave me a few to plant at my new home. They flourished, their bright-orange blooms fond reminders of him. When I moved to Vermont, I brought some with me and planted them next to the house that first autumn. The following spring, they emerged from the ground and bloomed in July, my one-year Vermont anniversary.

Completing the cairn, I whispered, "I love you. I miss you. Thank you." My shoulders relaxed, and I smiled at Finn and Conall. My father and my girls were now tangibly with me in my new home.

On July 8, 2023, I welcomed another Alaskan Malamute puppy into my life. I named him Chann, Irish for "young wolf."

Later that month, I finally received a corticosteroid injection for my sacroiliac joint and leg pain. I was running pain-free again.

In late October, Conall and I began introducing Chann to trail running. He loves it. His enthusiasm is infectious.

Small steps, one after another, toward reclaiming my life, my sense of gratitude and joy.

It's been twenty years since my first CSF leak and the discovery of my tethered spinal cord. My early reactions to the physical and emotional symptoms of leaking were a mix of fear, anger, denial, and grief. Today, I'm grateful for the entire, ongoing journey. Without the leaks, I may not have made the adjustments to my lifestyle that allowed me to move to Idaho, slow down, spend more time with my dogs, embrace my sensitive and introverted nature, explore the wilderness, and let the natural world work its healing magic on me. I've learned I'm more resilient than I thought. Now, I understand what Roman Emperor and Stoic Marcus Aurelius meant when, two thousand years ago, he wrote in his diary, "The impediment to action advances action. What stands in the way becomes the way."

The summer I lost both Maia and Meadow, I said to friends, "Dogs teach us how to grow old gracefully, how to accept whatever health challenges come our way with dignity." I was impressed with how the girls handled their pain, loss of mobility, and reduced energy. I vowed I would always try to follow their example.

Finn, at sixteen, is reminding me those lessons.

I try to have the same equanimity when facing my own health challenges, but I often fall short. Dogs are savvier than us, wiser in so many ways.

The Irish poet and philosopher John O'Donohue wrote about the concept of *anam cara*, a Gaelic term meaning "soul friend." He explained that the term originally referred to someone who acted as a teacher, companion, or spiritual guide, someone you could trust with your innermost confessions. "When you had an *anam cara*, your friendship cut across all convention, morality, and category. You were joined in an ancient and eternal way with the 'friend of your soul.'"

While O'Donohue wrote about *anam cara* as a relationship between two people, I think it applies just as beautifully to other relationships, such as mine with my dogs, wolves, and the natural world.

"When your affection is kindled," O'Donohue wrote, "the world of your intellect takes on a new tenderness and compassion... You look and see and understand differently. Initially, this can be disruptive and awkward, but it gradually refines your sensibility and transforms your way of being in the world. ...The *anam cara* perspective is sublime because it permits us to enter this unity of ancient belonging. ...A friend is a loved one who awakens your life in order to free the wild possibilities within you."

While walking in the neighbors' fields with all three boys this past summer, a raven flew overhead, the first I'd seen since leaving Idaho. "Prruk-prruk-prruk," it called to us.

Someday, along with the raven's call, I hope to once again hear a wolf's piercing howl drift across these forested hills on a chilly, moonlit night.

AFTERWORD:
GRAY WOLVES IN THE UNITED STATES:
A PRIMER

I offer this information with no small degree of trepidation, because what we know about ancient wolves and early humans is quickly evolving (pun intended). We've gone from examining bones and carbon dating to extracting and analyzing DNA from bones, hair, teeth, fur, and soil, placing discovered remains along a chronological continuum in specific locations, with information on age, sex, and diet. With each discovery, estimated dates for various events are pushed back and tomorrow is likely to bring more new evidence, new ways to analyze and interpret it, and new evolutionary milestones and timelines.

The following synopsis is what scientists say we currently know and what they speculate likely occurred, based on the best available information.

No definitive evidence has been found to establish when gray wolves first came to occupy the portion of the northern hemisphere known as North America, or when the dogs we know and love today (*Canis lupus familiaris*) first became a branch on the genetic tree that also contains gray wolves (*Canis lupus*).

What is known is that glacial and interglacial periods throughout the Pleistocene epoch (roughly 2.58 million to 11,700 years ago) accelerated substantial changes in species distributions. At times, most of northern North America was covered in glaciers, turning much of the world's water into ice. As a result, global sea levels dropped as much as 300-500 feet, revealing the floor of what otherwise was the Bering Sea, exposing a land connection between eastern Siberia and modern-day Alaska. This land bridge was part of the area we now call Beringia.

At various times, that land bridge was up to 620 miles wide covering an area as large as British Columbia and Alberta, facilitating the dispersal of both animals and early humans between Asia and North America.

To date, the earliest evidence of the gray wolf in North America is a fossil tooth discovered at Old Crow, Yukon, Canada. The specimen was embedded in sediment dated to one million years ago, although this geological attribution is a subject of dispute. Other specimens were discovered at Cripple Creek Sump, Fairbanks, Alaska, in strata dating to 810,000 years ago. Both specimens suggest an origin in east Beringia during the Middle Pleistocene epoch (781,000 to 126,000 years ago).

It is believed that as ice sheets retreated, gray wolves started crossing from Siberia at least 700,000 years ago, and populating mid-North America (including the area known today as Yellowstone National Park) some 15,000 years ago.

Some research has suggested that modern grey wolves can trace their origin to a single Late Pleistocene Beringian population that expanded both east toward North America and west into Europe starting about 25,000 years ago.

However, a study published in 2022 compared the demographic and phylogeographic histories of surviving populations around the Bering Strait with wolves from two inland regions of the Russian Far East and one coastal and two inland regions of northwestern North America. The study found that Russian Far East and northwestern North American wolves had a common ancestry until about 34,400 years ago, suggesting that these populations started to diverge before the previously proposed dispersal out of Beringia. Coastal and inland northwestern North American wolf populations diverged approximately 16,000 years ago, in keeping with the earliest proposed date for the ecological viability of a migration route along the Pacific Northwest coast.

When compared to modern-day wolves, mitochondrial DNA collected in the western US and Mexico in 1916 and earlier showed more than twice the genetic diversity. This suggests that a large population, perhaps several hundred thousand, existed before Europeans colonized that portion of the continent.

The first *Homo sapiens* are thought to have come from Eurasia, crossing the Bering land bridge and arriving in North America between 25,000 and 16,000 years ago. Domesticated dogs have been in North America for at least 9,000 years, and may have arrived alongside people as long as 15,000 years ago. According to Angela Perri, an archaeologist at Texas A&M University, "The first people to enter the Americas likely did so with their dogs. Where people went, dogs went," she and colleagues wrote in 2021 in the journal *Proceedings of the National Academy of Sciences*. The oldest dog bones discovered so far, dating to 10,000 years ago, were unearthed in what is today Illinois.

North American Indigenous cultures generally accepted wolves as integral to the landscape, often incorporating them into their origin stories, even engaging with them. Early European colonists noted that the dogs associated with Indigenous groups along the eastern portion of the Americas were wolflike in appearance and howled rather than barked.

One study found that in North America, early dogs (i.e., pre-European colonization) were not derived from North American wolves. Instead, these dogs comprised a single ancestral lineage that likely originated from now-extinct wolves in Siberia and dispersed into the Americas alongside people. "After the arrival of Europeans, native American dogs almost completely disappeared, leaving a minimal genetic legacy in modern dog populations."

For centuries, many Indigenous groups, including coastal tribes such as the Coast Salish in the Pacific Northwest, carefully bred and maintained distinct, long-haired, wooly coated dogs, using their fur to weave blankets and clothing. Genetic analysis of DNA extracted from the pelt of a wooly dog that died in 1859, preserved at the Smithsonian, shows that at that time, that dog had less than 20 percent genetic contribution from post-colonial dogs.

Colonists not only brought their own dogs from Europe, they also brought their strong bias and cultural animosity toward predators, especially wolves. As they moved westward, colonists removed what they perceived to be threats standing in their way, including bison, wolves, and Indigenous peoples. They also overhunted deer, elk, and other species; by the 1800s, elk were extinct across most of the US, small numbers surviving only in the remote Rocky Mountains and other western mountain ranges.

In 1915, at the request of ranchers and hunters, the Federal Bureau of Biological Survey (precursor to the US Fish and Wildlife Service, or USFWS) began shooting, trapping, and poisoning the West's remaining wolves. Between July 1, 1915, and June 20, 1942, when the program terminated, *24,132 wolves were killed*, most in Colorado, Wyoming, Montana, and the western Dakotas.

The National Park Service (formed in 1916), did its part to remove wolves from the federal lands it managed. Rangers and government-paid "wolfers" killed at least 136 wolves in Yellowstone National Park (YNP) between 1914 and 1926. In 1934, with wolves no longer keeping their numbers in balance, the elk population in YNP became the subject of an NPS active-management program.

The attitudes and deliberate actions of settlers and the US government ultimately led to the extirpation of wolves from all Lower 48 states, with the sole exception of northern Minnesota. (A handful of lone wolves killed in the 1940s to the 1970s in Montana, Idaho, and the Greater Yellowstone Ecosystem were likely Canadian, dispersing south.)

Coyotes, which initially thrived only in the southern US, quickly filled the void left by extirpated wolves and eventually inhabited the entire continental US. The same hatred, and methods used to kill wolves in the US, were transferred to coyotes, aka "brush wolves."

By the 1960s, scientists had begun studying remaining populations of wolves in Alaska, Canada, Minnesota, and on Isle Royale, Michigan (an isolated ecosystem near the Canadian border). In the 1970s and 1980s, that research, combined with popular literature, provided greater understanding and increased acceptance of wolves among the general public.

Reintroduction of Gray Wolves in the United States: A Timeline

1973: Congress passed the Endangered Species Act (ESA). Under the ESA, the USFWS became lead agency in recovering endangered species, including the wolves they once helped extirpate.

1974: Wolves once populating the northern Rockies were listed as endangered.

1975–1977: A survey of Yellowstone National Park by John Weaver confirmed that wolves no longer lived in the park.

Mid-1980s: A pair of dispersing Canadian wolves were found denning in Glacier National Park. Another pack was found preying on livestock east of Glacier. Because the species was protected by the ESA, ranchers demanded help from the federal government. Unprepared to respond, by the end of 1987, the USFWS had either killed or placed the entire pack in captivity. The presence of these packs suggested that dispersing wolves could eventually repopulate areas in the Lower 48, albeit slowly.

1987: After a 1983 amendment to the ESA gave the USFWS more

flexible management options, it signed a recovery plan that selected Yellowstone National Park as the most viable reintroduction location. For the next few years, wolf reintroduction to YNP became a political football.

1991: Congress passed a bill requiring an Environmental Impact Statement (EIS) on wolf recovery in Yellowstone and central Idaho, where wolves were already naturally dispersing. To comply, the USFWS, NPS, and US Forest Service (USFS) were directed to prepare a draft EIS.

1994: After two years of public meetings, information distribution, and analysis of some 180,000 public comments from every US state and 40 countries, the EIS recommended that wolves be reintroduced as "nonessential experimental populations" to both YNP and central Idaho. That designation allowed removal of "problem" wolves by the government or authorized citizens in specific situations.

In November, biologists captured and collared wolves in Alberta in order to transport them to YNP. At the same time, a Republican-majority Congress was voted in, to be seated in February 1995, risking future funding to the project. Federal lawsuits pending in 1994 slowed reintroduction efforts.

1995: Fourteen wolves were transported to YNP and fifteen to central Idaho. Despite cuts during the year to federal funding, the project proceeded with supplemental private funds from the Wolf Education and Research Center, Defenders of Wildlife, and the Yellowstone Association.

1996: More wolves were captured in British Columbia; seventeen were flown to YNP and twenty to Idaho.

1997: The Yellowstone ecosystem was occupied by eighty-six wolves self-organized into nine packs; YNP biologists deemed that no additional captured wolves were needed. The wolves were immensely popular with park visitors. Populations in both YNP and Idaho quickly increased, exceeding recovery goals by 2002.

The federal government was not the only entity involved in this effort. In the 1990s, the Nez Perce Tribe's approach to gray wolf reintroduction in Idaho was based on their cultural beliefs. In contrast to most Idahoans and Idaho Fish and Game, the Nez Perce were eager to help restore gray wolves to their lands and Idaho in general. "The gray wolf, or *hîmiin* in the Nez Perce language, occupies an important place within Nez Perce culture. Wolves have particular religious and spiritual significance to many Nez Perce. . . . Nez Perce leaders have pointed to similarities between Nez Perce culture and the social structure of wolves in terms of support for one another, the importance of family bonds, and use of the landscape. Others have noted similarities in the ways in which the Nez Perce and wolves were treated during Euro-American expansion into the Tribe's homeland. . . . Ultimately, our efforts to restore the gray wolf to the Nez Perce homeland and his rightful place in Nez Perce culture have been a resounding success. Today, many hundreds of wolves live within the Tribe's homeland in Idaho, Washington, and Oregon."

Wolves Today

Wolf Restoration and Management in the Contiguous United States, a position paper published by The Wildlife Society on March 24, 2020, provides a succinct picture of wolf recovery in the US over the past few decades, including estimated populations.

> Wolves were listed throughout the contiguous U.S. by the 1973 Endangered Species Act (ESA). Wolves were restored by a combination of natural recovery and translocations in the Northern Rocky Mountains. In 2011, there were >1,700 wolves in a 3-part meta-population in Montana, Idaho, Wyoming; eastern one-third of Oregon and Washington; and a small part of northern Utah.
>
> Wolves recovered naturally in the Western Great Lakes. In 2011, there were >4,500 wolves in a 3-part meta-population in Minnesota (the only area in the contiguous U.S. where wolves were not extirpated): Wisconsin, Michigan, and parts of surrounding states. Both distinct population segments (DPS) of wolves in the Northern Rocky Mountains and Western Great Lakes are well-connected southern extensions of the wolf population in Canada.
>
> Wolves in the Northern Rocky Mountains, except in Wyoming, were delisted by Congress in 2011 when it reinstated the 2009 U.S. Fish and Wildlife Service (FWS) delisting rule that had previously been overturned in federal court. Wolves in the Western Great Lakes were delisted in 2007, but were returned to ESA protections in 2008 by court order. In January 2012, the FWS announced that the Western Great Lakes DPS of wolves had fully recovered and was healthy, leading to these wolves again being delisted.

The wolf population in the southwestern U.S. resulted from translocations. For the past decade, the Southwest has contained about 50 wolves in a single isolated wild population, but several hundred others are maintained in captivity, all originating from only 7 founders. Recovery efforts in the Southwest are continuing but additional efforts over a larger area will be needed to achieve recovery. Suitable habitat exists in other areas of the Southwest and in Mexico.

Wolves will continue to disperse naturally beyond the Northern Rocky Mountain, Western Great Lakes, and Southwest populations, but currently there are no other established populations.

Most of us fall victim to something called shifting baseline syndrome, defined as follows: "In the absence of past information or experience with historical conditions, members of each new generation accept the situation in which they were raised as being normal." Most don't remember forests with wolves, so when wolves manage to reestablish themselves in an area, tolerance is low and fear and anxiety are high. Wolves are often described as invaders, their presence an abnormal and threatening event, just as the reintroduction of wolves to Yellowstone and Idaho was vilified as unnatural by many who had never lived in an environment in which wolves were present.

If you've grown up being told by people you trust and believe that wolves are evil, dangerous, and should be killed, to hear otherwise creates an uncomfortable cognitive dissonance. There's motivation to reduce that dissonance, and any guilt that goes with it, by doubling down on the beliefs and behaviors. Humans have a long history of mistreating and exploiting animals, including wolves; to justify ongoing exploitation and cruelty, many choose to deny that animals are sentient, that they have thoughts, emotions, feel pain, and deserve empathy. By refusing to see the animals as sentient, such people are protecting their *own* psychological wellbeing.

Delisting wolves as an endangered species in the Northern Rocky Mountains in 2011 and 2012 allowed the states of Idaho, Montana, and Wyoming to amp up management efforts within their borders. These states immediately broadened their wolf hunting and trapping regulations, with the goal of keeping wolf populations as low as possible without triggering a relisting by the federal government. (In Idaho, a population below 150 wolves would trigger relisting, a number considerably lower than the USFW's recommendation of 500 in a stable population.)

In May 2021, against the wishes of the state's Fish and Game Department, Idaho's governor signed a law that allowed up to 90 percent of the state's wolf population to be killed. A state fund compensates private contractors who kill wolves, with bounties as high as $2,000. Hunters and trappers can kill an unlimited number of wolves in any year. Hunting and trapping on private land are allowed year-round, and on federal land, during prescribed seasons. Wolves can be hunted by hounds and chased down with all-terrain vehicles, including snowmachines.

In Montana, those hunting wolves can now use night-vision scopes and spotlights on private land, strangulation snares on public and private land, and bait to lure wolves. The number of wolves a single hunter/trapper can take was increased to 20, the wolf-trapping season was extended by four weeks (late November to March 15), and a bounty program reimburses hunters and trappers for costs associated with killing wolves.

In Wyoming, the Game and Fish Department allows year-round wolf killing across 85 percent of the state, at any time and by virtually any means, including running them over with snowmobiles and incinerating pups and nursing mothers in dens.

Various animal welfare organizations have filed lawsuits seeking to have Rocky Mountain wolves relisted, citing the increase in hunting and trapping in Idaho, Montana, and Wyoming and the lack of verifiable numbers of wolves surviving efforts to manage them. Some lawsuits also point out that trapping impacts other endangered species, including grizzlies and lynx.

In *America's New War on Wolves and Why it Must Be Stopped*, an article published in YaleEnvironment360 (February 17, 2020), author Ted Williams noted that most wildlife biologists find such expanded hunting and trapping laws extreme and not based in science. Instead, they're political.

"It's about making 'snowflakes' cry," remarks Ed Bangs, who led wolf recovery for the Northern Rockies. "Wild-ass hysteria is driving public policy. Invent a nonissue like too many wolves. Fish and game departments had been doing a good job since delisting. Then the legislatures politicized everything and made wolves a symbol of liberals and outsiders. It's 1850s stuff — let's show how much we hate wolves and the people who like them, and let's stick it to the feds."

Recently, Colorado took a different approach regarding the reintroduction of gray wolves. In 2020, voters narrowly passed Proposition 114, which required the creation of a plan to reintroduce wolves to the state west of the Continental Divide by the end of 2023. Rather than reacting to the natural reappearance of wolves (as did Washington, Oregon, and California), voters required their state agencies to plan for the return of gray wolves to their historical habitat, and to protect them. On December 15 and 22, 2023, a total of ten gray wolves captured in Oregon were relocated to Colorado's Western Slope. Another five are expected to be reintroduced in early 2024.

Wolves have more value alive than dead. One analysis estimated that wolf recovery in the Yellowstone National Park area would lead to benefits of between $6.7 and $9.9 million per year, with total costs (defined as the value of foregone benefits to hunters, lost value due to livestock depredation, and wolf-management costs) of $0.7 to $0.9 million per year. Tourism by those wanting to see or hear wolves in the wild provided $65.5 million annually to Yellowstone and the communities on its borders in Idaho, Montana, and Wyoming. Because of that tourism, park officials estimate that each of Yellowstone's ninety or so remaining wolves is worth $1 million. Contrast that with the $200 to $2,000 a dead wolf outside the park in Montana, Idaho, or Wyoming is worth to a bounty hunter—a "reward" paid by taxpayers.

Wolf-management policies enacted in Montana, Idaho, and Wyoming after delisting are immensely unpopular with the general public, and particularly offensive to most Indigenous groups, who have been left out of the decision-making process. After taking office in 2021, the Biden administration agreed to undertake a year-long review of the status of wolf recovery across the country. As of the end of 2023, nothing has been published, no action has been taken. In 2021, various groups sent impassioned letters to Secretary of the Interior Deb Haaland urging the return of protections for wolves everywhere. Among others, letters came from 85 members of the U.S. House of Representatives, 21 U.S. senators, 634 Canadian First Nations, nearly 200 U.S. tribal leaders, 30 business leaders, 61 conservation groups, and 800-plus scientists.

In Minnesota, where wolves are currently under federal protection, the University of Minnesota's Voyageurs Wolf Project is studying the wolves in the Greater Voyageurs Ecosystem in the northern part of the state. The ongoing study focuses on how the wolves live in the summer, including what they eat, how many pups they have, and how many of those pups survive to adulthood. The project's research helps address questions including wolf impacts on prey populations such as deer, beaver, and even fish; where wolves hunt, and where they're most successful; and how wolf packs form and compete with each other. With the cooperation of Minnesota Department of Natural Resources Fish and Wildlife Division and a ranching family with land in the middle of the ecosystem, the project is testing the ability of fencing to keep wolves out, thereby preventing predation of calves.

What researchers are learning and sharing with the public is enlightening, often surprising, and frequently debunks long-held myths. And proof that scientific information can help inform wildlife management and conservation in the future, in Minnesota and elsewhere.

CODA: NEMOPHILIST

I haunt the forest.

I feel most alive there. The forest provides peace, quiet, comfort, and solitude. In grief, the forest offers solace. In good times, the forest is my playground.

The forest never haunts me.

Light: The rising sun's beams filtered first by distant peaks, then nearby tree trunks, eventually branches, casting bright orange-yellow rays that spill across the forest floor, highlighting dew-speckled wildflowers and snow crystals.

Footsteps and paws: Their rhythmic punch on moist dirt in spring. Their muffled scuffling on fallen pine and fir needles in summer. Their loud crackling on gold, fire-orange, and wine-red leaves in autumn. Their squeak on packed snow in frigid winter.

Dogs: Following ears, noses, and eyes. Finding something of interest with every step: squirrels, birds, deer, scat, tracks, bones. A source of immense joy. My heart rate slows. I smile. I laugh. A shared a sense of discovery and excitement. We're a pack, intrigued by the same things, yet in different ways.

Tracks: In the mud, dust, and snow. Riddles to be solved. My Malamutes know more than I ever can. They sniff, then look in a particular direction, scanning for the animal leaving the track.

Wolves: Ruby Meadows. Howls cutting through the night's mysterious darkness, floating over the forest treetops to my ears as I lay in bed.

Quiet: Deep forest silence. Peaceful. Invigorating. My footsteps, the dogs', our breathing. Birds singing and wings beating against the breeze. The sudden *thump, thump, thump* of deer bounding away through the trees. Psithurism: wind through trees, bringing hints of what it has caressed along the way.

Birds: Jays jeering, ravens cawing, great-horned owls hoo-hoo-whooing, male red-winged blackbirds heralding spring as they stake out territory for mates with their songs. A turkey hen running through the undergrowth, poults right behind. The heart-stopping, sudden burst of a startled grouse, wings furiously flapping. The ki-ki-ki-ki-ki-ker of a bald eagle circling high overhead. The loud, ancient cackle of Sandhill cranes.

Trails: Dirt, rocks, roots. Paths leading deeper into the forest, over a ridge or peak, across a stream, to a lake, through a lush meadow, toward a new discovery, a new memory.

Running: Breathing deeply, lungs and heart oxygenating blood to power muscles. Mind in the moment. Dogs, trees, rocks, wildflowers, water, wildlife tracks, blue sky above. *I want to stay out here forever.*

Wildflowers. So many. Dainty, bold, resilient, colorful, short, tall, fat, slender, fragrant, shy, showy, turning to the sun, closing tight at night. Hosts to bees, bugs, butterflies, hummingbirds. Brilliant beauty followed by seeds and berries feeding forest creatures before tiring, dropping, decomposing in autumn's chill and winter's snowflakes to remerge the next spring.

Trees: Ponderosa bark, gnarled and deeply-lined, a beloved elder's face, each crevice a story. Aspen, white peeling bark with black eyes, Basque shepherd carvings, spring's bright green leaves turning yellow and gold, cackling in the wind. Ancient whitebark pine, twisted, knotty, knowing.

Water: Snow melt becoming spring's wild gushing rivers, summer's flowing streams, autumn's trickling creeks. Sunlight sparkling on, and wind sculpting, surfaces. Respite on warm days.

Snow: Nature's playscape. Pristine, cleansing, hushing. Sparkling prisms in slanted morning sunlight. Revelator of wildlife tracks.

Cairns: Heaps of stones. Memorials to departed beloved.

Clouds: Cumulonimbus piling high against a wide blue sky, pushed by breezes. Memorial cairns in the sky.

Lessons: Play. Explore. Learn. Grow. Nap. Pace yourself. Show gratitude. Forgive. Be generous. Live like every day is your last. Love unconditionally. Dance. Feel deeply. Be strong, resilient, hopeful. One foot in front of the other.

Healing. Joy. Awe.

Do what you love. Know your own bone; gnaw at it, bury it, unearth it, and gnaw it still.
—Henry David Thoreau

NOTES AND REFERENCES (BY CHAPTER)

Prelude

Since the beginning of the millennium, dog ownership in the United States has grown. https://financesonline.com/number-of-dogs-in-the-us/ According to the American Veterinary Medical Association, (2017–2018 survey results), roughly 38 percent of US households have at least one dog, with an average of 1.6 dogs per household. That's 76,811,305 dogs. https://www.avma.org/resources-tools/reports-statistics/us-pet-ownership-statistics In 2022, Americans spent $136.8 billion on their pets, up 10.68 percent from 2021 ($123.6 billion). https://www.forbes.com/advisor/pet-insurance/pet-ownership-statistics/

Wild

The book that helped launch the running craze, Jim Fixx's *The Complete Book of Running*, came out in 1977.

Opus

Basal breeds: A 2010 study (vonHolt et al., 2010) identified thirteen breeds genetically divergent from modern breeds based on phenotype: Basenji, Saluki, Afghan hound, Samoyed, Canaan dog, New Guinea singing dog, dingo, Chow Chow, Chinese Shar Pei, Akita, Alaskan Malamute, Siberian husky, and American Eskimo dog. A 2012 study (Larson et al., 2012) added three more: Eurasier, Finnish Spitz, and Shiba Inu.

On the 2022 AKC most-popular-breed list, Alaskan Malamute was number fifty-seven (of 199 recognized breeds). https://www.akc.org/expert-advice/dog-breeds/most-popular-dog-breeds-2022/ In 1985, the year I got Opus, Siberian huskies ranked eighteenth in popularity (20,144 registered), and Malamutes, thirty-fifth (6,506 registered). Most years, Labrador retrievers have ranked number one in breed popularity.

Puppies

Information about Yellowstone National Park wolves and wolf-pack interactions in general: The National Park Service publishes an annual Yellowstone Wolf Project summary, starting with the year 2000. Articles also appeared touting the environmental benefits of wolf reintroduction (e.g., Peterson, 2020). I read everything I could find, including observations of wild pack dynamics. In "Back to the Future" (Cordoni and Palagi, 2019), the authors offer a nice overview of social characteristics of wolves and wolf sociobiology. This new information contrasted sharply with old "facts" about wolf-pack dynamics.

Communing

Machu Picchu: Abelardo said that during the winter solstice, the rising sun shines through a window in the Gateway to the Sun straight through a window in a Machu Picchu temple.

Long distance running and human evolution: "Long distance running was crucial in creating our current upright body form, according to a new theory. Researchers have suggested that our early ancestors were good endurance runners, and that their habit has left its evolutionary mark on our bodies, from our leg joints right up to our heads." (Hopkin, 2004).

Persistence

The *dura mater*—Latin for "tough mother"—is the outer of three layers of connective tissue surrounding and protecting the brain and spinal cord.

An "MRI with contrast" combines magnetic and radio-wave imaging with an injection of a contrast agent (dye). The dye highlights blood vessels, organs, and specific soft tissues so they show up more clearly.

I received those three blind blood patches in early 2004. At the time, little was known about SIH or blood patches as treatment, other than that they seemed to work in some patients. Afterward, I went home with no instructions and no list of things to avoid. Ecstatic to be headache-free, I went for a run the next morning, thrilled that my eyes weren't bouncing and my forehead didn't feel as if it was about to explode. The protocol is much different today. Several days (at least 72 hours flat), if not weeks, of bed rest are prescribed, along with instructions not to bend, lift, twist, or strain the back in any way for months. Even with all those precautions, the patches don't always work long-term. Or they succeed only after three or four tries with various volumes of blood injected in various locations along the spine, or with fibrin glue substituted for blood.

Introvert

Read Mary Oliver's poem, "How I Go Into the Woods," online here. https://apoemaday.tumblr.com/post/181173241895/how-i-go-into-the-woods

Barry Lopez, in his wonderful book *Of Wolves and Men*, provides this detailed comparison of wolf and Malamute: "I spent a couple of days south of the Alaska Range on the Susitna River one spring weighing and measuring wild wolves and when I returned home, a friend asked how wolves compared in size to his Alaskan malamute, which many people think of as a sort of carbon copy of the wolf. I took a tape measure, and using the figures from my notebook for a typical male of the same age and weight came up with the following differences: The wolf's head was wider, longer, and generally larger. Malamute and wolf were about the same in the neck, twenty inches around, but the malamute was bigger in the chest by a few inches. The wolf stood two inches taller, was three inches longer in the leg, and eight inches longer in the body. The wolf's tail was longer and had no tendency to curl over its back as the malamute's did. The wolf's track was nearly twice the size of the dog's. Both animals' weight was about 100 pounds."

Stones

Prosser, the cat I got while in law school and who tolerated Opus, was named after the ubiquitous first-year textbook, *Prosser on Torts*; she died at twelve following a sudden seizure.

Keeping my Idaho house was the second-to-last bit of good advice my father gave me. The last: "Don't fight Sara because Sara always wins." (Sara was his second wife.)

Seasons

Autumn: Western larch trees
https://idahoforests.org/content-item/western-larch/

Winter: Covid contributed to a significant increase in snowmobile use during the winter of 2020/21. Dirt bikes converted for travel over snow, front wheel replaced by a ski, back by a narrow snowmachine tread, were also appearing; they went faster, were louder than even the snowmobiles, and chewed up the groomed surface faster.

Illegal snowmobile trail: Snowmobiles are required to stay on Forest Service roads (groomed or ungroomed). A neighbor's son was the most likely suspect for running one up the wildlife trail; he'd lived there all his life and probably learned that trick from his father.

Spring: Early in my explorations, Sound of Music Hill (a name I bestowed) was a special place in the Payette: quiet, full of wildflowers in spring, with stunning views of distant peaks. Several old Ponderosa pines kept watch from the top of the hill. In later years, a young pine growing alone near the bottom of the open hillside became the object of target shooting. So much so that it eventually died and became a brown-needled reminder of human stupidity. Local kids began using the hillside as a party place, leaving trash and empty beer cans near the tree. People gathering firewood in the fall started driving trucks and off-road vehicles straight up the hillside, avoiding the Forest Service road with its tank traps designed to keep them out. Eventually, they created a permanent scar: a renegade two-track road that even wildflowers couldn't grow on. It broke my heart to see the destruction of such a beautiful place.

Taking photos of wildflowers helped me learn their names more quickly as I later edited the photos and searched for them in my favorite guidebook, *Wildflowers of the Mountain West* (by R. M. Anderson, J. D. Gunnell, and J. L. Goodspeed, published by the University Press of Colorado, 2002) and online at the US Wildflowers website's page for Idaho. https://uswildflowers.com/stateref.php?State=ID Later, Google Lens provided pretty accurate (and immediate) results.

Wolves

Spring: Rick McIntyre's books can be found at https://www.rickmcintyrebooks.com/ and Rick Lamplugh's at https://www.amazon.com/stores/author/B001H6S990?ingress=0&visitId=c8a6293f-5135-4503-a77d-c5ec8486283a

Wolf coat color: Gray wolves with black coats are rare in most places, but occur more frequently in parts of the western US, including Yellowstone National Park. The black coat color comes from a gene mutation that also confers immunity to canine distemper and other lung diseases. As more black-coated wolves survive, they pass that gene on to their offspring, resulting in more black-coated wolves. Only one copy of the gene is needed for coat color and disease immunity. "[B]lack coats were maintained through heterozygote advantage in, and mate choice preference for, black-coated wolves in areas where canine distemper is endemic even though gray-coated wolves have higher success when the virus is absent."(Cubaynes et al., 2022).

An article about research suggesting wolves were domesticated before livestock: Serpell, 2021.

Books putting forth the "garbage pit" theory of early wolf domestication: Lorenz, 1954; Coppinger and Coppinger, 2001.

Articles detailing findings of wolves, dogs, fox buried with early humans: Morey, 2006; Maher et al., 2011; Wong, 2015.

Winter: A study found that wolves infected with the parasite *Toxoplasma gondii* "were more likely to make high-risk decisions such as dispersing and becoming a pack leader, both factors critical to individual fitness and wolf vital rates." (Meyer et al., 2022).

Spring: Benefits of the human/companion-animal bond (Friedmann and Son, 2009); pets help with stress (American Heart Association, 2021).

The first quoted section is an excerpt from a letter to Secretary of the Interior Deb Haaland urging relisting for gray wolves and inclusion of Indigenous voices in the decision-making process. Dated September 14, 2021, it was signed by close to 200 US tribal leaders. https://www.relistwolves.org/_files/ugd/da04a3_dd7cadb4364f430cb8f0e63fa2b86f43.pdf

The second quoted section is from a similar letter also addressed to Secretary Haaland, dated September 28, 2021, and signed by 634 Canadian First Nation leaders. https://www.globalindigenouscouncil.com/_files/ugd/13fe3b_3924608bd4ae413186f7b47ab2e7d5e6.pdf

Dedicated breed-tweaking: Started in the Victorian era, especially for companion dogs.

Estimated lifetime trail mileage for my dogs: Using my training logs, I once calculated that in the dozen years I ran or walked trails with Maia and Meadow (roughly, 2000 to 2012), we covered nearly 10,000 miles together, an average of sixteen miles per week. Lots of time (some 2,250 hours) to observe their behaviors in wilderness settings as they used their instincts and intelligence to keep us safe. That time and distance investment has continued with Finn and Conall.

Empathy

Rick McIntyre's books can be found on Amazon.

Shattered

Repeated visits by two sheriff's deputies to discuss dead coyotes displayed on Wallace Lane: I laughed to myself at the rumors those visits would stir up among my neighbors in our otherwise quiet subdivision.

Naturalism

Some of my childhood TV favorites: *Mutual of Omaha's Wild Kingdom*, *The Undersea World of Jacques Cousteau*, and *The Wonderful World of Disney*.

Butch the harbor seal: He lived in the lake I grew up on, Lake Sammamish, east of Bellevue, Washington, and spent most of his time near our dock. He often played with Spot and Tar, two large neighborhood mutts, splashing them by slapping his tail against the water while they barked from the dock. They played that way for years. I loved watching from a distance that didn't spook Butch. How Butch started living in the lake was the subject of rumor and conjecture, but he may've been someone's pet at one time; he had a red collar around his neck, so tight that the skin under it was raw and irritated.

Origin stories offering different viewpoints: In her book *Braiding Sweetgrass* (Minneapolis: Milkweed Editions, 2015), botanist and member of the Citizen Potawatomi Nation Robin Wall Kimmerer compares her Starwoman heritage origin story to that of the Biblical Eve. Starwoman was cared for by the wildlife that helped her create the Earth on the back of a turtle so the seeds and plants she brought with her could thrive. Eve? Cast out for eating "forbidden fruit," gates locked behind her in anger, to forever toil in misery until (maybe) making it to heaven. Kimmerer imagines a conversation between the two women, in which Starwoman says, "Sister, you got the short end of the stick."

Naturalism is different than atheism: Sean Carroll, from a May 2016 interview with *Wired*, about his book, *The Big Picture: On the Origins of Life, Meaning and the Universe Itself* (New York: Dutton, 2016).
https://www.wired.com/2016/05/maybe-youre-not-atheist-maybe-youre-naturalist-like-sean-carroll/

Origin of the word "naturalist":
https://www.etymonline.com/word/naturalist

Masculinity

Idaho hunting regulations: "It is Unlawful To: [...] Shoot from or across the traveled portion, shoulders or embankments of any road maintained by any government entity." Idaho Fish & Game interpretation: https://idfg.idaho.gov/sites/default/files/file/ma/highway_rights-of-way_interpretation_1.pdf

Toxic masculinity: According to a piece in the *New York Times* ("What Is Toxic Masculinity?" January 22, 2019), researchers define toxic masculinity "as a set of behaviors and beliefs that include the following: Suppressing emotions or masking distress; maintaining an appearance of hardness; violence as an indicator of power (think: 'tough-guy' behavior)." https://www.nytimes.com/2019/01/22/us/toxic-masculinity.html

Quoted material: Lopez, 2004, p.166.

The American Redoubt: A political migration movement first proposed in 2011 by survivalist novelist and blogger James Wesley Rawles, which designated Idaho, Montana, and Wyoming (along with eastern parts of Oregon and Washington) as safe havens for conservative Christians. https://en.wikipedia.org/wiki/American_Redoubt

The Aryan Nation: Successfully sued by the Southern Poverty Law Center, declared bankruptcy to avoid paying monetary damages, lost their land after their leader died, and slinked away to form splinter groups. https://en.wikipedia.org/wiki/Aryan_Nations

Wolf-birds

In *Mind of the Raven*, zoologist Bernd Heinrich suggested that, as a basis for the relationship between ravens and wolves, ravens lead wolves to their prey, alert them to approaching dangers while they eat, and are rewarded by sharing the spoils after the wolves make the meat accessible for the ravens.

Steps

Idaho fires: In 2022, Idaho led the nation in the number of large fires. Reports were becoming the norm by the time I left Idaho in July 2021. https://idahonews.com/news/local/idaho-wildfires-leads-acres-burned

Vermont's forests: They cover 4,591,281 acres, equal to 78 percent of the state, a level that has remained steady since the 1980s; individuals and families own more than 80 percent of the forestlands. https://fpr.vermont.gov/forest/vermonts-forests

On Conall being mistaken for a coyote in Vermont: Not a farfetched scenario. Coyotes in Vermont are larger and more wolfish in appearance than those out west. DNA collected from hundreds of northeastern coyotes has been used in several studies; one, led by Stony Brook University, found that of 462 animals tested, the average genetic breakdown was 64 percent coyote, 13 percent gray wolf, 13 percent eastern wolf, and 10 percent domestic dog (National Park Service, November 2022). Conall would continue to wear his Do Not Hunt Me vest in Vermont.

John O'Donohue: More here. https://johnodonohue.com/anam-cara

Afterword: Gray Wolves in the United States: A Primer

Beringia: https://en.wikipedia.org/wiki/Beringia

Study re ancient wolf dispersal: Pacheco et al., 2022.

Observation and description by explorer and naturalist Samuel Hearne of an Alaskan Indigenous woman interacting with wolf pups in the late eighteenth century: "They always burrow underground to bring forth their young, and though it is natural to suppose them very fierce at those times, yet I have frequently seen the Indians go to their dens and take out the young ones and play with them. I never knew a Northern Indian to hurt one of them: on the contrary, they always put them carefully into the den again; and I have sometimes seen them paint the faces of the young wolves with vermillion, or red ochre." (Hearne, 1911)

Early colonists noted that dogs living with Indigenous groups howled rather than barked: Ruane, 2022.

Articles about early dogs in the Americas: Leathlobhair et al., 2018; Lin et al., 2023.

Sources for reintroduction of wolves to Yellowstone: Smith et al., 2020; Lopez, 2004.

The Nez Perce Tribe's approach to wolves and wolf reintroduction: The Homecoming of *Hîmiin* [Wildlife Division web page]. https://www.nezpercewildlife.org/gray-wolf

The Wildlife Society position paper: "Wolf Restoration and Management in the Contiguous United States" (March 2020). https://wildlife.org/tws-issues-statement-wolf-restoration-and-management-in-the-contiguous-united-states/

Humane Society of the United States press release: "Lawsuit Seeks to Restore Federal Protections to Northern Rockies Wolves After Government Misses Deadline" (August 9, 2022). https://www.humanesociety.org/news/lawsuit-seeks-restore-federal-protections-northern-rockies-wolves-after-government-misses

"America's New War on Wolves . . ." (T. Williams, 2020).

Colorado Proposition 114, Gray Wolf Reintroduction Initiative (2020): https://ballotpedia.org/Colorado_Proposition_114,_Gray_Wolf_ Reintroduction_Initiative_(2020)

Letters seeking relisting of the gray wolf under the Endangered Species Act came from 85 members of the U.S. House of Representatives, 21 U.S. senators, 634 Canadian First Nations, nearly 200 U.S. tribal leaders, 30 business leaders, 61 conservation groups, and 800-plus scientists.

Voyageurs Wolf Project: https://www.voyageurswolfproject.org/about-the-project

On the positive financial impact of Yellowstone wolves: Weiss et al., 2007; Smith et al., 2020.

RESOURCES AND SOURCES CITED

Books

Coppinger, R., and L. Coppinger. *Dogs: A Startling New Understanding of Canine Origin, Behavior and Evolution*. New York: Scribner, 2001.

Ferguson, G. *The Yellowstone Wolves:The First Year*. Helena, MT: Falcon Press, 1996.

Hearne, S. *A Journey from Prince of Wales's Fort in Hudson's Bay to the Northern Ocean in the Years 1769, 1770, 1771, 1772* (New edition with introduction, notes, and illustrations). Toronto: Champlain Society Publications, 1911. [Available at https://www.gutenberg.org/files/38404/38404-h/38404-h.htm]

Heinrich, B. *The Mind of the Raven: Investigations and Adventures with Wolf-birds*. New York: Harper Perennial, 2006.

Lamplugh, R. *In the Temple of Wolves: A Winter's Immersion in Wild Yellowstone*. [n.p.]: CreateSpace Independent Publishing Platform, 2014.

Lopez, B. *Of Wolves and Men*. New York: Scribner, 1978, 2004.

Lorenz, K. *Man Meets Dog*. Translated by M. K. Wilson. London: Methuen, 1954.

McIntyre, R. *The Reign of Wolf 21: The Saga of Yellowstone's Legendary Druid Pack*. Vancouver: Greystone Books, 2020.

McIntyre, R. *The Rise of Wolf 8: Witnessing the Triumph of Yellowstone's Underdog*. Vancouver: Greystone Books, 2019.

Mech, L. D., and L. Boitani, eds. *Wolves: Behavior, Ecology, and Conservation*. Chicago: University of Chicago Press, 2003.

Mowat, F. *Never Cry Wolf: The Amazing True Story of Life Among Arctic Wolves*. New York: Back Bay Books, 2001.

Niemeyer, C. *Wolf Land*. Boise, ID: Bottlefly Press, 2016.

Pierotti, R., and B. R. Fogg. T*he First Domestication: How Wolves and Humans Coevolved*. New Haven: Yale University Press, 2017.

Smith, D. W., D. R. Stahler, and D. R. MacNulty, eds. *Yellowstone Wolves: Science and Discovery in the World's First National Park*. Chicago: University of Chicago Press, 2020.

Articles and Podcasts

American Heart Association. "5 Ways Pets Help with Stress and Mental Health." *American Heart Association Online* (Reviewed May 20, 2021). https://www.heart.org/en/healthy-living/healthy-bond-for-life-pets/pets-as-coworkers/pets-and-mental-health

Andrews, R. G. "Oldest Dog Remains in Americas Discovered in Alaska." *National Geographic Newsletter* (February 21, 2021). https://www.nationalgeographic.com/history/article/oldest-dog-remains-in-americas-discovered-alaska

Bergström, A., D. W. G. Stanton, U. H. Taron et al. "Grey Wolf Genomic History Reveals a Dual Ancestry of Dogs." *Nature* 607: 313–320 (2022). https://doi.org/10.1038/s41586-022-04824-9

Bittel, J. "Humans and Dogs Have Been Sledding Together for Nearly 10,000 Years." *National Geographic Newsletter* (June 25, 2020). https://www.nationalgeographic.com/animals/article/humans-dogs-sledding-together-ten-thousand-years

Comeleo, R. "Using Coyotes to Protect Livestock—Wait. What?" *Oregon State University Small Farm News* XIII, no. 2 (Spring 2018). https://smallfarms.oregonstate.edu/using-coyotes-protect-livestock-wait-what/

Cordoni, G., and E. Palagi. "Back to the Future: A Glance Over Wolf Social Behavior to Understand Dog-Human Relationship." *Animals (Basel)* 9, no. 11 (2019): 991. https://doi.org/10.3390/ani9110991

Cubaynes, S., E. E. Brandell, D. R. Stahler et al., "Disease Outbreaks Select for Mate Choice and Coat Color in Wolves," *Science* 378, no. 6617 (2022): 300–303. https://www.science.org/doi/10.1126/science.abi8745

Dubner, S. J. "Can the Big Bad Wolf Save Your Life?" *Freak-o-Nomics* podcast (March 23, 2022). https://freakonomics.com/podcast/can-the-big-bad-wolf-save-your-life/

Friedmann, E., and H. Son. "The Human–Companion Animal Bond: How Humans Benefit." *Veterinary Clinics of North America: Small*

Animal Practice 39, no. 2 (2009): 293–326. https://doi.org/10.1016/j.cvsm.2008.10.015

Gehert, S. D., E. M. Muntz, E. C. Wilson et al. "Severe Environmental Conditions Create Severe Conflicts: A Novel Ecological Pathway to Extreme Coyote Attacks on Humans. *Journal of Applied Ecology* 60, no. 22 (2022): 353–364. https://besjournals.onlinelibrary.wiley.com/doi/10.1111/1365-2664.14333

Grimm, D. "How Dogs Tracked Their Humans Across the Ancient World." *Science* (October 29, 2020). doi: 10.1126/science.abf4882. https://www.science.org/content/article/how-dogs-tracked-their-humans-across-ancient-world

———. "Ice Age Siberian Hunters May Have Domesticated Dogs 23,000 Years Ago," *Science* (January 21, 2021). doi: 10.1126/science.abg7468. https://www.science.org/content/article/ice-age-siberian-hunters-may-have-domesticated-dogs-23000-years-ago

Handwerk, B. "How Accurate Is the Theory of Dog Domestication in 'Alpha?'" *Smithsonian Magazine* (August 15, 2018). https://www.smithsonianmag.com/science-nature/how-wolves-really-became-dogs-180970014/

Hopkin, M. "Distance Running 'Shaped Human Evolution.'" *Nature* (2004). https://doi.org/10.1038/news041115-9

Kelley, S. "Bring Back the Wolves—But Not as Heroes or Villains." *Cornell Chronicle* (July 5, 2022). https://news.cornell.edu/stories/2022/07/bring-back-wolves-not-heroes-or-villains

Kesselheim, A. "The Howling Wilderness." *The Sun* (January 2021). [Interview with Doug Smith about his work with Yellowstone wolves.] https://www.thesunmagazine.org/issues/541/the-howling-wilderness

Kirknen, T., O. López-Costas, A. M. Cortizas et al. "Preservation of Microscopic Fur, Feather, and Bast Fibers in the Mesolithic Ochre Grave of Majoonsuo, Eastern Finland." *PLoS One* 17, no. 9 (2022). https://doi.org/10.1371/journal.pone.0274849

Kotera, Y., M. Richardson, and D. Sheffield. "Effects of Shinrin-Yoku (Forest Bathing) and Nature Therapy on Mental Health: A Systemic Review and Meta-Analysis." *Journal of Mental Health and Addiction* 20 (2022): 337–361. https://doi.org/10.1007/s11469-020-00363-4

Larson, G., E. K. Karlsson, A. Perri, and M. T. Webster. "Rethinking Dog Domestication by Integrating Genetics, Archeology, and Biogeography." *Proceedings of the National Academy of Sciences of the United States of America* 109, no. 23 (2012): 8878-8883. https://doi.org/10.1073/pnas.1203005109

Leathlobhair, M. N., A. R. Perri, E. K. Irving-Pease et al. "The Evolutionary History of Dogs in the Americas." *Science* 361, no. 6397 (July 2018): 81–85. https://www.science.org/doi/10.1126/science.aao4776

Lightning, C. "Secretary Haaland, from One Indigenous Mother to Another: If Not Now, When Will You Reverse Trump on Wolves?" *Native News Online* (September 16, 2021). https://nativenewsonline.net/opinion/secretary-haaland-from-one-indigenous-mother-to-another-if-not-now-when-will-you-reverse-trump-on-wolves

Lin, A. T., L. Hammond-Kaarremaa, H. Liu et al. "The History of Coast Salish 'Woolly Dogs' Revealed by Ancient Genomics and Indigenous Knowledge." *Science* 382, no. 6676 (December 2023): 1303–1308. https://www.science.org/doi/10.1126/science.adi6549

Lishin, U. "Motivated Science: What Humans Gain from Denying Animal Sentience." *Animal Sentience* 31, no. 19 (2022). https://www.wellbeingintlstudiesrepository.org/animsent/vol6/iss31/19

Maher L. L., J. T. Stock, S. Finney et al. "A Unique Human-Fox Burial from a Pre-Natufian cemetery in the Levant (Jordan)." *PLoS ONE* 6, no. 1 (2001):e15815. https://doi.org/10.1371/journal.pone.0015815

Marti, R., M. Petignat, V. L. Marcar et al. "Effects of Contact with a Dog on Prefrontal Brain Activity: A Controlled Trial." *PLoS ONE* 17, no. 10 (2022). https://doi.org/10.1371/journal.pone.0274833

Meyer, C., K. A. Cassidy, E. E. Stahler et al. "Parasitic Infection Increases Risk-Taking in Social, Intermediate Host Carnivore." *Communications Biology* 5, no. 1180 (2022). https://doi.org/10.1038/s42003-022-04122-0

Molde, D. "Let's Talk Hunting." *Sierra Nevada Ally* (July 15, 2022). https://sierranevadaally.org/2022/07/15/lets-talk-hunting/

Morey, D. F. "Burying Key Evidence: The Social Bond Between Dogs and People." *Journal of Archaeological Science* 33, no. 2 (2006): 158–75. https://doi.org/10.1016/j.jas.2005.07.009

Nuwer, R. "Dogs That Should be Guarding Sheep Are Mating with Wolves Instead." *Smithsonian Magazine* (April 16, 2014). https://www.smithsonianmag.com/smart-news/some-dogs-meant-guard-sheep-wolves-are-instead-hybridizing-those-predators-180951122/

Pacheco C., A. V. Stronen, B. Jędrzejewska et al. "Demography and Evolutionary History of Grey Wolf Populations Around the Bering Strait." *Molecular Ecology* 31, no. 18 (2022): 4851–4865. https://doi.org/10.1111/mec.16613

Peterson, C. "25 Years After Returning to Yellowstone, Wolves Have Helped Stabilize the Ecosystem." *National Geographic Newsletter/Animals* (July 2020). https://www.nationalgeographic.com/animals/article/yellowstone-wolves-reintroduction-helped-stabilize-ecosystem

Ravisetti, M. "Scientists Now Know Why Coyotes Unexpectedly Killed a Human in 2009." *CNET* (December 18, 2022). [See also Gehert et al., for study on which this article was based.] https://www.cnet.com/science/biology/scientists-now-know-why-coyotes-unexpectedly-killed-a-human-in-2009

Ruane, M. E. "Bones of Ancient Native Dogs Found at Jamestown." *Washington Post* (12/29/2022). https://www.washingtonpost.com/history/2022/12/29/dogs-native-jamestown-discovered/

Serpell, J. "Commensalism or Cross-Species Adoption? A Critical Review of Theories of Wolf Domestication." *Frontiers in Veterinary Science* no. 8 (2021). https://doi.org/10.3389/fvets.2021.662370

Smith, P. "Study Sheds Light on Top Causes of Deer Mortality." *Milwaukee Journal Sentinel* (January 25, 2014.) [Wisconsin study (2011–2013) of deer mortality/causes, ranked.] https://archive.jsonline.com/sports/outdoors/study-sheds-light-on-top-causes-of-deer-mortality-b99190938z1-241992741.html

Stanley, G. "The State of Wolves." *Star Tribune* (July 10, 2022). https://www.startribune.com/minnesota-wolves-predators-research-survival-extinction-preservation/600184286

Starr, M. "The Color of Wolves Mysteriously Changes Across America. We Finally Know Why." *Science Alert* (January 1, 2023). [See also Cubaynes et al., for study on which this article was based.] https://www.sciencealert.com/the-color-of-wolves-mysteriously-changes-across-america-we-finally-know-why

Vendantam, S. "Made of Honor." *Hidden Brain* podcast (n.d.). ["Honor culture" and how it shaped the South and West.] https://hiddenbrain.org/podcast/made-of-honor/

vonHoldt, B. M., J. P. Pollinger, K. E. Lohmueller et al. "Genome-wide SNP and Haplotype Analyses Reveal a Rich History Underlying Dog Domestication." Nature 464, no. 7290 (2010): 898-902. https://doi.org/10.1038/nature08837

Weiss, A. E., T. Kroeger, J. C. Haney, and N. Fascione. "Social and Ecological Benefits of Restored Wolf Populations" (Session Five: Predator and Prey). *Transactions of the 72nd North American Wildlife and Natural Resources Conference* (March 20–24, 2007): 297-319. https://wildlifemanagement.institute/sites/default/files/2016-09/11-Social_and_Ecological.pdf

Williams, P. "Letter from Idaho: Killing Wolves to Own the Libs?" *New Yorker Magazine* (March 28, 2022). https://www.newyorker.com/magazine/2022/04/04/killing-wolves-to-own-the-libs-idaho

Williams, T. "America's New War on Wolves and Why It Must Be Stopped." *Yale Environment 360* (February 17, 2022). https://e360.yale.edu/features/americas-new-war-on-wolves-and-why-it-must-be-stopped

Wong, K. "From Wolf to Dog: What Siberian Burials Reveal about the Relationship between Humans and Dogs." Scientific American 313, no. 1 (2015). https://www.scientificamerican.com/article/dogs-what-siberian-burials-reveal-about-the-relationship-between-humans-and-dogs/

Zaske, S. "Women Influenced Coevolution of Dogs and Humans." *WSU Insider* (January 15, 2021). https://news.wsu.edu/press-release/2021/01/25/women-influenced-coevolution-dogs-humans/

Other Suggested Viewing/Reading

CSF leaks: Information about and resources for those dealing with CSF leaks: Spinal CSF Leak Foundation, https://spinalcsfleak.org/.

I Am 06, an animated video about Wolf 06 and the effort to create a no-hunt zone around Yellowstone. https://youtu.be/eAHo9khApJE?si=uX45DX6dewTCEH8b

Leopold, A. *A Sand County Almanac and Sketches Here and There.*

Oxford, UK: Oxford University Press, 1949 (commemorative paperback edition 1989).

My Octopus Teacher (Netflix). "People ask, 'Why are you going to the same place every day?' But that's when you see the subtle differences. That's when you get to know the wild." https://en.wikipedia.org/wiki/My_Octopus_Teacher

Voyageurs Wolf Project, for science-based information and research about wolves, including amazing videos and photos. https://www.voyageurswolfproject.org (Also on Facebook: https://www.facebook.com/VoyageursWolfProject)

Washington Department of Fish and Wildlife. *How to Count a Wolf, 2020*. A short documentary about wolf recovery in Washington state, highlighting methods for counting and collaring wolves. https://youtu.be/V9q2txY_FNY?si=ZYMJkwVzhFlzrJnx

Yong, E. *An Immense World: How Animal Senses Reveal the Hidden Realms Around Us.* New York: Random House, 2022. Here's a video of Ed talking about human vs. animal senses: https://aeon.co/videos/to-understand-the-limits-of-human-senses-look-to-the-wild-world-of-animal-cognition

"You're Not Going to Believe What I'm About to Tell You." Comic by The Oatmeal on why people believe what they do. https://theoatmeal.com/comics/believe

ACKNOWLEDGEMENTS

Deeply moved by the wolf encounter that opens this book, I knew someday I wanted to write about wolves. But first, I needed to finish the book I was working on. After publishing *Growing Up Boeing* in 2014, whenever a friend asked me what I was writing, I would reply, vaguely, "the wolf book." I didn't know *what* I would write or what sort of book it would be. I only knew it would feature dogs, and wolves.

From 2004 to 2020, *The Bark* magazine published my articles featuring the human-canine bond. Claudia Kawczynska and Cameron Woo, thank you both for taking on a rookie writer, mentoring me over those years, and making me a contributing editor. You provided a safe and supportive space for me to learn how to write for a broad audience, and I will always be proud of my minor role in your excellent magazine.

During the past ten years of researching, thinking, and trying to write the wolf book, many people encouraged me. Whether longtime friends or online acquaintances, they listened, asked questions, and offered insights. When I felt discouraged, unworthy, and unable to write, they buoyed me with their assurances. They checked in, occasionally asking, "How's the wolf book coming?" Perhaps they intuitively knew I work best under such gentle pressure. Miki Robinson, Shelle Singer, Laurie Carroll, Lee Lovelace, Suzanne Olson, and many others, thank you. Please know how much I value such steadfast encouragement and faith in my ability to ultimately write this book.

I'm grateful to the WordPress blogging community, where for several years I've found an inspiring family of fellow writers. A welcoming place to practice my craft. Three bloggers in particular agreed to help me with this book in concrete ways: Siobhan Sullivan, thank you for reading every draft chapter, providing feedback, edits, and endless cheering; Kim Clair Smith and Martha Kennedy, thank you for being early readers and offering valuable critiques.

Other early readers donating their time, vital comments, and sometimes a blurb: Laura Meuser, Sean Prentiss, Kristina Siladi, Sean Meissner,

Adrian Raeside, Kelly Beckwith Verduin, and members of the Burlington Writers Workshop Creative Nonfiction writing group. Huge thanks to all of you.

A wholehearted thank you to Thomas Gable, Project Lead, Voyageurs Wolf Project, who took time from his busy schedule studying the wolves of Minnesota to fact check my wolf vignettes in the WOLVES chapter.

Michael Metivier, you took on the daunting task of early developmental editing. With your suggestions, my messy manuscript eventually became a well-structured story. Thank you for your insights and advice. And Valentyn Smith, thank you for early line editing. Many of your non-editing comments in the manuscript allowed me to believe I was hitting the right notes, giving me confidence.

Jane Dixon-Smith, I'm grateful I found you! Your cover design is what I envisioned, even though I couldn't describe it in words. Thank you, also, for formatting all versions of the book and offering advice along the way. You're a dream to work with.

Last but most certainly not least: Susan Tasaki, you've been in my corner since the beginning. We've never met in person, yet I consider you one of my closest friends, one of those rare people who gets me. From the first article I submitted to *The Bark* magazine in 2004—which you edited, the start of a long and wonderful collaboration there—to now, you've not only made my words shine, you've been a *friend*. Over the years, you maintained a steady stream of encouragement for me to write "the wolf book," sending me article links and nonfiction books about the natural world as inspiration, sharing your own thoughts about dogs, wolves, and nature, even surprising me with figurines of a wolf family to set on my desk, constant reminders why I was writing this book. When you stepped in to copyedit, while also offering exceptional developmental editing suggestions, I knew I was safe. I was in expert and caring hands. The best possible version of *Wild Running* would make it to readers. My gratitude, for both your enduring friendship and your editing expertise, is boundless. If I ever get to meet you in person, expect happy tears and a heartfelt bear hug.

And of course, I'm grateful beyond words for every dog I've been fortunate to share my life with. They are my inspiration. Thanks, Dad, for introducing me to the joys and wisdom of dogs.

ABOUT THE AUTHOR

Rebecca Wallick is an author and runner currently living with her dogs in rural Vermont. Born and raised in the Seattle area, Rebecca spent 15 years living in Idaho's Salmon River Mountains before moving to Vermont in 2021. After a career as a family law attorney in both Washington and Idaho, in 2020 she retired to focus on running with her dogs and writing. She is the author of *Growing Up Boeing: The Early Jet Age Through the Eyes of a Test Pilot's Daughter* (2014). A contributing editor at *The Bark* magazine from 2004 to 2019, Wallick has also had articles published in *Aloft* (Museum of Flight), *Flight Journal, UltraRunner, Seattle,* and *City-Dog* magazines. She blogs at Wild Sensibility and maintains Facebook pages for *Growing Up Boeing* and *Wild Running*. (Photo: The author with Meadow and Maia, August 2012, by Shelle Singer.)

Made in United States
Troutdale, OR
04/19/2024